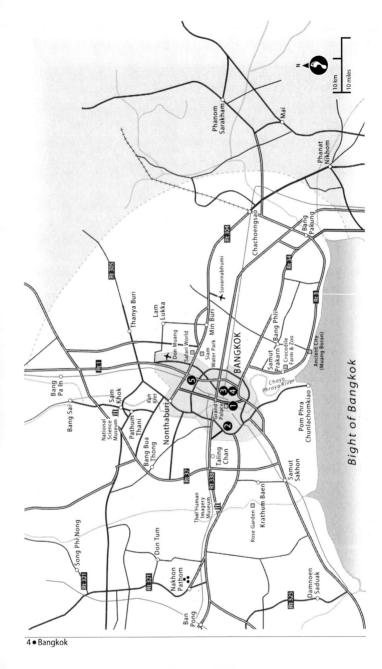

N

10 km
10 miles

Phanom Sarakham

Mai

Phanat Nikhom

Rt 304

Chachoengsao

Bang Pakung

Rt 34

Rt 305

Thanya Buri

Lam Lukka

Suvarnabhumi

Min Buri

Bang Phli

Rt 3

Bang Pa In

Siam Water Park

Don Muang

Safari World

BANGKOK

Samut Prakarn

Crocodile Farm & Zoo

Ancient City (Muang Boran)

Rt 31

Bang Sai

Sam Khok

Koh Kret

Nonthaburi

5

3

4

1

Grand Palace

2

Chao phraya River

National Science Museum

Pathum Thani

Pom Phra Chunlachomkiao

Bang Bua Thong

Bight of Bangkok

Song Phi Nong

Rt 37

Taling Chan

Rt 338

Samut Sakhon

Thai Human Imagery Museum

Don Tum

Rose Garden

Krathum Baen

Nakhon Pathom

Rt 321

Rt 321

Damnoen Saduak

Rt 325

Ban Pong

Dirty, dynamic, wild and sweaty, Bangkok is a heaving scrum of humanity blended with ancient beauty, booming youth culture and the rituals of a bygone age. The Thais call it the City of Angels but there's nothing angelic about Bangkok. Don't arrive expecting an exotic, languid, dreamy place trapped in some imagined, traditional past. What will hit you is the size, pace, endless olfactory cacophony, friendliness of the locals and interminable gridlocked traffic. The whole place resembles a giant, out-of-control car-boot sale whose pavements are humming with open-air kitchens, clothes stalls, hawkers and touts.

Some of the old King and I romanticism does persist. There are the khlongs, palaces and temples but ultimately, what marks Bangkok out from the imaginings of its visitors, is its thrusting modernity in open struggle with the ancient, rural traditions of Thai culture. Neon, steel and glass futuristic transport rubs shoulders with blind street bands, alms-collecting monks and crumbling teak villas. It's all here: poverty and wealth, smog-filled thoroughfares and backstreets smothered in alluring exotic aromas, cybercafés and barrows laden with fried bugs.

With your senses fully overloaded don't forget the sheer luxury that's on offer. Bangkok is home to some of the best, and most affordable, hotels in the world. Add the numerous spas, the futuristic super-hip nightlife and the incredibly diverse range of markets and shops selling everything from amulets and sarongs to Prada and hi-tech gadgets – your head will be spinning. And when the urban theatre of Bangkok finally overwhelms, take a day trip to the ancient summer residence of the Thai kings at Bang Pa In or drift upriver to Nonthaburi for its provincial charm.

Planning your trip

Getting to Bangkok

Air

The city's sleek but troubled Helmut Jahn-designed international airport, **Suvarnabhumi** (pronounced su-wan-na-poom), sits 25 km east of the city. Although travel links are considerably improved, it can still take well over an hour to get to the city centre by car Taking the expressway cuts the travel time down significantly and, outside rush-hour, the transit time to Central Bangkok should be 35-45 minutes. A cheaper (and depending on where you're staying, often quicker) option is the 28-km overhead monorail link. Opened in August 2010, it stops at seven stations, including one – Phaya Thai – that intersects with the city's Skytrain. ▸▸ *For further details of transport from the airport to the city centre, see page 117.*

Suvarnabhumi opened in September 2006, much later than originally promised. Controversy clung to the project from the start, with allegations of backhanders influencing the award of contracts for construction and ground services, and the troubled airport still sometimes makes the headlines due to cracked and sinking runways and creaking infrastructure. The Thai police report that pickpockets journey across Asia to descend on distracted passengers here.

Bangkok is Thailand's domestic transport hub, with flights to around 25 towns and cities throughout the country; trains head south to the Malaysian border (and onward to Kuala Lumpur and Singapore), north to Chiang Mai, and northeast to Nong Khai and Ubon Ratchathani; and buses of every kind make their way to all corners of the country. It is often necessary to transit through Bangkok if working your way north to south by whatever means of transport. The old airport, **Don Muang**, 25 km north of the city, was serving a few domestic routes until the late 2011 floods submerged its runways. At the time of writing, only one airline, budget carrier **Nok Air**, has resumed flights from there, though this may change as Suvarnabhumi gets more and more congested and surpasses its design capacity of 45 million passengers a year.

Flights from Europe The approximate flight time from London to Bangkok (non-stop) is 12 hours. From London Heathrow, airlines offering non-stop flights include **Qantas**, **British Airways**, **THAI** and **Eva Air**. You can easily connect to Thailand from the UK via most other European capitals. **Finnair** flies daily from Helsinki, **KLM** via Amsterdam and **Lufthansa** via Frankfurt. **SAS** flies from Copenhagen and **Swiss Air** from Zurich. Further afield, **Etihad** flies via Abu Dhabi, **Gulf Air** via Bahrain and **Qatar** via Muscat and Doha. Non-direct flights can work out much cheaper, so if you want a bargain, shop around. **Finnair**, www.finnair.com, often offers some of the cheapest fares. It is also possible to fly direct to Chiang Mai from Dusseldorf, Frankfurt and Munich in Germany, and to Phuket from Dusseldorf and Munich.

Flights from the USA and Canada The approximate flight time from Los Angeles to Bangkok is 21 hours. There are one-stop flights from Los Angeles on **THAI** and two-stops on **Delta**; one-stop flights from San Francisco on **Northwest** and **United** and two-stops on **Delta**; and one-stop flights from Vancouver on **Canadian**. **THAI** have now started a non-stop flight from New York to Bangkok, which takes 16 hours.

Don't miss…

Numbers relate to map on page 4.

Flights from Australasia There are flights from Sydney and Melbourne (approximately nine hours) daily with **Qantas** and **THAI**. There is also a choice of other flights with **British Airways**, **Alitalia**, **Lufthansa** and **Lauda Air**, which are less frequent. There are flights from Perth with **THAI** and **Qantas**. From Auckland, **Air New Zealand**, **THAI** and **British Airways** fly to Bangkok.

Flights from Asia THAI, **Air India** and **Indian Airlines**, **Air Lanka**, **THAI** and **Cathay Pacific** fly from Colombo. From Dhaka, there are flights with **Biman Bangladesh Airlines** and **THAI**. **PIA** and **THAI** fly from Karachi. **Balkan** flies from Male. **Royal Nepal Airlines** and **THAI** fly from Kathmandu. It is also possible to fly to Chiang Mai from Kunming (China) and Singapore and to Phuket from Hong Kong, Kuala Lumpur, Penang, Singapore, Taipei and Tokyo. Numerous airlines fly from Hong Kong, Tokyo, Manila, Kuala Lumpur, Singapore and Jakarta to Bangkok. There are daily connections from Singapore and Kuala Lumpur to Hat Yai and from Singapore and Hong Kong to Koh Samui. It is also possible to fly to Phuket from Hong Kong, Kuala Lumpur, Penang, Singapore, Taipei and Tokyo.

There has been a massive proliferation of budget airlines in Southeast Asia with Bangkok becoming one of the primary hubs. There are cheap fares available to/from Laos, Cambodia, Singapore, China, Macau, Maldives, Hong Kong and Malaysia. The pick of the bunch is Air Asia (www.airasia.com) which runs various routes to neighbouring countries. Bangkok has a concentration of tour companies specializing in Indochina and Burma and is a good place to arrange a visa (although most of these countries now issue visas on arrival).

Flights from the Middle East Etihad, flies from Abu Dhabi, **Gulf Air** flies from Bahrain, and **Egyptair** from Cairo.

Suvarnabhumi–city transport

Bus From Suvarnabhumi, an a/c Airport Express bus, T02-134 8030, operates every 15 minutes (0500-2400) and costs a flat fee of ฿150, whether you take the Silom Road service (AE1), Khaosan Road service (AE2), Sukhumvit-Ekkamai service (AE3) or Hualamphong train station service (AE4). Each one stops at between 10 to 12 popular tourist destinations and hotels. The airport offers full details at the stop located outside the Arrivals area on the pavement, and at the Airport Express Counter beside Gate 8. Some of the more popular stops on each line are: **Silom service (AE1)**: Central World Plaza, Lumpini Park, Silom Road, Sofitel Silom, BTS Sala Daeng Station. **Khaosan service (AE2)**: Pratunam, Democracy Monument, Phra Arthit Road, Khao San Road. **Sukhumvit-Ekkamai service (AE3)**: Phra Khanong, Ekkamai Bus Terminal, Sukhumvit Soi 38, 34, 24, 20, 18 and 10. **Hualamphong service (AE4)**: Victory Monument, Soi Rangnam, Asia Hotel Ratchathewi, Siam Discovery, MBK, Hualamphong train station.

Arrival advice

All facilities at Suvarnabhumi Airport are 24 hours so you'll have no problem exchanging money, getting a massage, finding something to eat or taking a taxi or other transport into the city at any time.

Very few buses arrive in Bangkok at night as nearly all long-distance services are timed to arrive in the morning. Bus stations are well served by meter taxis and if you do arrive late jump into one these.

Mo Chit and Ekamai bus stations are also linked to the Skytrain (BTS) which runs from 0600-2400. Mo Chit bus station and Hualamphong train station are linked to the Metro (MBK) which also runs from 0600-2400.

As Bangkok is a relatively safe city it is usually alright to walk around even the most deserted streets at night. However, be sensible, as you would anywhere else and don't display valuables or appear lost. The best bet late at night, if you're unsure where to go, is to flag down one of the capital's ubiquitous taxis.

Note: At all times of day and night airport flunkies are on hand inside the airport to try to direct passengers to the more expensive 'limousine' taxi service; for the public service walk through the exit to the well-signposted and helpful taxi desk.

Many visitors will see the ฿150 as money well spent (although note that, if there are three or more of you, a taxi is considerably cheaper). However, there will still be a hardened few who will opt for the regular Bangkok Mass Transit Authority bus service. These air-conditioned buses linking the airport to the city cost ฿24-35 but are just as slow as they ever were, 1½ to three hours (depending on time of day). The public bus station or 'public transportation centre' is linked to the airport by a free shuttle bus service which picks up passengers at the Arrivals area. Public buses are crowded during rush hours and there is little room for luggage. However, the new bus station is well signposted and organized with some English-speaking information services. Local bus services to Pattaya and Nong Khai are also available.

Courtesy car Many upmarket hotels will meet passengers and provide free transport to town. Check before arrival or contact the Thai Hotels Association desk in the terminal.

Taxi It can take over an hour to get to central Bangkok from either airport, depending on the time of day, the state of the traffic and how insane the driver is. Taking the expressway cuts the journey time significantly and, outside rush-hour, the transit time should be 35-45 minutes.

There are three sets of taxi/limousine services. First, **airport limos** (before exiting from the restricted area), next **airport taxis** (before exiting from the terminal building), and finally, a **public taxi counter** (outside, on the slipway). The latter are the cheapest. Airport flunkies in Suvarnabhumi's Arrival Hall often try to direct passengers to the more expensive 'limousine' service. Unless you fancy entering Bangkok in the back of a BMW 7 series or E-class Benz, and paying ฿1000 or more for the pleasure, ignore them, head down to Level 1 and walk outside to the public taxi desk on the slipway. Tell the booking desk your destination, and you'll be handed a coupon and assigned a taxi driver. Keep hold of the coupon as it details your rights and their obligations.

A public taxi to downtown should cost roughly ฿250-350. Note that tolls on the expressways are paid on top of the fare on the meter and should be no more than ฿45 per toll. There is also a ฿50 airport surcharge on top of the meter cost. If you've picked a hotel in advance, try to print out the map (or, failing that, have the phone number handy) as taxi drivers often do not know where the hotels are, especially the newer or remoter ones.

Suvarnabhumi regulars recommend going up to the Departures floor (Level 4) and flagging down a taxi that has just dropped passengers off. Doing it unofficially like this this will save you around ฿50 and possibly a long wait in a taxi queue. Secure an agreement to use the meter before you get in; many drivers refuse, in which case you'll have to negotiate a fare.

Train
On paper, the 28-km elevated airport rail link is now the cheapest and quickest route into the city. However, bear in mind that even if you're staying centrally, there is still likely to be an inconvenient journey by taxi, tuk-tuk or on foot from the station to your hotel. The Suvarnabhumi Airport City Line picks up commuters at four stations in the eastern suburbs before stopping at the inner city stations of Makkasan, Rajprarop and, finally, Phayathai. The whole journey takes about 30 minutes and costs ฿15-45. The Airport Express route runs from Suvarnabhumi straight through to Makkasan Station, or from Suvarnabhumi straight through to Phayathai, the only stop that intersects with a Skytrain station. It takes 15-17 mins and costs ฿90 one way, ฿150 return. 2 airlines – Thai Airways and Bangkok Airways – currently offer an early check-in and baggage-loading service out of Makkasan Station only; see the website for more, http://airportraillink.railway.co.th.

Don Muang–city transport
The same taxi services and charges apply from Don Muang as from Suvarnabhumi (see above). You can still get the old overground train from Don Muang to either Hualamphong in downtown Bangkok or north to Ayutthaya and beyond. It's cheap but very slow, and trains are often late.

Transport in Bangkok

Bangkok has the unenviable reputation for having some of the worst traffic in the world. However, the recently extended **Skytrain** (an elevated railway), along with the newer and still sparkling **Metro** underground system have made travel a lot easier in those areas of the city that they cover. Plentiful **buses** travel to all city sights and offer the cheapest way to get around; the website of the **Bangkok Mass Transit Authority**, www.bmta.co.th/en, has full listings and a route planner. There is an endless supply of metered **taxis**, which should charge ฿50-100 for a trip within the centre of town. All taxis now have meters, although some drivers develop an aversion to using them, the second a foreigner in shorts approaches. If this happens, either insist they turn the meter on or just get out of the car – most drivers will turn the meter on at this point. Alternatively, just wait for another cab. Bangkok's taxi drivers sometimes refuse to pick up fares at all, particularly if they feel your destination is troublesome. This can be frustrating, but try not to get angry with drivers, as aggression towards foreign passengers is not unknown. **Tuk-tuk** (motorized three-wheeled taxi) numbers are dwindling, and the negotiated fares often work out more expensive than a taxi, particularly as tuk-tuk drivers target tourists and have a deserved reputation for rip-offs and scams. What's more, riding in an open-sided tuk-tuk coats you in Bangkok's notorious smog by the time you arrive. **Walking** can be tough in the heat and fumes, although there are some parts of the city where this can be the best way to get around. For an alternative to the smog of Bangkok's streets, you can hop on board one of the express **river taxis** – more like river buses – which ply the Chao Phraya River (see www.chaophrayaexpressboat.com and box, page 53). Similar services on the city's khlongs (canals) were discontinued years ago, barring one along the putrid Klong Saen Saeb canal, which runs from the Old City's pretty Saphan Phan Fah bridge to the eastern suburbs. If you want to get from modern Bangkok to the Old City, or vice versa, these long-tailed boats are quicker and cheaper than a taxi (but not recommended for those with children). Private ruea hang yao, as they are known in Thai, can also be chartered from many river piers to whisk you along the cleaner khlongs of Thonburi, where glimpses of the fabled 'Venice of the East' survive. ▶ *For further information, see Transport, page 117. For boat tours, see pages 51 and 114.*

Maps and addresses

Traversing the city can be complicated, especially as there is no consistent romanization of Thai road names and no familiar 'block-style' street planning. Roads often lead to dead ends, and numbers can be confusing, with multiple slashes indicating streets and/or buildings off main roads, and street or house numbers that do not necessarily run consecutively. As a guide: main roads are known as *Thanon* (or *Th*) some of which, like Sukhumvit, span the entire city, so landmarks are useful. A *soi* is a street that runs off a main road, so Sukhumvit (Soi) 21 is the name of a smaller street off Sukhumvit Road. They may also have their own names – Sukhumvit 21 is also known as Soi Asoke – but the name is generally written in brackets after the *soi* number. In addresses, house and apartment numbers come first, so 123/1 Soi 1, Th Sukhumvit will be on Sukhumvit 1. If in doubt, ask hotel staff to write addresses out in Thai for taxi drivers.

As a guide to road names, multiple spellings to watch out for include Rachdamri Road (Rajdamri, Ratchadamri, Rachdameri), Phetburi (Phetchaburi), Aree (Ari) and Rama I-VI also known as Phra I-VI. Wireless Road next to Lumpini Park is also known as Thanon Witthayu).

Asia Books (see Shopping, page 102) has a good selection of Bangkok maps and A-Zs. **Periplus Editions** publish a very accurate map of Bangkok called *Bangkok Travel Map*, plus a Bangkok Street Atlas. The *Nancy Chandler Map of Bangkok* is a famous city resource. A lurid hand-drawn map with accompanying mini-guidebook, it crams in plenty of little known and quirky areas of interest, mainly shopping, eating and sightseeing, as well as all the main ones. The sections on Chinatown, the main strip of Sukhumvit and the Weekend Market are particularly detailed. Also recommended is the aptly titled *Groovy Map 'n' Guide Bangkok*, which combines colourful cartography with irreverent tips. If travelling by bus, a bus map of the city is an invaluable aid.

Where to stay in Bangkok

Thailand has a large selection of hotels, including some of the best in the world. Standards outside of the usual tourist areas have improved immensely over recent years and while such places might not be geared to Western tastes they offer some of the best-value accommodation in the country. Due to its popularity with backpackers, Thailand also has many small guesthouses, serving Western food and catering to the foibles of foreigners. These are concentrated in the main tourist areas.

Hotels and guesthouses

Hotels and guesthouses are listed under eight categories, according to the average price of a double/twin room for one night. It should be noted that many hotels will have a range of rooms, some with air conditioning (a/c) and attached bathroom facilities, others with just a fan and shared facilities. Prices can therefore vary a great deal. If a hotel entry lists 'some a/c', then these rooms are likely to be in the upper part of the range, perhaps even in the next range. Few hotels in Thailand provide breakfast in the price of the room. A service charge of 10% and government tax of 7% will usually be added to the bill in the more expensive hotels (categories **$$$$-$$**). Ask whether the quoted price includes tax when checking in. Prices in Bangkok are inflated.

During the off-season, hotels and guesthouses in tourist destinations may halve their room rates so it is always worthwhile bargaining or asking whether there is a special price. Given the fierce competition among hotels, it is even worth trying during the peak season. Over-building has meant that there is a glut of rooms in some towns and hotels are desperate for business.

Until 10 years ago, most guesthouses offered shared facilities with cold-water showers and squat toilets. Levels of cleanliness were also less than pristine. Nowadays, Western toilet imperialism is making inroads into Thai culture and many of the better-run guesthouses will have good, clean toilets with sit-down facilities and, sometimes, hot water. Some are even quite stylish in their bathroom facilities. Fans are the norm in most guesthouses although, again, to cash in on the buying power of backpackers with more disposable income more and more offer air-conditioned rooms as well. Check that mosquito nets are provided.

Security is a problem. Keep valuables with the office for safekeeping (although there are regular cases of people losing valuables that have been left in 'safekeeping') or on your person when you go out. Guesthouses can be tremendous value for money. With limited overheads, family labour and using local foods they can cut their rates in a way that larger hotels with armies of staff, imported food and expensive facilities simply cannot.

Food and drink in Bangkok

Thai food, for long an exotic cuisine distant from the average northerner's mind and tongue, has become an international success story. The Thai government, recognizing the marketing potential of their food, has instituted a plan called 'Global Thai' to boost the profile of Thai food worldwide as a means of attracting more people to visit its country of origin. Thai food has become, in short, one of Thailand's most effective advertisements.

Thai food is an intermingling of Tai, Chinese and, to a lesser extent, Indian cuisines. This helps to explain why restaurants produce dishes that must be some of the (spicy) hottest in the world, as well as others that are rather bland. *Larb* (traditionally raw – but now more

Price codes

Where to stay

$$$$ over US$100	**$$$** US$46-100
$$ US$20-45	**$** under US$20

Prices include taxes and service charge, but not meals. They are based on a double room, except in the **$** range, where prices are almost always per person.

Restaurants

$$$ over US$12	**$$** US$6-12	**$** under US$6

Prices refer to the cost of a two-course meal, not including drinks.

---

frequently cooked – chopped beef mixed with rice, herbs and spices) is a traditional 'Tai' dish; *pla priaw waan* (whole fish with soy and ginger) is Chinese in origin; while *gaeng mussaman* (beef 'Muslim' curry) was brought to Thailand by Muslim immigrants. Even satay, paraded by most restaurants as a Thai dish, was introduced from Malaysia and Indonesia (which themselves adopted it from Arab traders during the Middle Ages).

Despite these various influences, Thai cooking is distinctive. Thais have managed to combine the best of each tradition, adapting elements to fit their own preferences. Remarkably, considering how ubiquitous it is in Thai cooking, the chilli pepper is a New World fruit and was not introduced into Thailand until the late 16th century (along with the pineapple and the papaya).

A Thai meal is based around rice, and many wealthy Bangkokians own farms upcountry where they cultivate their favourite variety. When a Thai asks another Thai whether he has eaten he will ask, literally, whether he has 'eaten rice' (*kin khao*). Similarly, the accompanying dishes are referred to as food 'with the rice'. There are two main types of rice – 'sticky' or glutinous (*khao niaw*) and non-glutinous (*khao jao*). Sticky rice is usually used to make sweets (desserts) although it is the staple in the northeastern region and parts of the north. *Khao jao* is standard white rice.

In addition to rice, a meal usually consists of a soup like *tom yam kung* (prawn soup), *kaeng* (a curry) and *krueng kieng* (a number of side dishes). Thai food is spicy, and aromatic herbs and grasses (like lemongrass, coriander, tamarind and ginger) are used to give a distinctive flavour. *Nam pla* (fish sauce made from fermented fish and used as a condiment) and *nam prik* (*nam pla*, chillies, garlic, sugar, shrimps and lime juice) are two condiments that are taken with almost all meals. *Nam pla* is made from steeping fish, usually anchovies, in brine for long periods and then bottling the peatish-coloured liquor produced. Chillies deserve a special mention because most Thais like their food HOT! Some chillies are fairly mild; others – like the tiny, red *prik khii nuu* ('mouse shit pepper') – are fiendishly hot.

Isaan food – from the northeast of Thailand – is also distinctive, very similar to Lao cuisine and very popular. Most of the labourers and service staff come from Isaan, particularly in Bangkok, and you won't have to go far to find a rickety street stall selling sticky rice, aromatic *kai yang* (grilled chicken) and fiery *som tam* (papaya salad). *Pla ra* (fermented fish) is one of Isaan's most famous dishes but is usually found only in the most authentic Isaan dishes, its salty, pungent flavour being too much for effete Bangkokians.

Due to Thailand's large Chinese population (or at least Thais with Chinese roots), there are also many Chinese-style restaurants whose cuisine is variously 'Thai-ified'. Many of the snacks available on the streets show this mixture of Thai and Chinese, not to mention Arab and Malay. *Bah jang*, for example, are small pyramids of leaves stuffed with sticky rice, Chinese sausage, salted eggs, pork and dried shrimp. They were reputedly first created for the Chinese dragon boat festival but are now available 12 months a year – for around ฿20.

To sample Thai food it is best to go in a group to a restaurant and order a range of dishes. To eat alone is regarded as slightly strange. However, there are a number of 'one-dish' meals like fried rice and *phat thai* (fried noodles) and restaurants will also usually provide *raat khao* ('over rice'), which is a dish like a curry served on a bed of rice for a single person.

Strict non-fish-eating **vegetarians** and **vegans** are in for a tough time. Nearly every cooked meal you will eat in Thailand will be liberally doused in *nam pla* or cooked with shrimp paste. At more expensive and upmarket international restaurants you'll probably be able to find something suitable – in the rural areas, you'll be eating fruit, fried eggs and rice, though not all at once. There are a network of Taoist restaurants offering more strict veggie fare throughout the country – look out for yellow flags with red Chinese lettering. Also asking for 'mai sai nam pla' (no *nam pla* please)– when ordering what should be veggie food might keep the fish sauce out of harm's reach.

Restaurants

It is possible to get a tasty and nutritious meal almost anywhere – and at any time – in Thailand. Thais eat out a great deal so that most towns have a range of places. Starting at the top, in pecuniary terms at any rate, the more sophisticated restaurants are usually air-conditioned, and sometimes attached to a hotel. In places like Bangkok and Chiang Mai they may be Western in style and atmosphere. In towns less frequented by foreigners they are likely to be rather more functional – although the food will be just as good. In addition to these more upmarket restaurants are a whole range of places from **noodle shops** to **curry houses** and **seafood restaurants**. Many small restaurants have no menus. But often the speciality of the house will be clear – roasted, honeyed ducks hanging in the window, crab and fish laid out on crushed ice outside. Away from the main tourist spots, 'Western' breakfasts are commonly unavailable, so be prepared to eat Thai-style (noodle or rice soup or fried rice). Yet, the quality of much Thai food can be mixed, with many Thai restaurants and street stalls using huge amounts of sugar, MSG and oil in their cooking.

Towards the bottom of the scale are **stalls and food carts**. These tend to congregate at particular places in town – often in the evening, from dusk – although they can be found just about anywhere: outside the local provincial offices, along a cul-de-sac, or under a conveniently placed shady tree. Stall holders will tend to specialize in either noodles, rice dishes, fruit drinks, sweets and so on. Hot meals are usually prepared to order. While stall food may be cheap – a meal costs only around ฿15-20 – they are frequented by people from all walks of life. A well-heeled businessman in a suit is just as likely to be seen bent over a bowl of noodles at a rickety table on a busy street corner as a construction worker.

A popular innovation over the last 10 years or so has been the *suan a-haan* or **garden restaurant**. These are often on the edge of towns, with tables set in gardens, sometimes with bamboo furniture and ponds. Another type of restaurant worth a mention is the **Thai-style coffee shop**. These are sometimes attached to hotels in provincial towns and feature hostesses dressed in Imelda-esque or skimpy spangly costumes. The hostesses, when they are not crooning to the house band, sit with customers, laugh at their jokes and assiduously make sure that their glasses are always full.

In the north, *khantoke* dining is de rigueur – or so one might imagine from the number of restaurants offering it. It is a northern Thai tradition, when people sit on the floor to eat at low tables, often to the accompaniment of traditional music and dance.

Tourist centres also provide good European, American and Japanese food at reasonable prices. Bangkok boasts some superb restaurants. Less expensive Western **fast-food** restaurants can also be found, including **McDonald's** and **Kentucky Fried Chicken**.

The etiquette of eating

The Thai philosophy on eating is 'often', and most Thais will snack their way through the day. Eating is a relaxed, communal affair and it is not necessary to get too worked up about etiquette. Dishes are placed in the middle of the table where diners can help themselves. In a restaurant rice is usually spooned out by a waiter or waitress – and it is considered good manners to start a meal with a spoon of rice. While food is eaten with a spoon and fork, the fork is only used to manoeuvre food onto the spoon. Because most food is prepared in bite-sized pieces it is not usually necessary to use a knife. At noodle stalls chopsticks and china soup spoons are used while in the northeast most people – at least at home – use their fingers. Sticky rice is compressed into a ball using the ends of the fingers and then dipped in the other dishes. Thais will not pile their plates with food but take several small portions from the dishes arranged on a table. It is also considered good manners when invited out to leave some food on your plate, as well as on the serving dishes on the table. This demonstrates the generosity of the host.

Drink

Water in nearly every single restaurant and street stall now comes from large bottles of purified water but if you're unsure, buy your own.

Coffee is consumed throughout Thailand. In stalls and restaurants, coffee comes with a glass of Chinese tea. Soft drinks are widely available too. Many roadside stalls prepare fresh fruit juices in liquidizers while hotels produce all the usual cocktails.

Major brands of **spirits** are served in most hotels and bars, although not always off the tourist path. The most popular spirit among Thais is Mekhong – local cane whisky – which can be drunk straight or with mixers such as Coca-Cola. However, due to its hangover-inducing properties, more sophisticated Thais prefer Johnny Walker or an equivalent brand.

Beer drinking is spreading fast. The most popular local beer is Singha beer brewed by Boon Rawd. Singha, Chang and Heineken are the three most popular beers in Thailand. Leo and Cheers are agreeable budget options although they are seldom sold in restaurants. Beer is relatively expensive in Thai terms as it is heavily taxed by the government. It is a high status drink, so the burgeoning middle class, especially the young, are turning to beer in preference to traditional, local whiskies – which explains why brewers are so keen to set up shop in this traditionally non-beer drinking country. Some pubs and bars also sell beer on tap – which is known as *bier sot*, 'fresh' beer.

Thais are fast developing a penchant for **wine**. Imported wines are expensive by international standards but Thailand now has six wineries, mainly in the northeastern region around Nakhon Ratchasima. For tours around the wine regions (including to a vineyard where the workers use elephants) contact Laurence Civil (laurence@csloxinfo.com).

Entertainment in Bangkok

Bars and clubs

Thais are great clubbers and partygoers, although provincial nightclubs and coffee shops might not be to everyone's tastes. Karaoke is also very popular across the country. Unsurprisingly, the most sophisticated nightlife is to be found in the largest towns and in tourist centres. Jazz and blues, nightclubs, rock, discos, wine bars, gay and lesbian bars, cabaret, straight bars, beer gardens and more are all available. The ousted prime minister, Thaksin, brought in laws to close down most bars and clubs by midnight though special licences are granted for later hours. Nightclubs tend to close between 0200 and 0300 while opening hours are more variable, anywhere from 1800 to 2200. Bars tend to open and close earlier than nightclubs; happy hours are usually between 1700 and 1900. For the latest offerings, including music, dance and theatre check out the many free newspapers and magazines available in the country's tourist centres.

If you want a taste of tradition, then visit one of the upcountry coffee shops. Some of these are innocuous places where men gather to drink strong coffee, accompanied by Chinese tea, and chat about the price of rice and the latest political scandal. Others are really nightclubs where men drink prodigious quantities of whisky while accompanied by girls dressed in a weird assortment of dresses from figure-hugging little black numbers to Marie Antoinette extravagances. They also take it in turns to croon popular Thai ballads and rock songs to bad backing bands. Upstairs is, commonly, a brothel.

Cinema

In Bangkok, a range of cinemas show films either with an English soundtrack or English subtitles (listed in the *Bangkok Post* and *The Nation*). Up-country cinemas will often have a separate glass enclosed section where it is possible to listen to the English soundtrack of dubbed films. Generally films are screened at 1200, 1400, 1700, 1900, 2100, and at 1000 on Saturday and Sunday. In Bangkok, cultural centres such as the Alliance Française and the Goethe Institute show European films. It is also possible to rent videos in some towns. In the main tourist centres, bars and restaurants will often screen videos or DVDs on large-screen televisions, the night's offerings advertised in advance.

Shopping in Bangkok → *For VAT refunds, see Customs and duty free, page 20.*

Bangkok and Chiang Mai are the shopping 'centres' of Thailand. Many people now prefer Chiang Mai, as the shops are concentrated in a smaller area and there is a good range of quality products, especially handicrafts. Bangkok still offers the greatest variety and choice but it is difficult to find bargains any longer; the department stores and shopping malls contain high-price, high-quality merchandise (at a fixed price), much of which is imported.

Between shopkeepers competition is fierce. Do not be cajoled into buying something before having a chance to price it elsewhere – Thais can be very persuasive. Also, watch out for guarantees of authenticity – fake antiques abound, and even professionals find it difficult to know a 1990 Khmer sculpture from a 10th-century one.

Thailand has had a reputation as being a mecca for pirated goods: CDs and DVDs, Lacoste shirts, Gucci leather goods, Rolex watches, computer software and so on. These items are still available, but pressure from the US to protect intellectual copyright is leading to more enthusiastic crackdowns by the police. In Bangkok, genuine CDs can be bought at what are still bargain prices compared with the West; buying pirated DVDs often requires a retreat to some back room. Strangely though, most DVD sellers are quite honest and if your fake doesn't work they will replace it. When buying DVDs ask for 'master' copies – this way you should avoid purchasing a film shot from the back of a cinema.

The widest selection of **Thai silk** is available in Bangkok although cheaper silk, as well as good quality cotton, can be found in the northeast (the traditional centre of silk weaving). **Tailor-made clothing** is available although designs are sometimes outdated; it might be better for the tailor to copy an article of your own clothing. However, times are changing and there are now some top designers in Bangkok. **Leather goods** include custom-made crocodile skin shoes and boots (for those who aren't squeamish).

Bangkok is also a good place to buy **jewellery** – gold, sapphires and rubies – as well as **antiques**, **bronzeware** and **celadon**. (See Tricksters, below, and Safety page 27.) **Handicrafts** are best purchased up-country.

Bargaining

Bargaining is common, except in the large department stores (although they may give a discount on expensive items of jewellery or furniture) and on items like soap, books and most necessities. Expect to pay anything from 25-75% less than the asking price, depending on the bargainer's skill and the shopkeeper's mood.

Tricksters

Tricksters, rip-off artists, fraudsters, less than honest salesmen – call them what you will – are likely to be far more of a problem than simple theft. People may well approach you in the street offering incredible one-off bargains, and giving what might seem to be very plausible reasons for your sudden good fortune. Be wary in all such cases and do not be pressed into making a hasty decision. Unfortunately, more often than not, the salesman is trying to pull a fast one. Favourite 'bargains' are precious stones, whose authenticity is 'demonstrated' before your very eyes (see box, page 107). Although many Thais genuinely do like to talk to *farangs* and practise their English, in tourist areas there are also those who offer their friendship for pecuniary rather than linguistic reasons. Sad as it is to say, it is probably a good idea to be suspicious. For up-to-date information, visit www.bangkokscams.com.

Local customs and laws in Bangkok

Thais are generally very understanding of the foibles and habits of farangs (foreigners) and will forgive and forget most indiscretions. However, there are a number of 'dos and don'ts' that are worth observing.

Clothing In towns and at religious sights, it is courteous to avoid wearing shorts and sleeveless tops. Visitors who are inappropriately dressed may not be allowed into wats (temples); make sure your shoulders and knees are covered up and avoid wearing flip-flops. The same is true of mosques (in the Muslim-dominated far south). In the most expensive restaurants in Bangkok diners may well be expected to wear a jacket and tie. This does not apply on beaches and islands where (almost) anything goes and sarongs, flip-flops, etc are de rigueur. However, topless sunbathing or nudity is still very much frowned upon by Thais, especially in Muslim areas in the south. Most Thais always look neat and clean; *mai rieb-roi* means 'not neat' and is considered a great insult. Dirty, unkempt Westerns are sometimes given the pejorative, and decidedly racist, name of *kee nok farang* – or 'bird shit Westerners'.

Cool and hot hearts Among Thais, the personal characteristic of *jai yen* is very highly regarded; literally, this means to have a 'cool heart'. It embodies calmness, having an even temper and not displaying emotion. Although foreigners generally receive special dispensation, and are not expected to conform to Thai customs (all *farang* are thought to have *jai rawn* or 'hot hearts'), it is important to keep calm in any disagreement – losing one's temper leads to loss of face and loss of respect. An associated personal trait which Thais try to develop is *kreng jai*; this embodies being understanding of other people's needs, desires and feelings – in short, not imposing oneself.

Greeting people Traditionally, Thais greet one another with a *wai* – the equivalent of a handshake. In a *wai*, hands are held together as if in prayer, and the higher the *wai*, the more respectful the greeting. By watching Thai's *wai* it is possible to ascertain their relative seniority where a combination of class, age, wealth, power and gender all play a part. Juniors or inferiors should initiate a *wai*, and hold it higher and for longer than the senior or superior. Foreigners are not expected to conform to this custom – a simple *wai* at chest to chin height is all that is required. You should not *wai* to children or to waiters, waitresses and other people offering a service. When farangs and Thais do business it is common to shake hands. The respectful term of address is *khun*, which applies to both men and women. This is usually paired with a Thai's first name so that, for example, Somchai Bamruang would be greeted as Khun Somchai. The closest equivalent to the English Mr and Mrs/Miss are *Nai* and *Nang*, which are also used as formal terms of address. Thais also have nicknames like *Kai* (chicken), *Ooy* (sugar) or *Kung* (shrimp) while people from certain professions will also have respectful titles – like *ajaan* for a teacher or lecturer.

Heads and feet Try to not openly point your feet at anyone – feet are viewed as spiritually the lowest part of the body. At the same time, never touch anyone's (even a child's) head, which is the holiest as well as the highest part. Resting your feet on a table would be regarded as highly disrespectful while stepping over someone sitting on the floor is also frowned upon. If sitting on the floor, try to tuck your feet under your body – although Westerners unused to this posture may find it uncomfortable after a short time.

The monarchy Never criticize any member of the royal family or the institution itself. The monarchy is held in very high esteem and *lese-majesty* remains an offence carrying a sentence of up to 15 years in prison. More recently, the Abhisit-led Democrat Party government used the lese-majesty law to imprison a number of dissidents. You should treat coins and bank notes with respect as they bear the image of the king, as well as postage stamps, which are moistened with a sponge rather than the tongue. In cinemas, the national anthem is played before the show and the audience is expected to stand. At other events, take your lead from the crowd as to how to behave. A dying custom, but one which is still adhered to in smaller towns as well as certain parts of Bangkok, like Hualamphong railway station, is that everybody stops in their tracks at 0800 and 1800, when the national anthem is relayed over loudspeakers.

Monastery (wat) and monk etiquette Remove shoes on entering any monastery building, do not climb over Buddha images or have your picture taken in front of one, and when sitting in a *bot* or *viharn* ensure that your feet are not pointing towards a Buddha image. Wear modest clothing – women should not expose their shoulders or wear dresses that are too short (see Clothing, above). Ideally, they should be calf length although knee-length dresses or skirts are usually acceptable. Women should never touch a monk, hand anything directly to a monk or venture into the monks' quarters. They should also avoid climbing *chedis* (stupas). As in any other place of worship, visitors should not disturb the peace of a wat.

Open shows of affection Visitors will notice that men and women rarely show open, public signs of affection. It is not uncommon, however, to see men holding hands – this is usually a sign of simple friendship, nothing more. That said, in Bangkok, traditional customs have broken down and in areas such as Siam Square it is common to see young lovers, hand-in-hand.

Sanuk A quality of *sanuk*, which can be roughly translated as 'fun' or *joie de vivre*, is important to Thais. Activities are undertaken because they are *sanuk*, others avoided because they are *mai sanuk* ('not fun'). Perhaps it is because of this apparent love of life that so many visitors returning from Thailand remark on how Thais always appear happy and smiling. However, it is worth bearing in mind that the interplay of *jai yen* and *kreng jai* means that everything may not be quite as it appears.

Smoking This is now illegal in all air-conditioned areas. Fines are heavy, although not always enforced. Bangkok police regularly fine people up to ฿3000 for discarding cigarette butts anywhere other than in official ashtrays.

Essentials A-Z

Accident and emergency

Emergency services Police: T191, T123. **Tourist police:** T1155. **Fire:** T199. **Ambulance:** T02-2551134-6. **Tourist Assistance Centre:** Rachdamnern Nok Av, Bangkok, T02-356 0655.

Calling one of the emergency numbers will not usually be very productive as few operators speak English. It is better to call the tourist police or have a hotel employee or other English-speaking Thai telephone for you. For more intractable problems contact your embassy or consulate.

Children

Many people are daunted by the prospect of taking a child to Southeast Asia and there are disadvantages: travelling is slower and more expensive and there are additional health risks for the child or baby. But it can be a most rewarding experience and, with sufficient care and planning, it can also be safe. Children are excellent passports into a local culture. Thais love kids so are more than willing to accommodate, look after, feed, tolerate and adore your children. You will also receive the best service and help from officials and members of the public when in difficulty. A non-Asian child is still something of a novelty, especially in more remote areas, and parents may find their child frequently taken off their hands.

Disposable nappies can be bought in Thailand but remember that you're adding to the rubbish-disposal problem. Many Western baby products are available in Thailand: shampoo, talcum powder, soap and lotion. Baby wipes are expensive and not always easy to find. Other things worth packing are child paracetamol; first-aid kit; decongestant for colds; instant food for under one year olds; ORS (Oral Rehydration Salts) such as Dioralyte, widely available in Thailand, and the most effective way to alleviate diarrhoea (it is not a cure); sarong or backpack for carrying child (and/or lightweight collapsible buggy); sterilizing tablets (and container for sterilizing bottles, teats, utensils); cream for nappy rash and other skin complaints, such as Sudocrem; sunblock, factor 15 or higher; sun hat; thermometer; zip-lock bags for snacks, etc.

Eating

Be aware that even expensive hotels may have squalid cooking conditions; the cheapest street stall is often more hygienic. Where possible, try to watch food being prepared. Stir-fried vegetables and rice or noodles are the best bet; meat and fish may be pre-cooked and then left out before being re-heated. Fruit can be bought cheaply – papaya, banana and avocado are all excellent sources of nutrition. Western-style baby foods and products are widely available in good supermarkets. Powdered milk is also available throughout the region, although most brands have added sugar. If taking a baby, breast-feeding is strongly recommended. Powdered food, bottled water and fizzy drinks are also sold widely.

Health

More preparation is probably necessary for babies and children than for an adult, and particularly when travelling to remote areas where health services are primitive. A travel insurance policy which has an air ambulance provision is strongly recommended. When planning a route, try to stay within 24 hrs' travel of a hospital with good care and facilities. For advice about common problems, see Health, page 21. **Note** Never allow your child to be exposed to the harsh tropical sun without protection. A child can burn in minutes. Loose cotton clothing with long sleeves and legs and a sunhat are best. High-factor sun-protection cream is essential.

Vaccinations Children should already be properly protected against diphtheria, poliomyelitis and pertussis (whooping cough), measles and HIB, all of which can be more serious infections in Southeast Asia than at home. The measles, mumps and rubella vaccine is also given to children throughout the world, but those teenage girls who have not had rubella (German measles) should be tested and vaccinated. Hepatitis B vaccination for babies is now routine in some countries. See also Health, page 21.

Sleeping

At the hottest time of year, air conditioning may be essential for a baby or young child's comfort. This rules out many of the cheaper hotels, but air-conditioned accommodation is available in all but the most out-of-the-way spots. When the child is bathing, be aware that the water could carry parasites, so avoid letting him or her drink it.

Transport

Public transport may be a problem; trains are fine, but long bus journeys are restrictive and uncomfortable. Hiring a car is undoubtedly the most convenient way to see a country with a small child. It is possible to buy child-seats in larger cities.

Customs and duty free
Customs

Non-residents can bring in unlimited foreign and Thai currency although amounts exceeding US$10,000 must be declared. Maximum amount permitted to take out of Thailand is ฿50,000 per person.

Prohibited items

All narcotics; obscene literature, pornography; firearms (except with a permit from the Police Department or local registration office); and some species of plants and animals (for more information contact the **Royal Forestry Department**, Phahonyothin Rd, Bangkok, T02-561 0777).

Duty free

500 g of cigars/cigarettes (or 200 cigarettes) and one litre of wine or spirits.

Export restrictions

No Buddha or Bodhisattva images or fragments should be taken out of Thailand, except for worshipping by Buddhists, for cultural exchanges or for research. However, it is obvious that many people do – you only have to look in the antique shops to see the abundance for sale. A licence should be obtained from the **Department of Fine Arts**, Na Prathat Rd, Bangkok, T02-224 1370, from **Chiang Mai National Museum**, T02-221308, or from the **Songkhla National Museum**, Songkhla, T02-311728. 5-days' notice is needed; take 2 passport photos of the object and photocopies of your passport.

VAT refunds

Most of the major department stores have a VAT refund desk. Go to them on your day of purchase with receipts and ask them to complete VAT refund form, which you then present, with purchased goods, at appropriate desk in any international airport in Thailand. They'll give you another form that you exchange for cash in the departure lounge. You'll need to spend at least ฿4000 to qualify for a refund.

Disabled travellers

Disabled travellers will find Thailand a challenge. The difficulties that even the able bodied encounter in crossing roads when pedestrian crossings are either non-existent or ignored by most motorists are amplified for the disabled. Cracked pavements, high curbs and lack of ramps add to the problems for even the most wheelchair savvy. Buses and taxis are not designed for disabled access either and there are relatively few hotels and restaurants that are wheelchair-friendly. This is particularly true of cheaper and older establishments. This is not to suggest that travel in Thailand is impossible for the disabled. On the plus side, you will find Thais to be extremely helpful and because taxis and tuk-tuks are cheap it is usually not necessary to rely on buses. The **Global Access – Disabled Travel Network** website, www.globalaccess news. com, is useful. Another informative site, with lots of advice on how to travel with specific disabilities, plus listings and links, belongs to the **Society for Accessible Travel and Hospitality**, www.sath.org. Another site, www.access-able.com has a specific section for travel in Thailand.

Electricity
Voltage is 220 volts (50 cycles). Most first- and tourist-class hotels have outlets for shavers and hairdryers. Adaptors are recommended, as almost all sockets are 2-pronged.

Embassies and consulates
Thai embassies worldwide
www.thaiembassy.org is a useful resource.

Gay and lesbian travellers
On the surface, Thailand is incredibly tolerant of homosexuals and lesbians. In Bangkok and other major cities there's an openness that can make even San Francisco look tame. It is for this reason that Thailand's gay scene has flourished and, more particularly, has grown in line with international tourism. However, overt public displays of affection are still frowned upon (see Local customs and laws, page 18). Attitudes in the more traditional rural areas, particularly the Muslim regions, are far more conservative than in the cities. By exercising a degree of cultural sensitivity any visit should be hassle free.

Several of the free tourist magazines distributed through hotels and restaurants in Bangkok, Pattaya, Phuket and Koh Samui

provide information on the gay and lesbian scene, including bars and meeting points. The essential website before you get there is **www.utopia-asia.com** which provides good material on where to go, current events, and background information on the Thai gay scene in Bangkok and beyond. **Utopia tours** at Tarntawan Palace Hotel, 119/5-10 Suriwong Rd, T02-634 0273, www.utopia-tours.com, provides tours for gay and lesbian visitors. There's also a map of gay Bangkok. Gay clubs are listed in *Bangkok Metro* magazine (www.bkkmetro. co.th) and include **DJ Station** (by far the most famous Bangkok gay club) and its sister club **Freeman Dance Arena**, 60/18-21 Silom Rd, www.dj-station.com. The main centres of activity in Bangkok are Silom Rd sois 2 and 4 and Sukhumvit Soi 23. There is also a thriving gay scene in Pattaya and, to a lesser extent, on Phuket, Koh Samui and in Chiang Mai. See also the Thai section of **www.fridae.com**, one of Asia's most comprehensive gay sites.

Health
Hospitals/medical services are listed in the Directory sections of each chapter.

Staying healthy in Thailand is straightforward. With the following advice and precautions you should keep as healthy as you do at home. Most visitors return home having experienced no problems at all beyond an upset stomach. However, in Thailand the health risks, especially in the tropical areas, are different from those encountered in Europe or the USA. It also depends on how you travel and where. The country has a mainly tropical climate; nevertheless the acquisition of true tropical disease by the visitor is probably conditioned as much by the rural nature and standard of hygiene of the surroundings than by the climate. Malaria is common in certain areas, particularly in the jungle. There is an obvious difference in health risks between the business traveller who tends to stay in international class hotels in the large cities and the backpacker trekking through the rural areas. There are no hard and fast rules to follow; you will often have to make your own judgement on the healthiness or otherwise of your surroundings. Check with your doctor on the status of Avian flu before you go. At the time of writing, Thailand was clear of bird flu.

Before you go
Ideally, you should see your GP/practice nurse or travel clinic at least 6 weeks before your departure for general advice on travel risks, malaria and recommended vaccinations. Your local pharmacist can also be a good source of readily accessible advice. Make sure you have travel insurance, get a dental check (especially if you are going to be away for more than a month), know your own blood group and if you suffer a long-term condition such as diabetes or epilepsy make sure someone knows or that you have a **Medic Alert** bracelet/necklace with this information on it.

Recommended vaccinations No vaccinations are specifically required for Thailand unless coming from an infected area, but tuberculosis, rabies, Japanese B encephalitis and hepatitis B are commonly recommended. The final decision, however, should be based on a consultation with your GP or travel clinic. You should also confirm that your primary courses and boosters are up to date (diphtheria, tetanus, poliomyelitis, hepatitis A, typhoid).

A yellow fever certificate is required by visitors who have been in an infected area in the 10 days before arrival. Those without a vaccination certificate will be vaccinated and kept in quarantine for 6 days, or deported.

A-Z of health risks
Dengue fever This is a viral disease spread by mosquitoes that tend to bite during the day. The symptoms are fever and often intense joint pains, also some people develop a rash. Symptoms last about a week but it can take a few weeks to recover fully. Dengue can be difficult to distinguish from malaria as both diseases tend to occur in the same places. There are no effective vaccines or antiviral drugs though, fortunately, travellers rarely develop the more severe form of the disease (which can prove fatal). Rest, plenty of fluids and paracetamol (not aspirin) is the recommended treatment. **Note** The number of cases in Thailand has risen in the last year, consult your GP for further advice.

Diarrhoea and intestinal upset
Diarrhoea can refer either to loose stools or an increased frequency of bowel movement, both of which can be a nuisance. Symptoms should be relatively short-lived but if they persist beyond 2 weeks specialist medical attention should be sought. Also seek medical help if there is blood in the stools and/or fever.

Adults can use an anti-diarrhoeal medication such as loperamide to control the symptoms but only for up to 24 hrs. In addition keep well hydrated by drinking plenty of fluids and eat bland foods. Oral rehydration sachets taken after each loose stool are a useful way to keep hydrated. These should always be used when treating children and the elderly.

Bacterial traveller's diarrhoea is the most common form. Ciproxin (Ciprofloxacin) is a useful antibiotic and can be obtained by private prescription in the UK. You need to take one 500 mg tablet when the diarrhoea starts. If there are so signs of improvement after 24 hrs the diarrhoea is likely to be viral and not bacterial. If it is due to other organisms such as those causing giardia or amoebic dysentery, different antibiotics will be required.

The standard advice to prevent problems is be careful with water and ice for drinking. Ask yourself where the water came from. If you have any doubts then boil it or filter and treat it. There are many filter/treatment devices now available on the market. Food can also transmit disease. Be wary of salads (what were they washed in, who handled them), re-heated foods or food that has been left out in the sun having been cooked earlier in the day. There is a simple adage: wash it, peel it, boil it or forget it. Also be wary of unpasteurized dairy products as these can transmit a range of diseases.

Hepatitis Hepatitis means inflammation of the liver. Viral causes of the disease can be acquired anywhere in the world. The most obvious symptom is a yellowing of your skin or the whites of your eyes. However, prior to this all that you may notice is itching and tiredness. Pre-travel hepatitis A vaccine is the best bet. Hepatitis B (for which there is a vaccine) is spread through blood and unprotected sexual intercourse, both of which can be avoided.

Malaria Malaria can cause death within 24 hrs and can start as something just resembling an attack of flu. You may feel tired, lethargic, headachy, feverish; more seriously you may develop fits, followed by coma and then death. Have a low index of suspicion because it is very easy to write off vague symptoms, which may actually be malaria. If you have a temperature, visit a doctor as soon as you can and ask for a malaria test. On your return home, if you suffer any of these symptoms, have a test as soon as possible. Even if a previous test proved negative, this could save your life.

Treatment is with drugs and may be oral or into a vein depending on the seriousness of the infection. Remember ABCD: Awareness (of whether the disease is present in the area you are travelling in); Bite avoidance, Chemoprohylaxis; Diagnosis.

To prevent mosquito bites wear clothes that cover arms and legs, use effective insect repellents in areas with known risks of insect-spread disease and use a mosquito net treated with an insecticide. Repellents containing 30-50% DEET (Di-ethyltoluamide) are recommended when visiting malaria-endemic areas; lemon eucalyptus (Mosiguard) is a reasonable alternative. The key advice is to guard against contracting malaria by taking the correct anti-malarials and finishing the recommended course. If you are a popular target for insect bites or develop lumps quite soon after being bitten use antihistamine tablets and apply a cream such as hydrocortisone.

Remember that it is risky to buy medicine, and in particular anti-malarials, in some developing countries. These may be sub-standard or part of a trade in counterfeit drugs.

Rabies Rabies is prevalent in Thailand so be aware of the dangers of the bite from any animal. Rabies vaccination before travel can be considered but if bitten always seek urgent medical attention – whether or not you have been previously vaccinated – after first cleaning the wound and treating with an iodine-base disinfectant or alcohol.

Sun Take good heed of advice regarding protecting yourself against the sun. Overexposure can lead to sunburn and, in the longer term, skin cancers and premature skin aging. The best advice is simply to avoid exposure to the sun by covering exposed skin, wearing a hat and staying out of the sun if possible, particularly between late morning and early afternoon. Apply a high-factor sunscreen (at least SPF15) and also make sure it screens against UVB. A further danger in tropical climates is heat exhaustion or more seriously heatstroke. This can be avoided by good hydration, which means drinking water past the point of simply quenching thirst. Also when first exposed to tropical heat take time to acclimatize by avoiding strenuous activity in the middle of the day.

If you cannot avoid heavy exercise it is also a good idea to increase salt intake.

Water There are a number of ways of purifying water. Dirty water should first be strained through a filter bag and then boiled or treated. Bring water to a rolling boil for several minutes. There are sterilizing methods that can be used and products generally contain chlorine (eg Puritabs) or iodine (eg Pota Aqua) compounds. There are a number of water sterilizers now on the market available in personal and expedition size. Make sure you take the spare parts or spare chemicals with you and do not believe everything the manufacturers say.

Other diseases and risks There are a range of other insect-borne diseases that are quite rare in travellers, but worth finding out about if going to particular destinations. Examples are sleeping sickness, river blindness and leishmaniasis. Fresh water can also be a source of diseases such as bilharzia and leptospirosis and it is worth investigating if these are a danger before bathing in lakes and streams. Also remember that unprotected sex always carries a risk and extra care is required when visiting some parts of the world.

Useful websites
www.nathnac.org National Travel Health Network and Centre.
www.who.int World Health Organization.
www.fitfortravel.scot.nhs.uk Fit for Travel. This site from Scotland provides a quick A-Z of vaccine and travel health advice requirements for each country.

Books
Dawood R, editor. *Travellers' health* (3rd edition, Oxford University Press, 2002). *Expedition Medicine* (The Royal Geographic Society) Editors David Warrell and Sarah Anderson ISBN 1 86197 040-4.

Internet
Apart from a few remote islands Thailand has an excellent internet network. Tourist areas tend to be well catered for with numerous internet shops offering a connection for between ฿30-90 per hr. Some guesthouses and hotels have free wireless while the more expensive ones charge extortionate rates of up ฿1000 per day. You might also be able to pick up wireless for free from office blocks, etc. The cheapest internet options tend to be the small games rooms run primarily for Thai kids who eagerly play online games, usually ฿10-20 per hr, or by using your web-enabled mobile phone with a local simcard – see Mobiles, page 29.

Insurance
Always take out travel insurance before you set off and read the small print carefully. Check that the policy covers any activities that you may end up doing. Also check exactly what your medical cover includes, ie ambulance, helicopter rescue or emergency flights back home. And check the payment protocol; you may have to cough up first (literally) before the insurance company reimburses you. It is always best to dig out all the receipts for expensive personal effects like jewellery or cameras. Take photos of these items and note down all serial numbers. You are advised to shop around. **STA Travel** and other reputable student travel organizations offer good-value policies. Young travellers from North America can try the **International Student Insurance Service** (ISIS), which is available through STA Travel, T1-800-7814040, www.sta-travel.com. Other recommended travel insurance companies in North America include: Travel Guard, T1-800-8261300, www.noelgroup.com; **Access America**, T1-800-2848300; **Travel Insurance Services**, T1-800-9371387; and **Travel Assistance International**, T1-800-821 2828. Older

travellers should note that some companies will not cover people over 65 years old, or may charge higher premiums. The best policies for older travellers (UK) are offered by **Age Concern**, T0845-601 2234.

Language

English is reasonably widely spoken and is taught to all school children. Off the tourist trail, making yourself understood becomes more difficult. It is handy to buy a Thai/English road atlas of the country (most petrol stations sell them) – you can then point to destinations.

The Thai language is tonal and, strictly speaking, monosyllabic. There are 5 tones: high, low, rising, falling and mid-tone. These are used to distinguish between words which would otherwise be identical. For example: *mai* (low tone, new), *mai* (rising, silk), *mai* (mid-tone, burn), *mai* (high tone, question indicator), and *mai* (falling tone, negative indicator). Not surprisingly, many visitors find it hard to hear the different tones, and it is difficult to make much progress during a short visit. The tonal nature of the language also explains why so much of Thai humour is based around homonyms – and especially when *farangs* (foreigners) say what they do not mean. Although tones make Thai a challenge for foreign visitors, other aspects of the language are easier to grasp: there are no marked plurals in nouns, no marked tenses in verbs, no definite or indefinite articles, and no affixes or suffixes.

Visitors may well experience 2 oddities of the Thai language being reflected in the way that Thais speak English. An 'l' or 'r' at the end of a word in Thai becomes an 'n', while an 's' becomes a 't'. So some Thais refer to the 'Shell' Oil Company as 'Shen', a name 'Les' becomes 'Let', while 'cheque bill' becomes 'cheque bin'. It is also impossible to have 2 consonants after one another in Thai. If it occurs, a Thai will automatically insert a vowel (even though it is not written). So the soft drink 'Sprite' becomes 'Sa-prite', and the English word 'start', 'sa-tart'.

Despite Thai being a difficult language to pick up, it is worth trying to learn a few words, even if your visit to Thailand is short. Thais generally feel honoured that a *farang* is bothering to learn their language, and will be patient and helpful. If they laugh at some of your pronunciations do not be put off – it is not meant to be critical.

Media
Newspapers and magazines

There are 2 major English-language dailies – the *Bangkok Post* (www.bangkok post.net) and *The Nation* (www.nation multimedia.com), although journalistic standards in both newspapers are very low and they have a long-standing reputation of distorting the news. There are a number of Thai-language dailies and weeklies, as well as Chinese-language newspapers. The local papers are sometimes scandalously colourful, with gruesome pictures of traffic accidents and murder victims.

International newspapers are available in Bangkok, Chiang Mai, Pattaya and on Koh Samui.

Television and radio

CNN and BBC are available in most mid- or upper-range hotels. Local cable networks will sometimes provide English language films, while a full satellite package will give you English football and various movie and other channels. Programme listings are available in *The Nation* and *Bangkok Post*.

Short wave radio frequencies are **BBC**, London, Southeast Asian service 3915, 6195, 9570, 9740, 11750, 11955, 15360; Singapore service 88.9MHz; East Asian service 5995, 6195, 7180, 9740, 11715, 11750, 11945, 11955, 15140, 15280, 15360, 17830, 21715. **Voice of America** (VoA, Washington), Southeast Asian service 1143, 1575, 7120, 9760, 9770, 15185, 15425;

Indonesian service 6110, 11760, 15425.
Radio Beijing, Southeast Asian service
(English) 11600, 11660. **Radio Japan**
(Tokyo), Southeast Asian service (English)
11815, 17810, 21610. For information on
Asian radio and television broadcasts.

Internet
Recent events in Thailand have exposed the
vested interests hiding in the background
of papers such as *The Nation* and they are
no longer reliable news sources. See our list
of websites on page 31.

Money
Currency
Exchange rates: for up-to-the-minute
exchange rates visit www.xe.com.

The unit of Thai currency is the **baht** (฿),
which is divided into 100 **satang**. Notes
in circulation include ฿20 (green), ฿50
(blue), ฿100 (red), ฿500 (purple) and ฿1000
(orange and grey). Coins include 25 satang
and 50 satang, and ฿1, ฿2, ฿5, and ฿10.
The 2 smaller coins are disappearing
from circulation and the 25 satang coin,
equivalent to the princely sum of US$0.003,
is rarely found. The colloquial term for
25 satang is saleng.

Exchange
It is best to change money at banks or
money changers which give better rates
than hotels. The exchange booths at
Bangkok airport have some of the best
rates available. There is no black market.
First-class hotels have 24-hr money
changers. Indonesian rupiah, Nepalese
rupees, Burmese kyat, Vietnamese dong,
Lao kip and Cambodian riels cannot be
exchanged for baht at Thai banks. (Money
changers will sometimes exchange kyat,
dong, kip and riel and it can be a good
idea to buy the currencies in Bangkok
before departure for these countries as the
black-market rate often applies.) There is a
charge of ฿23 per cheque when changing
traveller's cheques (passport required)

so it works out cheaper to travel with large
denomination traveller's cheques (or avoid
them altogether).

Credit and debit cards
Plastic is increasingly used in Thailand and
just about every town of any size will have
a bank with an ATM. Visa and MasterCard
are the most widely taken credit cards, and
cash cards with the Cirrus logo can also
be used to withdraw cash at many banks.
Generally speaking, AMEX can be used at
branches of the **Bangkok Bank**; JCB at **Siam
Commercial Bank**; MasterCard at **Siam
Commercial** and **Bangkok Bank**; and Visa
at **Thai Farmers' Bank** and Bangkok Bank.
Most larger hotels and more expensive
restaurants take credit cards as well.
Because Thailand has embraced the ATM
with such exuberance, many foreign visitors
no longer bother with traveller's cheques or
cash and rely entirely on plastic. Even so, a
small stash of US dollars cash can come in
handy in a sticky situation.

Notification of credit card loss: **American
Express**, SP Building, 388 Phahonyothin Rd,
Bangkok 10400, T02-2735544; **Diners Club**,
Dusit Thani Building, Rama IV Rd, T02-233
5644, T02-238 3660; **JCB**, T02-256 1361,
T02-2561351; **Visa** and **MasterCard**, Thai
Farmers Bank Building, Phahonyothin Rd,
T02-251 6333, T02-273 1199.

Cost of living
One of the key pledges of the Yingluck
Shinawatra government elected in 2011
was to increase the minimum wage
to ฿300 a day (US$10). By mid-2012,
despite complaints by many of the richest
individuals and companies in Thailand, this
was coming into force. The average salary
of a civil servant is around US$250 a month.
Of course, Thailand's middle classes – and
especially those engaged in business in
Bangkok – will earn far more than this.
Thailand has appalling wealth distribution
yet Thai society is remarkably cohesive.
A simple but good meal out will cost ฿60;

the rental of a modern house in a provincial city will cost perhaps ฿4000 a month.

Cost of travelling

Visitors staying in the best hotels and eating in hotel restaurants will probably spend at least ฿2000 per day, conceivably much much more. Tourists staying in cheaper a/c accommodation and eating in local restaurants will probably spend about ฿600-900 per day. Backpackers staying in fan-cooled guesthouses and eating cheaply, should be able to live on ฿300 per day. In Bangkok, expect to pay 20-30% more.

Opening hours

Hours of business Banks: Mon-Fri 0830-1530. **Exchange**: daily 0830-2200 in Bangkok, Pattaya, Phuket and Chiang Mai. In other towns opening hours are usually shorter. **Government offices**: Mon-Fri 0830-1200, 1300-1630. **Shops**: 0830-1700, larger shops: 1000-1900 or 2100. **Tourist offices**: 0830-1630.

Safety

In general, Thailand is a safe country to visit. The vast majority of visitors to Thailand will not experience any physical threat what so ever. However, there have been some widely publicized murders of foreign tourists in recent years and the country does have a very high murder rate. It is best to avoid any situation where violence can occur – what would be a simple punch-up or pushing bout in the West can quickly escalate in Thailand to extreme violence. This is mostly due to loss of face. Getting drunk with Thais can be a risky business – Westerners visiting the country for short periods won't be versed in the intricacies of Thai social interaction and may commit unwitting and terrible faux pas. A general rule of thumb if confronted with a situation is to appear conciliatory and offer a way for the other party to back out gracefully. It should be noted that even some police officers in Thailand represent a threat –

at least 3 young Western travellers have been shot and murdered by drunken Thai policemen in the last few years. Confidence tricksters, touts, all operate, particularly in more popular tourist centres. Robbery is also a threat; it ranges from pick-pocketing to the drugging (and subsequent robbing) of bus and train passengers. Watchfulness and simple common sense should be employed. Women travelling alone should be careful (see also page 32). Always lock hotel rooms and place valuables in a safe deposit if available (if not, take them with you).

Areas to avoid

The UK Foreign and Commonwealth Office (www.fco.gov.uk/travel) advises against all but essential travel to the 4 provinces of **Yala**, **Pattani**, **Narathiwat** and **Songkhla** on the Thai-Malay border. The US State Department (www.travel.state.gov) does the same. These areas are the main base of Thailand's Muslim minority and are currently home to a slow-burning separatist insurgency. Car bomb explosions, shootings and other acts of politically motivated violence are weekly, often daily occurences.

If you plan to visit the Khmer temple, Preah Vihear, on the Thai-Cambodian border, check all travel warnings before travel; it has been the focus of fighting between troops on several occasions in the last few years. In light of events between Mar and May 2010, when political protests throughout Thailand resulted in the deaths of over 90 people, including several foreigners, and injuries to over 2200 people, it is also recommended that you avoid all political demonstrations, no matter how benign or carnival-like they seem.

If you do get any problems contact the tourist police rather than the ordinary police – they will speak English and are used to helping resolve any disputes, issues, etc. The country's health infrastructure, especially in provincial capitals and tourist destinations, is good.

For background information on staying healthy, see page 21. The UK's Foreign and Commonwealth Office's 'Know Before You Go' campaign, www.fco.gov.uk/travel, offers some advice.

Foreign and Commonwealth Office (FCO), T0845-850 2829, www.fco.gov.uk/travel. The UK Foreign and Commonwealth Office's travel warning section.

US State Department, www.travel.state.gov/travel_warnings.html. The US State Department updates travel advisories on its 'Travel Warnings and Consular Information Sheets'. It also has a hotline for American travellers, T202-647-5225.

Bribery

The way to make your way in life, for some people in Thailand, is through the strategic offering of gifts. A Chulalongkorn University report recently estimated that it 'costs' ฿10 million to become Bangkok Police Chief. Apparently this can be recouped in just 2 years of hard graft. Although bribing officials is by no means recommended, resident *farangs* report that they often resort to such gifts to avoid the time and hassle involved in filling in the forms and making the requisite visit to a police station for a minor traffic offence. As a visitor, it's best to play it straight.

Drugs and prostitution

Many prostitutes and drug dealers are in league with the police and may find it more profitable to report you than to take your custom (or they may try to do both). They receive a reward from the police, and the police in turn receive a bonus for the detective work. Note that foreigners on buses may be searched for drugs. Sentences for possession of illegal drugs vary from a fine or one year in jail for marijuana up to life imprisonment or execution for possession or smuggling of heroin. The death penalty is usually commuted.

Prisons

Thai prisons are very grim. Most foreigners are held in 2 Bangkok prisons – Khlong Prem and Bangkwang. One resident who visits overseas prisoners in jail wrote to us saying: "You cannot over-estimate the horrors! Khlong Prem has 7000 prisoners, 5 to a cell, with not enough room to stretch out, no recreation, one meal a day (an egg on Sundays) … ". One hundred prisoners in a dormitory is not uncommon, and prisoners on Death Row have waist chains and ankle fetters permanently welded on.

Tourist police

In 1982 the government set up a special arm of the police to deal with the demands of the tourist industry – the tourist police. Now, there is no important tourist destination that doesn't have a tourist police office. The Thai police have come in for a great deal of scrutiny over recent years, although most policemen are honest and only too happy to help the luckless visitor. **Tourist Police**, Bangkok, T02-2815051 or T02-2216206. Daily 0800-2400.

Traffic

Perhaps the greatest danger is from the traffic – especially if you are attempting to drive yourself. More foreign visitors are killed or injured in traffic accidents than in any other way. Thai drivers have a 'devil may care' attitude towards the highway code, and there are many horrific accidents. Be very careful when crossing the road – just because there is a pedestrian crossing, do not expect drivers to stop. Be particularly wary when driving or riding a motorcycle.

Student travellers

Anyone in full-time education is entitled to an **International Student Identity Card (ISIC)**. These are issued by student travel offices and travel agencies across the world and offer special rates on all forms of transport and other concessions and services. The ISIC head office is: **ISIC Association**, Box 9048, 1000 Copenhagen, Denmark, T45-3393 9303. Students are eligible for discounts at some museums but the use of student cards is not widespread so don't expect to save a fortune.

Tax
Airport tax is now included in the price of a ticket. For VAT refunds, see Customs and duty free, page 20.

Telephone → *Country code +66.*
From Bangkok there is direct dialling to most countries. To call overseas, you first need to dial the international direct dial (IDD) access code, which is 001, followed by the country code. Outside Bangkok, it's best to go to a local telephone exchange if calling internationally.

Local area codes vary according to province. Individual area codes are listed through the book; the code can be found at the front of the telephone directory.

Calls from a telephone box cost ฿1. All telephone numbers marked in the text with a prefix 'B' are Bangkok numbers.

Directory enquiries
For domestic long-distance calls including Malaysia and Vientiane (Laos): T101 (free), Greater Bangkok BMA T183, international calls T02-2350030-5, although hotel operators will invariably help make the call if asked.

Mobiles
Quite simply the cheapest and most convenient form of telephony in Thailand is the mobile/cell phone. Mobiles are common and increasingly popular – reflecting the difficulties of getting a landline as well as a desire to be contactable at all times and places. Coverage is good except in some border areas.

Sim cards and top-up vouchers for all major networks are available from every single 7-11 store in the country. You will need a sim-free, unlocked phone but you can pick up basic, second-hand phones for A600 from most local markets. Unfortunately for smart-phone users, most of Thailand has yet to acquire 3G, although cheap GPRS packages are available from all providers and coverage is pretty good.

AIS and *Happy D Prompt* sim cards and top ups are available throughout the country and cost ฿200 with domestic call charges from ฿3 per min and international calls from ฿8 per min. This is a very good deal and much cheaper than either phone boxes or hotels.

Internet
GPRS data deals are also incredible cheap – the AIS network offers 100 hrs of mobile internet connection for ฿300 per month. Speeds are slow though the network is perfectly adequate for text emails, basic web-browsing and social sites such as Facebook.

Time
GMT plus 7 hrs.

Tipping
Tipping is generally unnecessary. However, a 10% service charge is now expected on room, food and drinks bills in the smarter hotels as well as for any personal service. Increasingly, the more expensive restaurants add a 10% service charge; others expect a small tip.

Tour operators
UK
Asean Explorer, PO Box 82, 37 High St, Alderney, GY9 3DG, T01481-823417, www.asean-explorer.com. Holidays for adventurers and golfers in Thailand.
Buffalo Tours, the Old Church, 89b Quicks Rd, Wimbledon, London SW19 1EX, T020-8545 2830, www.buffalotours.com. Arrange tours throughout Southeast Asia. Also has office in Bangkok, Phuket and Chiang Mai.
Exodus Travels, 9 Weir Rd, London, T020-9500039, T020-8673 0859, www.exodus.

co.uk. Small group travel for walking and trekking holidays, adventure tours and more.
Magic of the Orient, 14 Frederick Pl, Bristol, BS8 1AS, T0117-3116050, www.magicofthe orient.com. Tailor-made holidays to the region. Established in 1989 the company's philosophy is to deliver first-class service from knowledgeable staff at good value.
Silk Steps, Compass House, Rowdens Rd, Wells, Somerset, BA5 1TU, T01749-685162, www.silk steps.co.uk. Tailor-made and group travel.
STA Travel, 33 Bedford St, Covent Garden, London, WC2E 9ED, T0871-468 0612, www.statravel.co.uk. Specialists in low-cost student/youth flights and tours, also good for student IDs and insurance.
Steppes Travel, 51 Castle St, Cirencester, GL7 1QD, T01285-880980, www.steppestravel.co.uk.
Symbiosis Expedition Planning, Holly House, Whilton, Daventry, Northamptonshire, T0845-1232844, www.symbiosis-travel.com. Specialists in tailor-made and small group adventure holidays for those concerned about the impact of tourism on environments.
Trailfinders, 194 Kensington High St, London, W8 7RG, T020-7938 3939, www.trailfinders.co.uk.
Trans Indus, 75 St Mary's Rd and the Old Fire Station, Ealing, London, W5 5RW, T020-8566 2729, www.transindus.co.uk. Tours to Thailand and other Southeast Asian countries.

North America
Global Spectrum, 3907 Laro Court, Fairfax, VA 22031, USA, T1800-419 4446, www.globalspectrumtravel.com.
Nine Dragons Travel & Tours, 1476 Orange Grove Rd, Charleston, SC 29407, USA, T1317-281 3895, www.nine-dragons.com. Guided and individually customized tours.
STA Travel, 920 Westwood Blvd, Los Angeles, CA 90024, T1-310-824 1574, www.statravel.com.

Thailand
Luxury Travel Thailand, c/o East West Siam, 40/83 Intramara Soi 8, Suthisan Rd, Samseannai, Payathai, Bangkok 104000, T66-266007, www.luxurytravelvietnam. com. Asian award-winning specialist in luxury privately guided and fully bespoke holidays in Vietnam, Laos, Cambodia, Myanmar and Thailand.

Tourist information
Tourist Authority of Thailand (TAT), 1600 New Phetburi Rd, Makkasan, Ratchathewi, T02-2505500, www.tourism thailand.org; also at 4 Rachdamnern Nok Av (intersection with Chakrapatdipong Rd), Mon-Fri 0830-1630; in addition there are 2 counters at Suvarnabhumi Airport, in the Arrivals halls of Domestic and International Terminals, T02-134 0040, T02-134 0041, 0800-2400. Local offices are found in most major tourist destinations in the country. Most offices open daily 0830-1630. TAT offices are a useful source of local information, often providing maps of the town, listings of hotels/guesthouses and information on local tourist attractions. The website is a useful first stop.

Tourism authorities abroad
Australia, Suite 2002, 2nd floor, 56 Pitt St, Sydney, NSW 2000, T9247-7549, www. thailand.net.au.
France, 90 Ave des Champs Elysées, 75008 Paris, T5353-4700, tatpar@wanadoo.fr.
Germany, Bethmannstr 58, D-60311, Frankfurt/Main 1, T69-1381390, tatfra@t-online.de.
Hong Kong, 401 Fairmont House, 8 Cotton Tree Drive, Central, T2868-0732, tathkg@hk.super.net.
Italy, 4th floor, Via Barberini 68, 00187 Roma, T06-487 3479.
Japan, Yurakucho Denki Building, South Tower 2F, Room 259, 1-7-1, Yurakucho, Chiyoda-ku, Tokyo 100-0006, T03-218 0337, tattky@criss cross.com.

Malaysia, c/o Royal Thai Embassy 206 Jalan Ampang, 50450 Kuala Lumpur, T26-23480, sawatdi@po.jaring.my.

Singapore, c/o Royal Thai Embassy, 370 Orchard Rd, Singapore 238870, T2357901, tatsin@mbox5.singnet.com.sg.

UK, 1st floor, 17-19 Cockspur St, Trafalgar Sq, London SW1Y 5BL, T0870-900 2007, www.tourismthailand.co.uk.

USA, 1st floor, 611 North Larchmont Blvd, Los Angeles, CA 90004, T461-9814, tatla@ix.netcom.com.

Useful websites

www.asiancorrespondent.com Regional news website featuring guest blogs on Thai politics by writers who dig deep rather than toe the line. A better source of unbiased analysis than either the *Bangkok Post* or *The Nation*.

www.bangkokpost.com Homepage for the country's most widely read English-language daily.

www.bk.asia-city.com The online version of Bangkok's weekly freebie BK Magazine offers instant access to the hipper side of city life, from upcoming events to comment, chat and lifestyle features.

www.fco.gov.uk/travel The UK Foreign and Commonwealth Office's travel warning section.

www.paknamweb.com Umbrella website for the Paknam Network, expat Richard Barrow's assorted websites and blogs covering all facets of Thai culture.

www.thaifolk.com Good site for Thai culture, from folk songs and handicrafts through to festivals like Loi Kratong, and Thai myths and legends. Information posted in both English and Thai – although the Thai version of the site is better.

www.thai-language.com An easy-to-use Thai-English online language resource with an excellent dictionary, thousands of audio clips, lessons and a forum.

www.tourismthailand.org A useful first stop.
www.travel.state.gov/travel The US State Department updates travel advisories on its Travel Warnings & Consular Information Sheets.

Visas and immigration

For the latest information on visas and tourist visa exemptions, see the consular information section of the **Thai Ministry of Foreign Affairs** website, www.mfa. go.th. Having relocated from its central location on Soi Suan Plu, the immigration department that deals with tourists is now on the outskirts: Immigration Bureau, Government Complex Chaeng Wattana, B Building, Floor 2 (South Zone), Chaengwattana Rd Soi 7, Laksi, Bangkok 10210, T02-141 9889, www.immigration. co.th. Mon-Fri 0830-1200, 1300-1630, closed Sat, Sun, official hols.

For tourists from 41 countries (basically all Western countries, plus some Arabic and other Asian states – see www.mfa. go.th), Thai immigration authorities will issue a 30-day visa-exemption entry permit if you arrive by plane. If you enter at a land crossing from any neighbouring country, the permit is for 15 days.

Visas on arrival

Tourists from 28 countries (most of them developing countries) can apply for a 15-day visa on arrival at immigration checkpoints. Applicants must have an outbound (return) ticket and possess funds to meet living expenses of ฿10,000 per person or ฿20,000 per family. The application fee is ฿1000 and must be accompanied by a passport photo.

Tourist visas

These are valid for 60 days from date of entry and must be obtained from a Thai embassy before arrival in Thailand.

Visa extensions

These are obtainable from the Immigration Bureau (see above) for ฿1900. Applicants must bring 2 photocopies of their passport ID page and the page on which their tourist visa is stamped, together with a passport photograph. It is also advisable to dress neatly. Visas are issued by all Thai embassies and consulates. The length of time a visa is extended varies according to the office and the official.

Weather

For daily weather reports visit the website www.thaimet.tmd.go.th.

Weights and measures

Thailand uses the metric system, although there are some traditional measures still in use, in particular the *rai*, which equals 0.16 ha. There are 4 *ngaan* in a *rai*. Other local measures include the krasorp (sack) which equals 25 kg and the *tang* which is 10-11 kg. However, for most purchases (for example fruit) the kg is the norm. Both kg and km are often referred to as lo – as in ki-lo.

Women travellers

Compared with neighbouring East and South Asia, women in Southeast Asia enjoy relative equality of opportunity. While this is a contentious issue, scholars have pointed to the lack of pronouns in Southeast Asian languages, the role of women in trade and commerce, the important part that women play in reproductive decisions, the characteristically egalitarian patterns of inheritance and so on. This is not to suggest that there is complete equality between the sexes. Buddhism, for example – at least as it is practised in Thailand – accords women a lower position and it is notable how few women are in positions of political power.

The implications for women travellers, and especially solo women travellers, is that they may face some difficulties not encountered by men – for example the possibility of some low-key sexual harassment. Women should make sure that rooms are secure at night and if travelling in remote regions, should try to team up with other travellers.

Working in Thailand
Most visitors to Thailand who wish to work take up a post teaching English. Some guest-houses will provide free accommodation for guests who are willing to allot a portion of the day to English conversation classes. Those with a qualification, for example a TEFL certificate, can usually command a higher salary. There are also various NGOs/voluntary organizations that employ people. See www.thaivisa.com or www.goabroad. com. The former provides background information on getting a visa while the latter has information on language schools, volunteer work and more.

Volunteering
Projects range from conservation and teaching English to looking after elephants. They vary in length from 2 weeks and beyond and generally need to be organized before you arrive. The application process almost always involves submitting a statement of intent, although generally no formal qualifications or experience are required; usually volunteers need to be over 18 and will pay fees upfront. Consult individual organizations about visas and lodgings – most include basic shared accommodation in the price but not travel to and from Thailand. The following international organizations run projects in Thailand.

British Trust for Conservation Volunteers, Sedum House, Mallard Way, Potteric Carr, Doncaster, DN4 8DB, T01302-388888, www. btcv.org. Mangrove conservation and turtle monitoring from 2 weeks in duration.

Cross Cultural Solutions, 2 Clinton Pl, New Rochelle, NY 10801, USA, T1800 3804777 (US only), T191 4632 0022, www.cross culturalsolutions.org. Community work and research into local development.

Earthwatch, 267 Banbury Rd, Oxford, OX2 7HT, T01865-318838, www.earthwatch.org.

Elephant Nature Park, 209/2 Sridorn Chai Rd, Chiang Mai 50100, Thailand, T053-272855, www.thaifocus.com/elephant/. Under 1 month, office work and working with elephants.

Global Services Corps, 300 Broadway, Suite 28, San Francisco, CA 94133-3312, USA, T415-788-3666, ext128, www.global service corps.org. Volunteers must be over 18 with an interest in international issues and sustainable development.

Involvement Volunteers, PO Box 218, Port Melbourne, Vic 3207, Australia, T613-9646 5504, www.volunteering.org.au. Australian network with international reach, organic farming, teaching and community work.

VSO, 317 Putney Bridge Rd, London, SW15 2PN, UK, T0208-780 7200, www.vso.org.uk. Worldwide voluntary organization.

Contents

Bangkok

Places in Bangkok

Wats and palaces, markets and shopping, traditional dancing and Thai boxing, glorious food, tuk-tuks and water taxis fill Bangkok. Get over the pace and pollution and you'll have a ball in Bangkok. This is one of the most engaging cities on the planet and its infectious, amiable energy soon wears down even the staunchest tree-hugger. Begin your sojourn in the bejewelled beauty of the Old City. Here you'll find the regal heart of Bangkok at the stupendous Grand Palace. The charming Golden Mount is a short hop to the east, while to the south are the bewildering alleyways and gaudy temples of Bangkok's frenetic Chinatown. Head west over the Chao Phraya River to the magnificent spire of Wat Arun and the *khlongs* of Thonburi. To the north sits the broad, leafy avenues of Dusit, the home of the Thai parliament and the king's residence. Carry on east and south and you'll reach modern Bangkok. A multitude of mini-boutiques forms Siam Square and the Thai capital's centre of youth fashion; Silom and Sukhumvit roads are vibrant runs of shopping centres, restaurants and hotels while the Chatuchak Weekend Market (known to locals as JJ), in the northern suburbs, is one of Asia's greatest markets.

Old City

Filled with palaces and temples, this is the ancient heart of Bangkok. These days it is the premium destination for visitors and controversial plans are afoot to change it into a 'tourist zone'. This would strip the area of the usual chaotic charm that typifies Bangkok, moving out the remaining poor people who live in the area and creating an ersatz, gentrified feel.

Wat Phra Chetuphon (Wat Pho)

ⓘ *The entrance is on the south side of the monastery, www.watpho.com. 0900-2100. ฿100. From Tha Tien pier at the end of Thai Wang Rd, close to Wat Pho, it is possible to get boats to Wat Arun (see page 51).*

Wat Phra Chetuphon, or Wat Pho, is the largest and most famous temple in Bangkok. 'The Temple of the Reclining Buddha' – built in 1781 – houses one of the largest reclining Buddhas in the country; the soles of the Buddha's feet are decorated with mother-of-pearl displaying the 108 auspicious signs of the Buddha.

Now open until 2100 each night, the bustling grounds of the wat display more than 1000 bronze images, mostly rescued from the ruins of Ayutthaya and Sukhothai, while the *bot* contains the ashes of Rama I. The *bot* is enclosed by two galleries, which house 394 seated bronze Buddha images. They were brought from the north during Rama I's reign and are of assorted periods and styles. Around the exterior base of the bot are marble reliefs telling the story of the *Ramakien* (see box, page 42) as adapted in the Thai poem *Maxims of King Ruang*. They recount only the second section of the *Ramakien*: the abduction and recovery of Ram's wife Seeda.

There are 95 *chedis* of various sizes scattered across the 8-ha (20-acre) complex. To the left of the bot are four large *chedis*, memorials to the first four Bangkok kings. The library nearby is richly decorated with broken pieces of porcelain. The large top-hatted stone figures, the stone animals and the Chinese pagodas scattered throughout the compound came to Bangkok as ballast on the royal rice boats returning from China. Rama III wanted Wat Pho to become known as a place of learning, a kind of exhibition of all the knowledge of the time, and it is regarded as Thailand's first university.

One of Wat Pho's biggest attractions is its role as a respected centre of **traditional Thai massage** (see box, page 113). Thousands of tourists, powerful Thai politicians, businessmen and military officers come here to seek relief from the tensions of modern life. The Burmese destroyed most medical texts when they sacked Ayutthaya in 1776. In 1832, to help preserve the ancient medical art, Rama III had what was known about Thai massage inscribed onto a series of stones which were then set into the walls of Wat Pho. If you want to come here for a massage then it is best to arrive in the morning; queues in the afternoon can be long. ▸ *See What to do, page 113.*

Grand Palace and Wat Phra Kaeo

ⓘ *The main entrance is the Viseschaisri Gate on Na Phralan Rd, T02-623 5500, www.palaces. thai.net. Admission to the Grand Palace complex costs ฿400 (ticket office open daily 0830-1530 except Buddhist holidays when Wat Phra Kaeo is free but the rest of the palace is closed). The cost of the admission includes a free guidebook to the palace (with plan) as well as a ticket to the Coin Pavilion, with its collection of medals and 'honours' presented to members of the Royal Family, and to the Vimanmek Palace in the Dusit area (see page 55). No photography is allowed inside the bot. The Royal Pantheon is only open to the public once a year on Chakri Day, 6 Apr (the anniversary of the founding of the present Royal Dynasty). All labels in Thai. Free guided tours in English throughout the day. There are plenty of touts offering to guide tourists around the palace. Personal audio guides, ฿100 (2 hrs), available in English, French, German and some other languages. Decorum of dress means no shorts, short skirts, no sleeveless shirts, no flip flops or sandals. There are plastic shoes and trousers for hire near the entrance. Close to the Dusit Hall is a small café selling refreshing coconut drinks and other soft drinks.*

The Grand Palace is situated on the banks of the Chao Phraya River and is the most spectacular – some might say 'gaudy' – collection of buildings in Bangkok. The complex covers an area of over 1.5 sq km and the architectural plan is almost identical to that of the Royal Palace in the former capital of Ayutthaya. It began life in 1782.

The buildings of greatest interest are clustered around **Wat Phra Kaeo**, or the **Temple of the Emerald Buddha** (see box, page 41). The glittering brilliance of sunlight bouncing

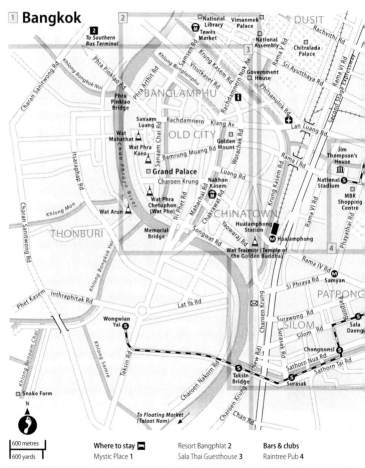

| Where to stay ▣ | Resort Bangphlat 2 | Bars & clubs |
| Mystic Place 1 | Sala Thai Guesthouse 3 | Raintree Pub 4 |

off the coloured glass mosaic exterior of Wat Phra Kaeo creates a gobsmacking first impression for visitors to the Grand Palace. Built by Rama I in imitation of the royal chapel in Ayutthaya, Wat Phra Kaeo was the first of the buildings within the Grand Palace complex to be constructed. While it was being erected the king lived in a small wooden building in the palace compound. Numbers in the following text refer to the map on page 40.

The **ubosoth (1)** is raised on a marble platform with a frieze of gilded *garudas* holding *nagas* running round the base. Mighty, bronze *singhas* (lions) act as door guardians. The inlaid mother-of-pearl door panels date from Rama I's reign (late 18th century) while the doors are watched over by Chinese door guardians riding on lions. Inside the temple, the Emerald Buddha peers down on the gathered throng from a lofty, illuminated position above a large golden altar. Facing the Buddha on three sides are dozens of other gilded Buddha images, depicting the enlightenment of the Buddha when he subdues the evil demon Mara, the final temptation of the Buddha and the subjugation of evil spirits.

Around the walls of the shaded **cloister**, which encompasses Wat Phra Kaeo, is a continuous mural depicting the *Ramakien* – the Thai version of the Indian *Ramayana* (see box, page 42). There are 178 sections in all, which were first painted during the reign of King Rama I but have since been restored on a number of occasions.

To the north of the *ubosoth* on a raised platform are the **Royal Pantheon (2)**, the **Phra Mondop (3)** (the library), two gilt stupas, a **model of Angkor Wat (4)** and the **Golden Stupa (5)**. At the entrance to the Royal Pantheon are gilded *kinarees*. On the same terrace there are two gilt stupas built by King Rama I in commemoration of his parents. The Mondop was also built by Rama I to house the first revised Buddhist scriptural canon. To the west of the Mondop is the large Golden Stupa or *chedi*, with its circular base. To the north of the Mondop is a model of Angkor Wat constructed during the reign of King Mongkut (1851-1868) when Cambodia was under Thai suzerainty.

Saxophone **5**

➡ **Bangkok maps**
1 Bangkok, page 38
2 Old City, Banglamphu & Chinatown, page 44
3 Bangkok's river & khlongs, page 52
4 Siam Square & Ploenchit Road, page 57
5 Silom & Lumpini Park, page 60
6 Sukhumvit Road, page 62

To the north again from the Royal Pantheon is the **Supplementary Library** and two viharns – **Viharn Yod (6)** and **Phra Nak (7)**. The former is encrusted with pieces of Chinese porcelain.

To the south of Wat Phra Kaeo are the buildings of the **Grand Palace**. These are interesting for the contrast that they make with those of Wat Phra Kaeo. Walk out through the cloisters. On your left is the French-style **Boromabiman Hall (8)**, which was completed during the reign of Rama VI. The **Amarinda Hall (9)** has an impressive, airy interior, with chunky pillars and gilded thrones. The **Chakri Mahaprasart (10)** – the Palace Reception Hall – stands in front of a carefully manicured garden with topiary. It was built and lived in by Rama V shortly after he had returned from a trip to Java and Singapore in 1876, and it shows: the building is a rather unhappy amalgam of colonial and traditional Thai styles of architecture. King Chulalongkorn (Rama V) found the overcrowded Grand Palace oppressive and after a visit to Europe in 1897 built himself a new home at Vimanmek (see page 55) in Dusit where the present king, Bhumibol, lives in the Chitralada Palace. The Grand Palace is now only used for state occasions. Next to the Chakri Mahaprasart is the raised **Dusit Hall (11)**, a cool, airy building containing mother-of-pearl thrones. Near the Dusit Hall is a **museum** ① *0900-1600, ฿50*, which has information on the restoration of the Grand Palace, models of the palace and many more Buddha images. There is a collection of old cannon, mainly supplied by London gun foundries.

Wat Phra Kaeo & Grand Palace

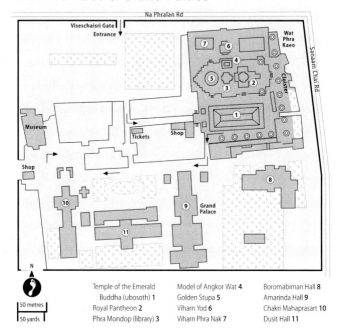

Temple of the Emerald Buddha (ubosoth) 1	Model of Angkor Wat 4	Boromabiman Hall 8
Royal Pantheon 2	Golden Stupa 5	Amarinda Hall 9
Phra Mondop (library) 3	Viharn Yod 6	Chakri Mahaprasart 10
	Viharn Phra Nak 7	Dusit Hall 11

The Emerald Buddha

Wat Phra Kaeo was specifically built to house the Emerald Buddha, the most venerated Buddha image in Thailand. It is carved from green jade (the emerald in the name referring only to its colour), a mere 75 cm high, and seated in an attitude of meditation. It is believed to have been found in 1434 in Chiang Rai, and stylistically belongs to the Late Chiang Saen or Chiang Mai schools. Since then, it has been moved on a number of occasions – to Lampang, Chiang Mai and Laos (both Luang Prabang and Vientiane). It stayed in Vientiane for 214 years before being recaptured by the Thai army in 1778 and placed in Wat Phra Kaeo on 22 March 1784.

The image wears seasonal costumes of gold and jewellery; one each for the hot, cool and the rainy seasons. The changing ceremony occurs three times a year in the presence of the king.

Buddha images are often thought to have personalities. The Phra Kaeo is no exception. It is said that such is the antipathy between the Phra Bang image in Luang Prabang (Laos) and the Phra Kaeo that they can never reside in the same town.

Turn left outside the Grand Palace and a five-minute walk leads to **Tha Chang pier and market**. The market sells fruit and food, cold drinks and the like. There is also a small amulet (lucky charm) and second-hand section. From Tha Chang pier it is possible to get a boat to Wat Arun for about ฿150 return; alternatively take a water-taxi.

Sanaam Luang

To the north of the Grand Palace, across Na Phralan Road, lies the large open space of the Pramane Ground (Royal Cremation Ground), better known as Sanaam Luang. Now open again after a lengthy revamp, this area is historically significant, having originally been used for the cremation of kings, queens and important princes. Later, foreigners began to use it as a race track and as a golf course. Today, Sanaam Luang is used for the annual **Royal Ploughing Ceremony**, held in May. This ancient Brahmanistic ritual, resurrected by Rama IV, signals the auspicious day on which farmers can begin to prepare their rice paddies, the time and date of the ceremony being set by Royal Astrologers. Bulls decorated with flowers pull a red and gold plough, while the selection of different lengths of cloth by the Ploughing Lord predicts whether the rains will be good or bad.

Sanaam Luang has several other claims to fame. Traditionally, it is also the place in Bangkok to fly kites, eat charcoal-grilled dried squid and have your fortune told. The *mor duu* ('seeing doctors') would sit in the shade of the tamarind trees along the inner ring of the southern footpath. Prior to 1987, the weekend market at Chatuchak was located here. Political protests, some of them bloody, have also been been staged here over the decades, though these, like many of the other activities, have been banned as part of the recent 'improvements'. At the northeast corner of Sanaam Luang, opposite the **Royal Hotel**, is a statue of the **Goddess of the Earth** erected by King Chulalongkorn to provide drinking water for the public.

Lak Muang

ⓘ *Open daily, 24 hrs; there is no entrance charge to the compound although touts sometimes insist otherwise; donations can be placed in the boxes within the shrine precincts.*

Thai Ramayana: the Ramakien

The Ramakien – literally the "Story of Rama" – is an adaptation of the Indian Hindu classic, the Ramayana, which was written by the poet Valmiki about 2000 years ago. This 48,000-line epic odyssey – often likened to the works of Homer – was introduced into mainland Southeast Asia in the early centuries of the first millennium. The heroes were simply transposed into a mythical, ancient, Southeast Asian landscape. In Thailand, the Ramakien quickly became highly influential, and the name of the former capital of Siam, Ayutthaya, is taken from the legendary hero's city of Ayodhia in the epic. Unfortunately, these early Thai translations of the Ramayana were destroyed following the sacking of Ayutthaya by the Burmese in 1767. The earliest extant version was written by King Taksin in about 1775, although Rama I's rather later rendering is usually regarded as the classic interpretation.

In many respects, King Chakri's version closely follows that of the original Indian story. It tells of the life of Ram (Rama), the King of Ayodhia. In the first part of the story, Ram renounces his throne following a long and convoluted court intrigue, and flees into exile. With his wife Seeda (Sita) and trusted companion Hanuman (the monkey god), they undertake a long and arduous journey. In the second part, his wife Seeda is abducted by the evil king Ravana, forcing Ram to wage battle against the demons of Langka Island (Sri Lanka). He defeats the demons with the help of Hanuman and his monkey army,

and recovers his wife. In the third and final part of the story – and here it diverges sharply from the Indian original – Seeda and Ram are reunited and reconciled with the help of the gods (in the Indian version there is no such reconciliation). Another difference with the Indian version is the significant role played by the Thai Hanuman – here an amorous adventurer who dominates much of the third part of the epic.

There are also numerous sub-plots which are original to the Ramakien, many building upon events in Thai history and local myth and folklore. In tone and issues of morality, the Thai version is less puritanical than the Indian original. There are also, of course, differences in dress, ecology, location and custom.

In the southeast corner of Sanaam Luang, opposite the Grand Palace, is Bangkok's Lak Muang, housing the City Pillar and horoscope, originally placed there by Rama I in 1782. The shrine is believed to grant people's wishes, so it is a hive of activity all day. In a small pavilion to the left of the main entrance, Thai dancers are hired by supplicants to dance for the pleasure of the resident spirits – while providing a free spectacle for everyone else.

Wat Mahathat

ⓘ *Daily 0900-1700.*

North along Na Phrathat Road, on the river side of Sanaam Luang, is Wat Mahathat (the Temple of the Great Relic), a temple famous as a meditation centre; walk under the archway marked 'Naradhip Centre for Research in Social Sciences' to reach the wat. For those interested in learning more about Buddhist meditation, contact monks in section five within the compound (see Meditation, page 112). The wat is a royal temple of the first grade and a number of Supreme Patriarchs of Bangkok have based themselves here.

On Maharaj Road, a narrow *soi* (lane) leads down towards the river and a large daily **market** selling exotic herbal cures, false teeth, old religious texts, amulets, clothes and food. At weekends, the market spills out onto the surrounding streets (particularly Phra Chan Road) and amulet sellers line the pavement, their magical and holy talismens carefully displayed, see box, page 49.

Thammasat University

Further north along Na Phrathat Road is Thammasat University, the site of viciously suppressed student demonstrations in 1973. Sanaam Luang and Thammasat University remain a popular focus of discontent, the last being mass demonstrations in May 1992 demanding the resignation of Prime Minister General Suchinda which led to a military crackdown. In the grounds of Thammasat, there is a new monument to the victims of 1973, 1976 and 1992.

National Museum

ⓘ *www.nationalmuseums.finearts.go.th. Wed-Sun 0900-1600 (last tickets sold 1530), ฿200.*

Opposite the northwest rim of Sanam Luang, beside Thammasat University, is the National Museum. Reputedly the largest museum in Southeast Asia, it's an excellent place to visit before exploring the ancient Thai capitals, Ayutthaya and Sukhothai. A palace during the reign of King Rama V, it showcases a vast assortment of Thai Buddhist art and artefacts from all of the country's main historical periods, including the reigning Rattanakosin dynasty.

Each of the complex's buildings exhibits a different kind of relic: weapons, old scriptures, musical instruments, Buddhist sculptures, royal elephant tusks, and more. The **Buddhaisawan Chapel**, to the right of the ticket office, contains some of the finest Bangkok period murals in Thailand. The chapel was built in 1795 to house the famous Phra Sihing Buddha. Legend has it that this image originated in Ceylon and, when the boat carrying it to Thailand sank, it floated off on a plank to be washed ashore in southern Thailand, near the town of Nakhon Si Thammarat. The chapel's magnificent murals were painted between 1795 and 1797 and depict stories from the Buddha's life.

Good information is lacking, so it's recommended that interested visitors join one of the free tours conducted in English, French, German and Japanese by the National Museum Volunteers at 0930 every Wednesday and Thursday (meet at the ticket office). Tailor-made tours in these and other languages can also be arranged by contacting the chairman of this non-profit organization; see www.museumvolunteersbkk.net for details.

National Theatre and National Art Gallery

ⓘ *National Theatre programmes can be checked by calling T02-224 1342, Mon-Fri 0830-1630. National Art Gallery, T02-281 2224, Wed-Sun 0900-1600, ฿30.*

Next to the National Museum, on the corner of Na Phrathat and Phra Pinklao Bridge roads, is Thailand's National Theatre. Thai classical drama and music are staged here on the last Friday of each month at 1730 as well as periodically on other days.

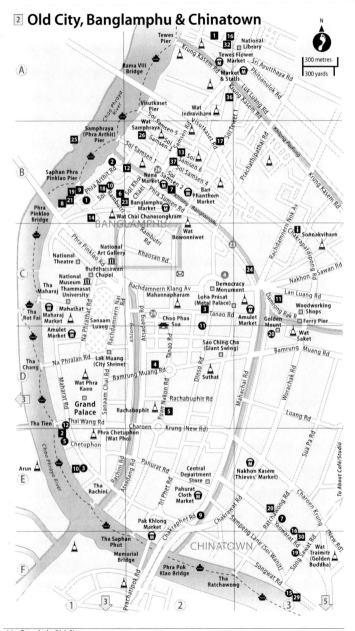

2 Old City, Banglamphu & Chinatown

N

300 metres
300 yards

Tewes Pier

National Library

Krung Kasem Rd

Sri Ayutthaya Rd

Tewes Flower Market

Phitsanulok Rd

Luk Luang Rd

Market & Stalls

Rama VIII Bridge

Chao Phraya River

Visutkaset Pier

Wat Indraviharn

Krung Kasem Rd

Soi Thewet

Khlong Padung

Samphraya (Phra Arthit) Pier

Wat Samphraya

Soi Samsen 5

Visutkaset Rd

Prachathipathai Rd

Samsen 3

Soi Samsen

Soi Samsen 6

Saphan Phra Pinklao Pier

Phra Arthit Rd

Soi Samsen 2

Soi Samsen 4

Krung Kasem Rd

Banglamphu

Nana Market

Soi Rambutri

Phra Sumen Rd

Chakrabongse

Ban Phanthom Market

Rachadamnoen Nok Av

Sonnakviharn

Soi Khlong

Khlong

Phra Pinklao Bridge

Banglamphu Market

Wat Chai Chanasongkram

Rambutri Rd

Wat Bowonniwet

BANGLAMPHU

Nakhon Sawan Rd

Phra Pinklao Rd

National Art Gallery

Khaosan Rd

Lan Luang Rd

Rachadamnoen Klang Av

Woodworking Shops

National Theatre

Buddhaisawan Chapel

Mahannapharam

Democracy Monument

Golden Mount

Ferry Pier

Tha Maharaj

National Museum

Rachadamnern Nai Rd

Atsadang Rd

Loha Prasat (Metal Palace)

Tanao Rd

Amulet Market

Wat Saket

Tha Rot Fai

Thammasat University

Mahathat

Chao Phaa Sua

Damrong Rak Rd

Amulet Market

Sanaam Luang

Khlong

Sao Ching Cha (Giant Swing)

Bamrung Muang Rd

Na Phralan Rd

Lak Muang (City Shrine)

Tha Chang

Wat Phra Kaeo

Bamrung Muang Rd

Suthat

Rachabuphit Rd

Mahachai Rd

Worachat Rd

Luang Rd

Grand Palace

Sanaam Chai Rd

Tuan Nakon Rd

Dinso Rd

Maharat Rd

Tha Tien

Thai Wang Rd

Phra Chetuphon (Wat Pho)

Rachabophit

Charoen Krung (New Rd)

Sua Pa Rd

Chetuphon

Chao Phraya River

Arun

Tha Rachini

Ratchini Rd

Atsadang Rd

Tri Phet Rd

Pahurat Rd

Central Department Store

Pahurat Cloth Market

Nakhon Kasem (Thieves' Market)

Charoen Krung (New Rd)

Pak Khlong Market

Chakraphet Rd

Chakrawat Rd

Sampeng Lane (Soi Wanit)

Ratchawong Rd

Yaowarat Rd

Song Sawat Rd

Wat Traimitr (Golden Buddha)

Tha Saphan Phut

Memorial Bridge

CHINATOWN

Songwat Rd

Phra Pok Klao Bridge

Tha Ratchawong

Prachathipok Rd

Khaosan Road detail

Opposite the National Theatre is the National Art Gallery on Chao Fa Road. It exhibits traditional and contemporary work by Thai artists in a peeling Italianate mansion.

Museum Siam

ⓘ *4 Sanaam Chai Rd, T02-622 2599, http:// en.museumsiam.com. Tue-Sun 1000-1800. Entry ฿300 for foreigners; free for children under 15. Free entry 1600-1800.*

Just a short walk from Wat Pho, this slick museum is located in a beautifully restored historical building once occupied by the Commerce Ministry. It is aimed, first and foremost, at the attention-deficient younger generation and features a permanent exhibition about Thai identity and its roots. Hands-on activities and games that will appeal to kids – and big kids – include dressing up as an early 20th-century Thai noblemen, or playing a computer game in which you blast cannonballs at rampaging Burmese war elephants in a futile bid to prevent the fall of Ayutthaya, among many others. Cultural exhibitions and, occasionally, concerts on the lawns out front are also held here. Come at 1600 to get in free.

Banglamphu and Khaosan Road

Northeast of the National Art Gallery is the district of Banglamphu and the legendary Khaosan Road, backpacker haunt and epi-centre of Bangkok's travellers' culture. It all began when the **Viengtai Hotel** opened in 1962, giving the area a reputation for budget accommodation. Local families began to rent out rooms to travellers and by the mid-1970s the Khaosan Road we love/ hate was firmly established. Much has been said and written about the strip. Thai purists look down their noses at it while many locals like the money it brings in but feel threatened by the loose Western culture it brings to the capital. For some younger Thais, it's a hip, liberal hang-out, a space and place apart from the constrictions of traditional Thai culture. There is no doubting Khaosan Road's sustained popularity, though the quality of food, accommodation, goods and services are easily surpassed in other parts of the city. As well as the expensive Thai food being of a very low standard, souvenirs are overpriced, while the minibuses that take unsuspecting backpackers to the popular beaches and islands tend to be falling apart and driven by Red Bull-fuelled maniacs. Taking public buses from the respective bus stations tends to be cheaper and safer. So why stay here? If you're travelling on a budget and it's your first time in Asia there are few better places to connect with other travellers and get into the swing of things. More seasoned travellers may find Khaosan Road a homogeneous spread of tie-dyed, penny-pinching backpackers and every bit as challenging as staying in a packaged resort.

Phra Arthit Road

Running north from the National Theatre, following the river upstream, is Phra Arthit Road. The community along this narrow, leafy street is recognised as one of the most cohesive in Bangkok, and a centre for artists and intellectuals as well as traditional shop owners. The nearby addition of a park and Thai *sala* on the river has created a pleasant place to sit and watch the boats. There are interesting shops and restaurants, and the traffic is relatively sedate compared with other parts of the city.

Wat Indraviharn

Wat Indraviharn (see map, page 44) is rather isolated from the other sights, lying just off Visutkaset Road (not too far north of Phra Arthit Road and the traveller nexus of Banglamphu). It contains a 32-m standing Buddha encrusted in gold tiles that can be seen from the entrance to the wat. The image is impressive only for its size. The topknot contains a relic of the Buddha brought from Ceylon.

Golden Mount and around

This is where ancient Bangkok begins to give way to the modern thrust of this engagingly bewildering city. Apart from the obvious sights listed below there's little reason to hang around here but with its history of demonstrations and cries for democracy it beats a defining pulse in the hearts of most Thais. ►► *See Old City map, page 44.*

Democracy Monument

The Democracy Monument is a 10- to 15-minute walk from the north side of Sanaam Luang, in the middle of Rachdamnern Klang Avenue. Designed by Italian artist and sculptor Corrado Feroci, and completed in 1940 to commemorate the establishment of Siam as a constitutional monarchy, its dimensions signify, in various ways, the date of the 'revolution' – 24 June 1932. For example, the 75 buried cannon which surround the structure denote the Buddhist year (BE – or Buddhist Era) 2475 (AD 1932). In May 1992, the monument was the focus of the anti-Suchinda demonstrations, so brutally suppressed by the army. Scores of Thais died here, many others fleeing into the nearby **Royal Hotel** which also became an impromptu hospital to the many wounded. On the night of 10 April 2010, it witnessed bloodshed again, when government troops dispersed Red Shirt protestors from the area using live ammunition.

Golden Mount

From the Democracy Monument, across Mahachai Road, at the point where Rachdamnern Klang Avenue crosses Khlong Banglamphu, the Golden Mount can be seen (also known as the

Royal Mount), an impressive artificial hill nearly 80 m high. The climb to the top is exhausting but worth it for the fabulous views of Bangkok. On the way up, the path passes holy trees, memorial plaques and Chinese shrines. The construction of the mount was begun during the reign of Rama III who intended to build the greatest *chedi* in his kingdom. The structure collapsed before completion, and Rama IV decided merely to pile up the rubble in a heap and place a far smaller golden *chedi* on its summit. The *chedi* contains a relic of the Buddha placed there by the present king after the structure had been most recently repaired in 1966.

Wat Saket
① *Daily 0800-1800.*
Wat Saket lies at the bottom of the mount, between it and Damrong Rak Road – the mount actually lies within the wat's compound. Saket means 'washing of hair' and Rama I is reputed to have stopped here and ceremoniously washed himself before being crowned King in Thonburi (see Festivals, page 100). The only building of real note is the *hor trai* (library) which is Ayutthayan in style. The door panels and lower windows are decorated with wood carvings depicting everyday Ayutthayan life, while the window panels show Persian and French soldiers from Louis XIV's reign.

Wat Rachanada and Loha Prasat
① *Daily 0900-1700.*
Also in the shadow of the Golden Mount but to the west and on the corner of Rachdamnern Klang Avenue and Mahachai Road, lies Wat Rachanada and the Loha Prasat, a strange-looking 'Metal Palace' with 37 spires. Built by Rama III in 1846 as a memorial to his beloved niece, Princess Soammanas Vadhanavadi, it is said to be modelled on the first Loha Prasat built in India 2500 years ago. The 37 spires represent the 37 Dharma of the Bodhipakya.

Next to the Loha Prasat is the much more traditional Wat Rachanada. The principal Buddha image is made of copper mined in Isaan – the ordination hall also has some fine doors. What makes the wat particularly worth visiting is the **Amulet Market** (see box, page 49) to be found close by, between the Golden Mount and the wat. The market also contains Buddha images and other religious artefacts.

Wat Mahannapharam and Chao Phaa Sua
West of the Democracy Monument on Tanao Road is Wat Mahannapharam in a large, tree-filled compound. A peaceful place to retreat to, it contains some good examples of high-walled, Bangkok-period architecture decorated with woodcarvings and mother-of-pearl inlay. Just south of here is the bustling Chao Phaa Sua, a Chinese temple with a fine tiled roof surmounted with mythological figures.

Giant Swing
A five-minute walk south of Wat Rachanada, on Bamrung Muang Road, is the Sao Ching Cha (Giant Swing), consisting of two tall red pillars linked by an elaborate cross piece, set in the centre of a square. A familiar emblem of the city, the Giant Swing was originally the centre for a Brahman festival in honour of Siva. Young men on a giant 'raft' would be swung high into the air to grab pouches of coins, hung from bamboo poles, between their teeth. Because the swinging was from east to west, it has been said that it symbolized the rising and setting of the sun. The festival was banned in the 1930s because of the injuries that occurred; prior to its banning, thousands would congregate around the Giant Swing for two days of dancing and music.

Wat Suthat

ⓘ *Bamrung Muang Rd. Daily 0900-1700; viharn only opens on weekends and Buddhist holidays.*
The magnificent Wat Suthat faces the Giant Swing. The wat was begun by Rama I in 1807, and his intention was to build a temple that would equal the most glorious in Ayutthaya. The wat was not finished until the end of the reign of Rama III in 1851. Surrounded by Chinese pagodas, the *viharn's* six pairs of doors are each made from a single piece of teak, deeply carved with animals and celestial beings. Inside is the bronze Phra Sri Sakyamuni Buddha, while just behind is a very fine gilded stone carving from the Dvaravati period (second-11th centuries AD), 2.5 m in height and showing the miracle at Sravasti and the Buddha preaching in the Tavatimsa heaven. The bot is the tallest in Bangkok and one of the largest in Thailand.

Wat Rachabophit

ⓘ *Atsadang Rd. Daily 0800-1700.*
The little-visited Wat Rachabophit is close to the Ministry of the Interior on Rachabophit Road, a few minutes' walk south of Wat Suthat down Ti Thong Road. It is recognizable by its distinctive doors carved in high relief with jaunty-looking soldiers wearing European-style uniforms and is peculiar in that it follows the ancient temple plan of placing the Phra Chedi in the centre of the complex.

The 43-m-high gilded *chedi's* most striking feature are the five-coloured Chinese glass tiles which encrust the lower section. The ordination hall has 10 door panels and 28 window panels each decorated with gilded black lacquer on the inside and mother-of-pearl inlay on the outside showing royal insignia.

Pahurat Indian market 'Little India' and Pak Khlong market

From Wat Rachabophit, it is only a short distance to the Pahurat Indian textile market on Pahurat Road. Here you'll find a mesmerizing array of spangly fabrics and Indian trinkets as well as plenty of Indian restaurants/foodstalls (see **Royal India**, page 85). Tucked down an alley off Chakraphet Road is **Sri Guru Singh Sabha**, supposedly the second largest Sikh temple outside of India. To get to Pahurat, walk south on Ti Thong Road which quickly becomes Tri Phet Road. After a few blocks, Pahurat Road crosses Tri Phet Road. **Pak Khlong Market** is to be found a little further south on Tri Phet Road at the foot of the Memorial Bridge. A charming, authentic market specializing in fresh flowers, it is best visited between 2200 and dawn for an alternative, but still bedazzling taste of Thai nightlife. The market slows down by 1000 but never really stops.

Chinatown

Chinatown covers the area from Charoen Krung (or New Road) down to the river and leads on from Pahurat market; cross over Chakraphet Road and immediately opposite is the entrance to Sampeng Lane. Few other places in Bangkok match Chinatown for atmosphere. The warren of alleys, lanes and tiny streets are cut through with an industrious hive of shops, temples and restaurants. Weird food, neatly arranged mountains of mechanical parts, gaudy temple architecture, gold, flowers and a constant frenetic bustle will lead to hours of happy wandering. This is an area to explore on foot, getting lost in the miasma of nooks and crannies, and grazing as you go. A trip through Chinatown can start at the Thieves' Market or at Wat Traimitr, the Golden Buddha, to the southeast.

Magic designs and tokens: tattoos and amulets

Many, if not most, Thai men wear khruang (amulets). Some Thai women do so too. In the past tattooing was equally common, although today it is usually only in the countryside that males are extensively tattooed. In the case of both tattoos and amulets the purpose is to bestow power, good luck or protection on the wearer.

Amulets have histories: those believed to have great powers sell for millions of baht and there are several magazines devoted to amulet buying and collecting. Vendors keep amulets with their takings to protect against robbery and put them into food at the beginning of the day to ensure good sales. An amulet is only to be handled by the wearer – otherwise its power is dissipated and might even be used against the owner.

Amulets can be obtained from spirit doctors and monks and come in a variety of forms. Most common are amulets of a religious nature, known as Phra khruang. These are normally images of the Buddha or of a particularly revered monk. (The most valuable are those fashioned by the 19th-century monk Phra Somdet – which are worth more than their weight in gold).

Khruang rang are usually made from tiger's teeth, buffalo horn or elephant tusk and protect the wearer in very specific ways – for example from drowning. Khruang rang plu sek, meanwhile, are magic formulas which are written down on an amulet, usually in old Khmer script (khom), and then recited during an accident, attack or confrontation.

Tattooing is primarily talismanic: magic designs, images of powerful wild beasts, texts reproduced in ancient Khmer and religious motifs are believed to offer protection from harm and give strength. (The word tattoo is derived from the Tahitian word tattau, meaning 'to mark'.

It was introduced into the English language by Captain James Cook in 1769.) Tattoos are even believed to deflect bullets, should they be sufficiently potent. A popular design is the takraw ball, a woven rattan ball used in the sport of the same name. The ball is renowned for its strength and durability, and the tattoo is believed to have the same effect on the tattooed.

The purpose of some tattoos is reflected in the use of 'invisible' ink made from sesame oil – the talismatic effects are independent of whether the tattoo can be seen. Most inks are commercial today (usually dark blue) although traditionally they were made from secret recipes incorporating such ingredients as the fat from the chin of a corpse (preferably seven corpses, taken during a full moon).

The tattooist is not just an artist and technician. He is a man of power. A master tattooist is highly respected and often given the title ajarn (teacher) or mor phi (spirit doctor). Monks can also become well known for their tattoos. These are usually religious in tone, often incorporating sentences from religious texts. The tattoos are always beneficial or protective and always on the upper part of the body (the lower parts of the body are too lowly for a monk to tattoo). Tattoos and amulets are not only used for protection, but also for attraction: men can have tattoos or amulets instilled with the power to attract women; women, alternatively, can buy amulets which protect them from the advances of men. Khruang phlad khik ('deputy penis') are phallic amulets carved from ivory, coral or rare woods, and worn around the wrist or the waist – not around the neck. Not surprisingly, they are believed to ensure sexual prowess, as well as protection from such things as snake bites.

Nakhon Kasem (Thieves' Market)
Nakhon Kasem, strictly speaking Woeng Nakhon Kasem (Thieves' Market), lies between Charoen Krung and Yaowarat Road, to the east of the *khlong* that runs parallel to Mahachai Road. Its boundaries are marked by archways. As its name suggests, this market used to be the centre for the fencing of stolen goods. It is not quite so colourful today, but there remain a number of second-hand and antique shops that are worth a browse – such as the **Good Luck Antique Shop**. Items commonly for sale include musical instruments, brass ornaments and antique coffee grinders.

Yaowarat Road
Just to the southeast of the Thieves' Market are two roads that run parallel with one another: Yaowarat Road and Sampeng Lane. Yaowarat Road, a busy thoroughfare, is the centre of the country's gold trade. The trade is run by seven shops, the **Gold Traders Association**, and the price is fixed by the government. Sino-Thais often convert their cash into gold jewellery. The jewellery is bought by its 'baht weight' which fluctuates daily with the price of gold. It's at its busiest and best at night, when food stalls abound, and the neon signs flicker to life.

Sampeng Lane
The narrower Sampeng Lane, also called Soi Wanit, is just to the south of Yaowarat Road. This road's history is shrouded in murder and intrigue. It used to be populated by prostitutes and opium addicts and was fought over by Chinese gangs. Today, it is still an interesting commercial centre, although rather less illicit. There is not much to buy here – it is primarily a wholesale centre specializing in cloth and textiles although it is a good place to go for odd lengths of material, buttons of any shape and size, costume jewellery, and such like.

Wat Traimitr (Temple of the Golden Buddha)
ⓘ *Daily 0900-1700, ฿20.*
The most celebrated example of the goldsmiths' art in Thailand sits within Wat Traimitr (Temple of the Golden Buddha) which is located at the eastern edge of Chinatown, squashed between Charoen Krung, Yaowarat Road and Traimitr Road (just to the south of Bangkok's Hualamphong railway station). The Golden Buddha is housed in a small, rather gaudy and unimpressive room. Although the leaflet offered to visitors says the 3-m-high, 700-year-old image is 'unrivalled in beauty', be prepared for disappointment; it's featureless. What makes it special, drawing large numbers of visitors each day, is that it is made of 5½ tonnes of solid gold. Apparently, when the East Asiatic Company was extending the port of Bangkok, they came across a huge stucco Buddha image, which they obtained permission to move. However, whilst being moved by crane in 1957, it fell and the stucco cracked to reveal a solid gold image within. During the Ayutthayan period it was the custom to cover valuable Buddha images in plaster to protect them from the Burmese, and this particular example stayed that way for several centuries. In the grounds of the wat there is a school, crematorium, foodstalls and the excellent **Yaowarat Chinatown Heritage Centre** (฿100). Entertaining and informative, this museum traces the history of mainland Chinese immigrants in the Kingdom and the rise of Chinatown through their grit and hard work.

Between the river and Soi Wanit 2 is a warren of lanes, too small for traffic – this is the Chinatown of old. From here it is possible to thread your way through to the River City shopping complex, which is air-conditioned and a good place to cool off.

Thonburi, Wat Arun and the khlongs

Thonburi is Bangkok's little-known alter ego. Few people cross the Chao Phraya to see this side of the city, and if they do it is usually only to catch a glimpse from the seat of a speeding *hang yaaw* (long-tailed boat) and then climb the steps of Wat Arun. But Thonburi, during the reign of King Taksin, was once the capital of ancient Siam. King Rama I believed the other side of the river – present-day Bangkok – would be more easily defended from the Burmese and so, in 1782, he switched river banks. ▸▸ *See Bangkok's river and khlongs map, page 52. For boat tours, see page 114.*

Long-tailed boat tours, the Floating Market and Snake Farm

One of the most enjoyable ways to see Bangkok is by boat – and particularly by the fast and noisy long-tailed boats or *hang yaaws*: powerful, lean machines that roar around the river and the *khlongs* at breakneck speed. There are innumerable tours around the *khlongs* of Thonburi taking in a number of sights, which include the Floating Market, Snake Farm and Wat Arun. Boats go from the various piers located along the east bank of the Chao Phraya River. The journey begins by travelling downstream along the Chao Phraya, before turning 'inland' after passing beneath Krungthep Bridge. The route skirts past laden rice-barges, squatter communities on public land and houses overhanging the canals. This is a very popular route with tourists, and boats are intercepted by vendors selling everything from cold beer to straw hats. You may also get caught in a boat jam; traffic snarl-ups are not confined to the capital's roads. Nevertheless, the trip is a fascinating insight into what Bangkok must have been like when it was still the 'Venice of the East', and around every bend there seems to be yet another stunning wat.

On private tours, a common stop at weekends is the **Taling Chan** floating market (Khlong Chak Pra). Those expecting hundreds of boats, à la Damnoen Saduak (see page 66), will be disappointed, but the local grub, prepared in boats moored alongside a wooden platform, is superb.

Another popular stop is the **Snake Farm** (Khlong Sanaam Chai) ① *฿70, shows every 20 mins, refreshments available.* Here visitors can pose with pythons, and poisonous snakes are incited to burst balloons with their fangs, 'proving' how dangerous they are. There is also a rather motley zoo with a collection of crocodiles and sad-looking animals in small cages. Our advice is to avoid it. The other snake farm in Central Bangkok (see page 61) is cheaper and much more professional. After speeding past the snake farm, boats enter Khlong Bangkok Yai at the site of the large **Wat Paknam**. Just before re-entering the Chao Phraya itself, the route passes the impressive **Wat Kalaya Nimit**. Another popular stop is the Royal Barges Museum, further north, on Khlong Bangkok Noi (see below).

Wat Prayoon Wong

To the south of Wat Kalaya Nimit, on the Thonburi side of the river, is **Wat Prayoon Wong**, virtually in the shadow of the Saphan Phut bridge. The quirky wat is famous for its **Khao Tao (Turtle Mountain)** ① *0830-1730.* This is a concrete fantasy land of grottoes and peaks, with miniature *chedis* and *viharns*, all set around a pond teeming with turtles. These are released to gain merit and the animals clearly thrive in the murky water. This wat, which can be reached by taking a cross-river shuttle boat from Tha Saphan Phut (฿4), is rarely visited by tourists but its imposing white *chedi*, surrounded by 18 satellite *chedis* and a small museum filled with Buddhist statues and amulets, is clearly visible from Bangkok.

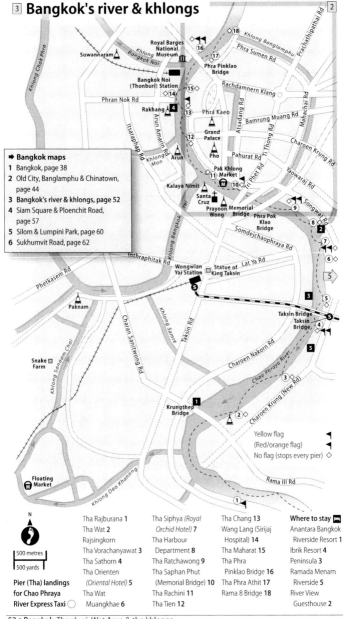

③ Bangkok's river & khlongs

Royal Barges National Museum

Suwannaram

Khlong Bangkok Noi

Bangkok Chak Phra

Khlong Banglamphu

Phra Sumen Rd

Prachathipathai Rd

② ◇ 18 ◀◀

◇ 16 ◀

17 ◀

Phra Pinklao Bridge

Phra Pinklao Bridge

Rachdamnern Klang

Bangkok Noi (Thonburi) Station

◇ 14 ◀

15 ◀

Phran Nok Rd

Atsadang Rd

Rakhang ▲ 4

13 ◀

Phra Kaeo

Bamrung Muang Rd

Mahachai Rd

Arun Amarin Rd

12 ◀

Grand Palace

Pho

Charoen Krung Rd

Itsaraphap Rd

Arun ▲

Pahurat Rd

Ti Thong Rd

Tri Phet Rd

Yaowarat Rd

Khlong Mon

Pak Khlong Market

11 ◀ 🏠

10 ◀

Songwat Rd

◇ 9

② ◀

◇ 8

Kalaya Nimit

Santa Cruz

Prayoon Wong

Memorial Bridge

Phra Pok Klao Bridge

⑦ ◀◀

◇ 6 ◇

⑤

➤ **Bangkok maps**
1 Bangkok, page 38
2 Old City, Banglamphu & Chinatown, page 44
3 Bangkok's river & khlongs, page 52
4 Siam Square & Ploenchit Road, page 57
5 Silom & Lumpini Park, page 60
6 Sukhumvit Road, page 62

Somdejchaophraya Rd

Khlong Bangkok Yai

Inthraphitak Rd

Lat Ya Rd

Wongwian Yai Station

☐ **Statue of King Taksin**

⑤

③ ▶

⑤

Phetkasem Rd

Charan Sanitwong Rd

Taksin Rd

Khlong Sanam

Taksin Bridge

Taksin Bridge

④ ◀

⑤

Paknam ▲

Charoen Nakorn Rd

Chao Phraya River

Snake 🏠 Farm

Khlong Sanam Chai

③

Charoen Krung (New Rd)

① ▲

Krungthep Bridge

② ▲

Yellow flag ◀

(Red/orange flag) ◀

No flag (stops every pier) ◇

Rama III Rd

🏠 **Floating Market**

Khlong Dao Khanong

① ◇

N 🧭

500 metres
500 yards

Pier (Tha) landings for Chao Phraya River Express Taxi ◯

Tha Rajburana **1**
Tha Wat Rajsingkorn
Tha Vorachanyawat **3**
Tha Sathorn **4**
Tha Orienten *(Oriental Hotel)* **5**
Tha Wat Muangkhae **6**

Tha Siphya *(Royal Orchid Hotel)* **7**
Tha Harbour Department **8**
Tha Ratchawong **9**
Tha Saphan Phut *(Memorial Bridge)* **10**
Tha Rachini **11**
Tha Tien **12**

Tha Chang **13**
Wang Lang (Sirijaj Hospital) **14**
Tha Maharat **15**
Tha Phra Pinklao Bridge **16**
Tha Phra Athit **17**
Rama 8 Bridge **18**

Where to stay 🛏
Anantara Bangkok Riverside Resort **1**
Ibrik Resort **4**
Peninsula **3**
Ramada Menam Riverside **5**
River View Guesthouse **2**

Chao Phraya River Express

One of the most relaxing – and one of the cheapest – ways to see Bangkok is by taking the Chao Phraya River Express. *Rua duan* (boats) link almost 40 piers (*tha*) along the Chao Phraya River from Tha Rajburana (Big C) in the south to Tha Nonthaburi in the north.

The entire route entails a journey of about 1¼-1½ hours, and fares are ฿9-15. At peak periods, boats leave every 10 minutes, off-peak about every 15-25 minutes. Boats flying red/orange (downriver) or yellow (upriver) pennants are Special Express boats which only run 0600-0900, 1200-1900 and do not stop at every pier (see map opposite). Also, boats will only stop if passengers wish to board or alight, so make your destination known.

Selected piers and places of interest, travelling upstream:

Tha Sathorn The pier with the closest access to the Skytrain (Taksin Bridge, S6).
Tha Orienten By the Oriental Hotel; access to Silom Road.
Tha Harbour Department In the shadow of the Royal Orchid Hotel, on the south side and close to River City shopping centre.

Tha Ratchawong Rabieng Ratchawong Restaurant; access to Chinatown and Sampeng Lane.
Tha Saphan Phut Under the Memorial Bridge and close to Pahurat Indian Market.
Tha Rachini Pak Khlong Market.
Tha Tien Close to Wat Pho; Wat Arun on the opposite bank; and, just downstream from Wat Arun.
Tha Chang Just downstream is the Grand Palace peeking out above whitewashed walls; Wat Rakhang with its white corn-cob prang lies opposite.
Tha Maharaj Access to Wat Mahathat and Sanaam Luang.
Tha Phra Arthit Access to Khaosan Road.
Tha Visutkasat Just upstream is the elegant central Bank of Thailand.
Tha Thewes Just upstream are boat-sheds with royal barges; close to the National Library.
Tha Wat Chan Just upstream is the Singha Beer Samoson brewery.
Tha Wat Khema Wat Khema in large, tree-filled compound.
Tha Wat Khian Wat Kien, semi-submerged.
Tha Nonthaburi Last stop on the express boat route.

Santa Cruz Church

A five-minute walk upstream from here is **Santa Cruz Catholic Church**. Cross-river shuttles run between here and Tha Rachini, close to the massive Pak Khlong fresh produce market, facing the river. The church, washed in pastel yellow with a domed tower, was built to serve the Portuguese community and is fully functioning.

Wat Arun

ⓘ *0830-1730, ฿20. Climbing the wat is not permitted. It is possible to get to Wat Arun by water-taxi from Tha Tien pier (at the end of Thai Wang Rd near Wat Pho), or from Tha Chang (at the end of Na Phralan near Wat Phra Kaeo) ฿3.*

Facing Wat Pho across the Chao Phraya River is the famous Wat Arun (Temple of the Dawn). Wat Arun stands 81 m high, making it the highest *prang* (tower) in Thailand. It was built in the early 19th century on the site of Wat Chaeng, the Royal Palace complex when Thonburi was briefly the capital of Thailand. The wat housed the Emerald Buddha before the image was transferred to Bangkok and it is said that King Taksin vowed to restore the wat after passing it one dawn. The *prang* is completely covered with fragments of Chinese porcelain and includes some delicate gold and black lacquered doors. The temple is really meant to be viewed from across the river; its scale and beauty can only be appreciated from a distance. The best view of Wat Arun is in the evening from the Bangkok side of the river when the sun sets behind the *prang*.

Royal Barges National Museum

① 0830-1630, ฿30, children free, ฿100 for cameras, ฿200 for video cameras.

After visiting Wat Arun, some tours then go further upstream to the mouth of Khlong Bangkok Noi where the Royal Barges are housed in a hangar-like boathouse. These ornately carved boats, winched out of the water in cradles, were used by the king at Krathin to present robes to the monks in Wat Arun at the end of the rainy season. The ceremony ceased in 1967 but the Royal Thai Navy restored the barges for the revival of the spectacle, as part of the extensive celebrations for the 60th anniversary of the king's succession to the throne in June 2006. The oldest and most beautiful barge is the *Sri Supannahong*, built during the reign of Rama I (1782-1809) and repaired during that of Rama VI (1910-1925). It measures 45 m long and 3 m wide, weighs 15 tonnes and was created from a single piece of teak. It required a crew of 50 oarsmen and two coxswains, along with such assorted crew members as a flagman, a rhythm-keeper and singer. Its gilded prow was carved in the form of a *hansa* (or goose) and its stern, in the shape of a naga (a mythical serpent-like creature).

Wat Rakhang

① Daily 0500-2100, ฿20. The river ferry stops at the wat.

Two rarely visited wats are Wat Suwannaram, see below, and Wat Rakhang. The royal Wat Rakhang is located just upstream from Wat Arun, almost opposite Tha Chang landing, and is identifiable from the river by the two plaster sailors standing to attention on either side of the jetty. Dating from the Ayutthaya period, the wat's **Phra Prang** is considered a particularly well proportioned example of early Bangkok architecture (late 18th century). The **Ordination Hall** (not always open – the abbot may oblige if he is available) was built during the reign of Rama III and contains a fine gilded Buddha image. The beautiful red-walled wooden **Tripitaka Hall** (originally a library built in the late 18th century), to the left of the *viharn*, was the residence of Rama I while he was a monk and Thonburi was still the capital of Siam. Consisting of two rooms, it is decorated with faded but nonetheless highly regarded murals of the *Ramakien* (painted by a monk-artist), black and gold chests, a portrait of the king, and some odd bits of old carved door.

Wat Suwannaram

Wat Suwannaram is a short distance further on from the Royal Barges National Museum on Khlong Bangkok Noi, on the other side of the canal. The main buildings date from Rama I's reign (late 18th century), although the complex was later extensively renovated by Rama III. There was a wat on this site even prior to Rama I's reign, and the original name, Wat Thong (Golden Wat), remains in popular use. On the right-hand wall, as you enter from the riverside door, is a representation of a boat foundering with the crew being eaten by sharks and sea monsters as they thrash about in the waves. Closer inspection shows that these unfortunates are wearing white skull-caps – presumably they are Muslims returning from the *haj* to Mecca. The principal image in the *bot* is made of bronze and shows the Buddha calling the Earth Goddess to witness. Wat Suwannaram is elegant and rarely visited and is a peaceful place to escape after the bustle of Wat Arun and the Floating Market.

Almost opposite Wat Suwannaram, on the opposite bank of the river, is the home of an unusual occupational group – Chao Phraya's divers. The men use traditional diving gear – heavy bronze helmets, leaden shoes, air pumps and pipes – and search the bed of the murky river for lost precious objects, sunken boats, and the bodies of those who have drowned or been murdered.

Dusit area

Dusit, the present home of the Thai Royal family and the administration, is an area of wide tree-lined boulevards – the rationalized spaces more in keeping with a European city. It is grand but lacks the usual bustling atmosphere found in the rest of Bangkok. ➜ *See map, page 38, for sights in the Dusit area.*

Vimanmek Palace
① *T02-281 1569, www.palaces.thai.net. 0930-1600 (last tickets sold at 1500), ฿100. Visitors are not free to wander, but must be shown around by one of the charming guides who demonstrate the continued deep reverence for King Rama V (tour approximately 1 hr). Note that tickets to the Grand Palace include entrance to Vimanmek Palace. Dance shows are held twice a day at 1030 and 1400. Visitors to the palace are required to wear long trousers or a long skirt; sarongs available for hire (฿100, refundable). Refreshments available. Buses do go past the palace, but from the centre of town it is easier to get a tuk-tuk or taxi (฿50-60).*
The Vimanmek Palace, just off Rachvithi Road, to the north of the National Assembly, is the largest golden teakwood mansion in the world, but don't expect to see huge expanses of polished wood – the building is almost entirely painted. It was built in 1901 by Rama V, who was clearly taken with Western style. It seems like a large Victorian hunting lodge and is filled with china, silver and paintings from all over the world (as well as some gruesome hunting trophies). The photographs are fascinating – one shows the last time elephants were used in warfare in Thailand. Behind the palace is the Audience Hall, which houses a fine exhibition of crafts made by the Support Foundation, an organization set up and funded by Queen Sirikit. Also worth seeing is the exhibition of the king's own photographs and the clock museum.

Amporn Gardens area
From Vimanmek, it is a 10- to 15-minute walk to the Dusit Zoo, skirting around the **Ananda Samakhom Throne Hall**, a huge, white Italian Renaissance-style structure in Carrara marble. Its interior was off-limits but currently there's an exhibition on display inside. '**Arts of the Kingdom**' ① *Tue-Sun 1000-1800, ฿150*, showcases heavily gilded regalia (elephant howdahs, throne pavilions, palanquins, etc) but, in truth, the exquisite Italian frescoes of Chakri Dynasty Kings that line the hall's recessed ceiling domes are the highlight.

In the centre of the square in front of the National Assembly stands an equestrian statue of the venerated King Chulalongkorn. To the left lie the Amporn Gardens, the venue for royal social functions and fairs. Southwards from the square runs the impressive **Rachdamnern Nok Avenue**, a Siamese Champs Elysées. Enter the **Dusit Zoo** ① *0800-1800, ฿100, ฿50 children*, through Uthong Gate, just before the square. A pleasant walk through the zoo leads to the Chitralada Palace and Wat Benchamabophit. Compared to zoos in the West (and even to others in Thailand), it's average at best, but the kids will enjoy themselves. There is a children's playground, plenty of space for them to run wild (unlike many of the listless animals) and pedal-boats can be hired on the lake.

From the Dusit Zoo's Suanchit Gate, a right turn down the tree-lined Rama V Road leads to the present King Bhumibol's residence – **Chitralada Palace**. It was built by Rama VI and is not open to the public. Evidence of the king's forays into agricultural research may be visible. He has a great interest and concern for the development of the poorer, agricultural parts of his country, and invests large sums of his own money in royal projects. To the right of the intersection of Rama V and Sri Ayutthaya roads are the gold and ochre roofs of Wat Benchamabophit – a 10-minute walk from the zoo.

Wat Benchamabophit
ⓘ *0800-1700, ฿20.*
Wat Benchamabophit (the Marble Temple) is the most modern of the royal temples and was only finished in 1911. Designed by Rama V's half brother, Prince Naris, it is an unusual display of carrara marble pillars, a marble courtyard and two large *singhas* guarding the entrance to the *bot*. The interior is magnificently decorated with crossbeams of lacquer and gold, and in shallow niches in the walls are paintings of important stupas from all over the kingdom. The door panels are faced with bronze sculptures and the windows are of stained-glass, painted with angels. The cloisters around the assembly hall house 52 figures – a display of the evolution of the Buddha image in India, China and Japan.

Government House and Wat Sonnakviharn
ⓘ *Government House only open on Wan Dek – a once-yearly holiday for children on the 2nd Sat in Jan; Wat Sonnakviharn open daily.*
Government House is south of here on Nakhon Pathom Road. The building is a weird mixture of cathedral Gothic and colonial Thai. The little-visited Wat Sonnakviharn is on Krung Kasem Road, located behind a car park and schoolyard. Enter by the doorway in the far right-hand corner of the schoolyard, or down Soi Sommanat. It is peaceful, unkempt and rather beautiful, with fine gold lacquer doors and a large gold tile-encrusted *chedi*.

Siam Square area

Shop, shop and then shop some more. Head for Siam Square if you want to be at the apex of Thai youth culture and the biggest spread of shopping opportunities in the city. From the hi-tech market at Panthip Plaza, the massive MBK complex, the host of upmarket stores at one of Southeast Asia's largest malls, Siam Paragon and neighbour Siam Discovery, pure silk at Jim Thompson's House or the warren of tiny boutiques in Siam Square, you should leave with a big hole in your bank account.

Suan Pakkard Palace (Lettuce Garden Palace)
ⓘ *352-354 Sri Ayutthaya Rd, south of the Victory Monument, 0900-1600, ฿100 – including a fan to ward off the heat; all profits go to a fund for artists. To get there, take the skytrain to Phaya Thai.*
This is a beautiful, relaxing spot. The five raised traditional Thai houses amid lush gardens were built by Princess Chumbhot, a great granddaughter of King Rama IV. They contain her collection of fine, rare but badly labelled antiquities. The rear pavilion is lovely, decorated in black and gold lacquerwork panels. Prince Chumbhot discovered this temple near Ayutthaya and reassembled and restored it here for his wife's 50th birthday.

Jim Thompson's House

ⓘ *Soi Kasemsan Song (2), opposite the National Stadium, www.jimthompsonhouse.com. Mon-Sat 0900-1700 by compulsory guided tour only, ฿100, concessions ฿50 (profits to charity). Shoes must be removed before entering; no photography allowed. Take the Skytrain to National Stadium; the house is well signposted from here. Alternatively, take a bus, taxi or tuk-tuk along Rama I Rd, or take a public canal boat. To get to the jetty from Jim Thompson's, walk down to the canal, turn right and along to the jetty by the bridge. Boats travelling to the Grand Palace will be coming from the right.*

Jim Thompson's House is an assemblage of traditional teak northern Thai houses, some more than 200 years old (these houses were designed to be transportable, consisting of five parts – the floor, posts, roof, walls and decorative elements constructed without the use of nails). Bustling Bangkok only intrudes in the form of the stench from the *khlong* that runs behind the house. Jim Thompson arrived in Bangkok as an intelligence officer attached to the United States' OSS (Office of Strategic Services) and then made his name by reinvigorating the Thai silk industry after the Second World War. He disappeared

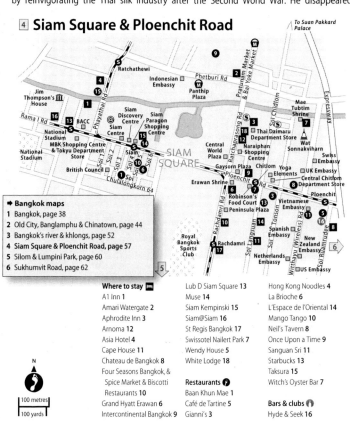

4 Siam Square & Ploenchit Road

Where to stay 🛏

A1 Inn 1
Amari Watergate 2
Aphrodite Inn 3
Arnoma 12
Asia Hotel 4
Cape House 11
Chateau de Bangkok 8
Four Seasons Bangkok, &
  Spice Market & Biscotti
  Restaurants 10
Grand Hyatt Erawan 6
Intercontinental Bangkok 9

Lub D Siam Square 13
Muse 14
Siam Kempinski 15
Siam@Siam 16
St Regis Bangkok 17
Swissotel Nailert Park 7
Wendy House 5
White Lodge 18

Restaurants 🍴
Baan Khun Mae 1
Café de Tartine 5
Gianni's 3

Hong Kong Noodles 4
La Brioche 6
L'Espace de l'Oriental 14
Mango Tango 10
Neil's Tavern 8
Once Upon a Time 9
Sanguan Sri 11
Starbucks 13
Taksura 15
Witch's Oyster Bar 7

Bars & clubs 🍸
Hyde & Seek 16

mysteriously in the Malaysian jungle on 27 March 1967, but his silk industry continues to thrive. Jim Thompson chose this site for his house partly because a collection of silk weavers lived nearby on Khlong Saensaep. The house contains an eclectic collection of antiques from Thailand and China, with work displayed as though it was still his home. Walking barefoot around the house adds to the appreciation of its cool teak floorboards. There is a little café attached to the museum, as well as a shop and rotating exhibition space upstairs.

The head office of the **Jim Thompson Silk Emporium**, selling fine Thai silk, is at the northeast end of Surawong Road, and there are numerous branches in the top hotels around the city. This shop is a tourist attraction in itself. Shoppers can buy high-quality bolts of silk and silk clothing here (from pocket handkerchiefs to suits). Prices are top of the scale.

Siam Square

A 10-minute walk east along Rama I Road is the biggest, busiest modern shopping area in the city. Most of it centres on a maze of tiny boutiques and covered market area known as Siam Square. Thronged with young people, Siam Square plays host to Bangkok's burgeoning youth culture: cutting-edge contemporary and experimental fashions, live music, pavement craft markets, Thai-style fast food, retro cineplexes and dozens of urban stylists keep the kids entertained. Needless to say, it epitomizes older Thais' fears about the direction their country is taking – young people aping East Asian and Western mores and irreverent modern values. Despite this, the area is distinctly Thai, albeit with a contemporary face and the groups of vibrant, self-confidently style-conscious youth will unsettle visitors who'd prefer Bangkok to remain a museum of teak villas and traditional temples. Just across Rama 1 are the shiny bright shopping centres of the enormous Siam Paragon, Siam Centre and Discovery – an elevated walkway connects Siam with Chitlom further down Rama 1 (see Deparment stores and shopping malls, page 102).

On the corner of Rama 1 and Phayathai Road is **MBK**, Bangkok's largest indoor shopping area. Crammed with bargains and outlets of every description this is one of the Thai capital's most popular shopping spots. Opposite MBK is the 11-storey **Bangkok Art and Culture Centre** ① *939 Rama I Rd, T02-214 6630, T02-214 6631, www.bacc.or.th, Tue-Sun 1000-2100*, worth visting for contemporary arts and cultural activities.

Madame Tussauds

① *6th floor, Siam Discovery Center, Rama 1 Rd, T02-658 0060, www.madametussauds.com/ bangkok. Daily 1000-2100. ฿800, ฿600 children (15% off for online bookings).*
Barack Obama, Madonna and most of the Hollywood A-listers are here, but so are loads of local heroes, too. Asia's first branch of the famous waxwork museum, located on the top floor of Siam Discovery, is a good place to acquaint yourself with Thailand's movers and shakers, from modern icons, such as boxing champ, Khaosai Galaxy, and 1960s movie stars, Mitr Chaibancha and Petchara Yaowarat, to famous poet, Sunthorn Phu, and more controversial figures like military dictator Field Marshal Plaek Pibulsongkram. Aung San Suu Kyi is also here, as are lots of fun interactive games to ward of waxwork-fatigue. Good fun but somewhat pricey.

Chulalongkorn University

This is the country's most prestigious university. While Thammasat University on Sanaam Luang is known for its radical politics, Chulalongkorn is more conservative. Just south of Siam Square, on the campus itself (off Soi Chulalongkorn 12, behind the **MBK** shopping centre; ask for *sa-sin*, the houses are nearby) is a collection of **traditional Thai houses**. Also on campus is the **Museum of Imaging Technology** ① *Mon-Fri 1000-1530, ฿100; to*

*get to the museum, enter the campus by the main entrance on the east side of Phaya Thai Rd
and walk along the south side of the playing field, turn right after the Chemistry 2 building
and then right again at the entrance to the Mathematics Faculty; the museum is at the end
of this walkway in the Department of Photographic Science and Printing Technology*, with
a few hands-on photographic displays. The Art Centre on the seventh floor of the Centre
of Academic Resources (central library) next to the car park, hosts regular exhibitions of
contemporary art and discussions in English and Thai.

Erawan Shrine
East of Siam Square is the Erawan Shrine, on the corner of Ploenchit and Rachdamri roads,
at the Rachprasong intersection. This is Bangkok's most popular shrine, attracting not just
Thais but also large numbers of other Asian visitors. The spirit of the shrine, the Hindu
god Thao Maha Brahma, is reputed to grant people's wishes. In thanks, visitors offer three
incense sticks, a garland, a candle and a piece of gold leaf to each of its four faces. Some
also pay to have dances performed for them accompanied by the resident Thai orchestra.
The shrine is a hive of activity at most hours, incongruously set on a noisy, polluted
intersection tucked into a corner, and in the shadow of the Zen Department Store.

Panthip Plaza
Sited on Phetburi Road (parallel to Rama I, 800 m to the north), Panthip Plaza, otherwise
known as 'geek's paradise', is home to one of the best hi-tech computer markets in Asia.
Motherboards, chips, drives and all manner and make of devices are piled high and sold
cheap over six floors. You'll be constantly hustled to buy copied software, DVDs, games,
most of which make excellent and affordable alternatives to the real thing. There's a great
foodhall on the second floor. Many of the named-brand goods are cheaper than back
home, but be aware that these are likely to be 'grey market' goods, imported through
unofficial channels, and so are unlikely to have the usual manufacturer warranty.

Silom area

Hi-tech, high-rise and clad in concrete and glass, Silom is at the centre of booming Bangkok.
Banks, international business and many media companies are based in this area as is the
heart of Bangkok's gay community on Patpong 2, one of two infamous *sois*. Patpong 1
now houses a famous night market and is largely recognized as the eponymous home
of Bangkok's notorious girly shows. Stylish, tacky and sweaty, head down the length of
Silom for a slice of contemporary Bangkok life. ▸▸ *See Silom and Surawong map, page 60.*

Patpong
ⓘ *Catch the Skytrain to the Sala Daeng station.*
The seedier side of Bangkok life has always been a crowd-puller to the Western tourist.
Most people flock to the red-light district of Patpong, which runs along two lanes
(Patpong 1 and 2) linking Silom to Surawong. These streets were transformed from a
street of 'tea houses' (brothels serving local clients) into a hi-tech lane of go-go bars in
1969 when an American entrepreneur made a major investment. Patpong 1 is the larger
and more active of the streets, with a host of stalls down the middle at night; Patpong 2
supports cocktail bars, pharmacies and clinics for STDs, as well as a few go-go bars. There
are also restaurants and bars here. Expats and locals (gay and straight) in search of less
sleazy surrounds, tend to opt for the middle ground of Patpong 4, still essentially a gay

enclave but more sophisticated than seedy, see Bars and clubs, page 93. Patpong is also home to a night market infamous for its line in copied designer handbags, some of which are better made than the originals.

Lumpini Park
ⓘ Take a Skytrain to Sala Daeng station or Metro to Lumpini station.

Lumpini Park, or 'Suan Lum' as it is affectionately known, is Bangkok's oldest, largest and most popular public park. It lies between Wireless Road and Rachdamri Road, just across from the entrance to Silom and Sathorn roads. Activity at the park starts early with large numbers of elderly and not so elderly Thais practising t'ai chi under the trees at dawn and dusk. This is also the time to join in the free en-mass aerobics sessions, jog along with the

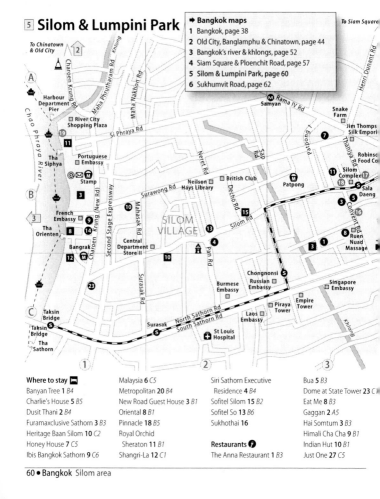

5 Silom & Lumpini Park

➡ Bangkok maps
1 Bangkok, page 38
2 Old City, Banglamphu & Chinatown, page 44
3 Bangkok's river & khlongs, page 52
4 Siam Square & Ploenchit Road, page 57
5 Silom & Lumpini Park, page 60
6 Sukhumvit Road, page 62

Where to stay 🛏
Banyan Tree 1 *B4*
Charlie's House 5 *B5*
Dusit Thani 2 *B4*
Furamaxclusive Sathorn 3 *B3*
Heritage Baan Silom 10 *C2*
Honey House 7 *C5*
Ibis Bangkok Sathorn 9 *C6*

Malaysia 6 *C5*
Metropolitan 20 *B4*
New Road Guest House 3 *B1*
Oriental 8 *B1*
Pinnacle 18 *B5*
Royal Orchid
  Sheraton 11 *B1*
Shangri-La 12 *C1*

Siri Sathorn Executive
  Residence 4 *B4*
Sofitel Silom 15 *B2*
Sofitel So 13 *B6*
Sukhothai 16

Restaurants 🍴
The Anna Restaurant 1 *B3*

Bua 5 *B3*
Dome at State Tower 23 *C*
Eat Me 8 *B3*
Gaggan 2 *A5*
Hai Somtum 3 *B3*
Himali Cha Cha 9 *B1*
Indian Hut 10 *B1*
Just One 27 *C5*

colourful crowds or lift some weights with the oiled beefcakes at the open-air gyms – all of which make great spectator sports too. Lumpini also has a lap pool, but it's for members only. At the weekend, it is a popular place for family picnics. In the evening, couples stroll along the lake and people jog or work out along the paths. Lumpini is also the site of the Bangkok Symphony Orchestra concerts that run during the cool season (November to February). Check the *Bangkok Post* for performances.

Thai Red Cross Snake Farm
ⓘ *Within the Science Division of the Thai Red Cross Society at the corner of Rama IV and Henri Dunant roads. Mon-Fri 0830-1730 (shows at 1100 and 1430), weekends and holidays 0930-1200 (show at 1100). ฿200.*

The Snake Farm of the Thai Red Cross is very central and easy to reach from Silom or Surawong roads (see map opposite). It was established in 1923 and raises snakes for the production of serum, which is distributed worldwide. The farm also has a collection of non-venomous snakes. During showtime (which lasts a mesmerizing half an hour) various snakes are exhibited, venom extracted and visitors can fondle a python. The farm is well maintained. There is also a small adjoining museum.

Sukhumvit Road

With the Skytrain running its length, Sukhumvit Road has developed into Bangkok's most vibrant strip. Shopping centres, girly bars, some of the city's best hotels and awesome places to eat have been joined by futuristic nightclubs. The grid of *sois* that run off the main drag are home to a variety of different communities including Arab, African and Korean as well as throngs of pasty Westerners. Sordid and dynamic, there's never a dull moment on Sukhumvit Road.

Siam Society
ⓘ *131 Soi Asoke, T02-6616470, www.siam-society.org, Tue-Sat 0900-1700, ฿100.*
Just off Sukhumvit Road, within the grounds of the Siam Society, a learned society established in 1904, is **Kamthieng House**, a 120-year-old northern Thai building. Donated to the society in 1963 the house was transported to Bangkok from Chiang

Krua Aroy Aroy **4** *B2*
La Table de Tee **6** *B4*
Le Bouchon **11** *B3*
Ruen Urai **7** *B3*
Silom Village **13** *B2*
Soi Polo Fried Chicken **12** *A5*
Tongue Thai **14** *B1*

Zanotti **15** *B4*

Bars & clubs 🍸
Molly Mallone's **16** *B3*
O'Reilly's **17** *B3*
Tapas **18** *B3*
Viva Aviv **19** *A1*

Mai and then reassembled a few years later. It now serves as an ethnological museum, devoted to preserving the traditional technologies and folk arts of northern Thailand. It makes an interesting contrast to the fine arts displayed in Suan Pakkard Palace and Jim Thompson's House. The Siam Society houses a library, organizes lectures and study trips and publishes books, magazines and pamphlets.

Science Museum and Planetarium
ⓘ *Tue-Sun 0900-1600, closed public holidays, ฿40, ฿20 children. Skytrain to Ekkamai.*
The Science Museum and Planetarium is just past Sukhumvit Soi 40, next to the Eastern bus terminal. As well as the planetarium, there are aeroplanes and other exhibits, but don't expect many of them to work. As one report put it, there are lots of interactive buttons, but nothing much happens when you press them. ➤➤ *For information on the newer and much better National Science Museum, see page 67.*

Bangkok suburbs

Phayathai Palace
ⓘ *Phramongkutklao Hospital, 315 Rachawithi Rd, T02-354 7987, www.phyathaipalace.org. Tours in English must be booked at least 7 days in advance; allow 2 hrs, ฿500. Tours in Thai Sat*

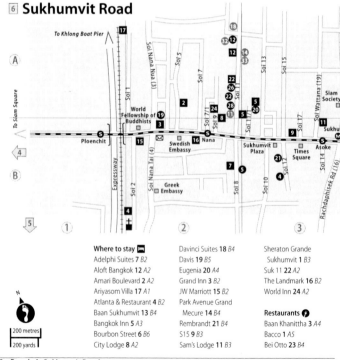

6 **Sukhumvit Road**

Where to stay 🛏
Adelphi Suites **7** *B2*
Aloft Bangkok **12** *A2*
Amari Boulevard **2** *A2*
Ariyasom Villa **17** *A1*
Atlanta & Restaurant **4** *B2*
Baan Sukhumvit **13** *B4*
Bangkok Inn **5** *A3*
Bourbon Street **6** *B6*
City Lodge **8** *A2*

Davinci Suites **18** *B4*
Davis **19** *B5*
Eugenia **20** *A4*
Grand Inn **3** *B2*
JW Marriott **15** *B2*
Park Avenue Grand
  Mecure **14** *B4*
Rembrandt **21** *B4*
S15 **9** *B3*
Sam's Lodge **11** *B3*

Sheraton Grande
  Sukhumvit **1** *B3*
Suk 11 **22** *A2*
The Landmark **16** *B2*
World Inn **24** *A2*

Restaurants 🍴
Baan Khanittha **3** *A4*
Bacco **1** *A5*
Bei Otto **23** *B4*

0930 and 1500, by donation only (if there are enough English speakers, one of the guides will break off from the main group and talk to you in English).

A 10-minute stroll west of Victory Monument roundabout sits Wang Phayathai, a palace built by King Rama V as a royal retreat back in 1909. After his premature death in 1910, his successor, King Vajiravudh, remodelled it into the palace visitors still enjoy today. An incongruous site, surrounded on both sides by a hulking city hospital, it has a charming Sino-Portuguese beige exterior, punctuated by a gothic turret and fringed by a lush lawn. The ground floor's open-sided corridors feature ageing frescoes and original floor tiling and, at the back, there's a neo-classical Roman garden of marble statues and geometric Corinthian columns, and an animist and Buddhist shrine. The lawn here was once home to one of the world's most bizarre manifestations of political thought: a miniature city that served as a fully-functioning model democratic society. You can explore these areas by yourself (and enjoy a cup of coffee in the stunning restaurant, Café de Norasingha, see Restaurants, page 92) but a guided tour is the only way to see all the rooms and to learn about the palace's many incarnations (between 1926 and 1932 it served as a luxury hotel) and European-style period motifs.

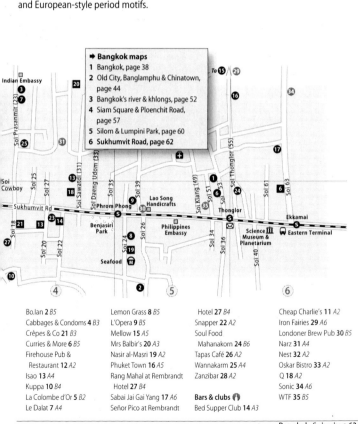

➜ **Bangkok maps**
1 Bangkok, page 38
2 Old City, Banglamphu & Chinatown, page 44
3 Bangkok's river & khlongs, page 52
4 Siam Square & Ploenchit Road, page 57
5 Silom & Lumpini Park, page 60
6 Sukhumvit Road, page 62

Bo.lan **2** *B5*
Cabbages & Condoms **4** *B3*
Crêpes & Co **21** *B3*
Curries & More **6** *B5*
Firehouse Pub & Restaurant **12** *A2*
Isao **13** *A4*
Kuppa **10** *B4*
La Colombe d'Or **5** *B2*
Le Dalat **7** *A4*

Lemon Grass **8** *B5*
L'Opera **9** *B5*
Mellow **15** *A5*
Mrs Balbir's **20** *A3*
Nasir al-Masri **19** *A2*
Phuket Town **16** *A5*
Rang Mahal at Rembrandt Hotel **27** *B4*
Sabai Jai Gai Yang **17** *A6*
Señor Pico at Rembrandt

Hotel **27** *B4*
Snapper **22** *A2*
Soul Food Mahanakorn **24** *B6*
Tapas Café **26** *A2*
Wannakarm **25** *A4*
Zanzibar **28** *A2*

Bars & clubs 🍸
Bed Supper Club **14** *A3*

Cheap Charlie's **11** *A2*
Iron Fairies **29** *A6*
Londoner Brew Pub **30** *B5*
Narz **31** *A4*
Nest **32** *A2*
Oskar Bistro **33** *A2*
Q **18** *A2*
Sonic **34** *A6*
WTF **35** *B5*

Chatuchak Weekend Market

ⓘ *At the weekend, the market is officially open from 0800-1800 (although some shops open earlier around 0700, some later around 0900). It's best to go early in the day or after 1500. Beware of pickpockets. Take the Skytrain to Mo Chit station.*

North of Bangkok, the Chatuchak Weekend Market is just off Phahonyothin Road, opposite the Northern bus terminal, near the Mo Chit Skytrain and Chatuchak Park and Kampaeng Phet Metro stations. Until 1982 this market was held at Sanaam Luang in central Bangkok, but was moved after it outgrew its original home. Chatuchak is a huge conglomeration of around 15,000 stallholders spread over an area of 14 ha, selling virtually everything under the sun, and an estimated 200,000 to 300,000 people visit the market each day. There are antique stalls, basket stalls, textile sellers, shirt vendors, carvers and painters along with the usual array of fishmongers, vegetable hawkers and butchers. A huge number of bars and foodstalls have also opened to cater for the crowds, so it is possible to rest and recharge before foraging once more. The head office and information centre, along with the police, first aid, banks and left-baggage facilities, can all be found opposite Gate 1, off Kampaengphet Road. The clock tower serves as a good reference point should visitors become disorientated.

Also here, in the north section of Chatuchak Park adjacent to Kamphaeng Phet Road, is the **Railway Museum** ⓘ *0900-1800, free,* with a small collection of steam locomotives as well as miniature and model trains. Later on, if you still have some energy and money, visit the relatively new **Talad Rot Fai** nearby. Located west of Chatuchak, just off Kampaengphet Road, this excellent night-time flea market is full of antiques, junk and faux-vintage pieces. It takes place on a squalid plot of land owned by the State Railway of Thailand and gets its moniker, the 'train market', from the row of rusting decommissioned rail carriages that flank it. There are also converted warehouses housing antique shops and cool bars, making it a great spot to browse or just hangout. It gets going at sundown every Saturday and Sunday.

Mansion 7

ⓘ *Ratchada Rd (mouth of Ratchada Soi 14), T02-692 6311, www.themansion7.com. Sun-Thu 1200-0000, Fri-Sat 1200-0200. ฿320 for entry to the Dark Mansion.*

Something different: a boutique shopping mall that peddles food, fashion and fear. Owned by the same company behind Hua Hin's faux-vintage market, Plearn Wan, this huge, lair-like hangar is just the sort of place you can imagine Tim Burton or The Munsters spending time at the weekend, with restaurants that casually ask for your blood group when you order, eerie (and not-so-eerie) shops and a Victorian Gothic-style haunted house at the back. The latter is called the Dark Mansion and is a real jump-a-minute fright fest, worth the entrance fee, just. It's only a short walk from MRT Huay Kwang station.

Safari World

ⓘ *99 Panyaintra Rd, Klongsamwa district, T02-518 1000, www.safariworld.com. Daily 0900-1700, ฿900, ฿650 children. Take bus Nos 26, 71, 60, 96 or 501 to Minburi, whence a minibus service runs to the park.*

Safari world is a 120-ha complex in Minburi, 9 km northeast of Bagnkok's city centre, with animals, a marine park and an amusement park. Most of the animals are African – zebras, lions, giraffes – and visitors can either drive through in their own (closed) vehicles or take one of the park's air-conditioned coaches. The marine park features dolphin and sea lion shows as well as a small aviary, restaurant and landscaped gardens.

Siam Park City

ⓘ *203 Suan Siam Rd, Kannayao district, T02-919 7200, www.siamparkcity.com. Daily 1000-1800. Day passes ฿900, ฿120 children under 130 cm; water park only ฿320, ฿120 children; you can also pay per ride. Take bus No60 from Rachdamnern Klang Rd, or No 96 from Victory Monument (both stop at the park's gate), 1 hr, or 30 mins by car.*

The sprawling Siam Park City combines a water park (with artificial surf, fountains, waterfalls and chutes), a theme park, zoo, botanical gardens and fair, all rolled into one.

Around Bangkok

If the heat and sprawl becomes too much, then do what any self-respecting Bangkokian does and get the hell out. You don't have to travel far to see ancient palaces, dreamy rivers and bizarre museums. Travel a little further and you'll be taking in sweeping green vistas amid thick forests or dipping your tootsies into warm sand.

Bang Krachao

ⓘ *Samut Prakarn; most cycle tour companies go there regularly (see What to do, page 116).*

Peer off the top of one of Bangkok's taller hotels or rooftop bars and, to the south, you should spot a dark mass of land that's surrounded on three sides by the Chao Phraya River and appears to be free of the concrete sprawl. This is Bang Krachao, a peninsula of marshy land that has managed to dodge the development free-for-all. Technically, it's in Samut Prakarn province but it's easily accessible from Bangkok as long as you can find the right ferry pier, which is hidden at the end of Klong Toey port. Alternatively, first-timers are better off taking a cycle tour, since the tour operator will meet you in a downtown location and then ship you, along with your mountain bike, to Bang Krachao. Few regret making the effort: this almost island (considered Bangkok's 'green lung') is criss-crossed with raised concrete paths that cut through the thick palm-studded foliage and are perfect for two wheels. It's also dotted with gorgeously dilapidated temples, friendly locals, a weekend-only floating market (Baan Nam Phung) and a quiet park called Sri Nakhon Keun Kan, among other rustic delights. If you fancy staying the night, check in at the **Bangkok Treehouse**, a new eco-resort (see Where to stay, page 82).

Muang Boran (Ancient City)

ⓘ *296/1 Sukhumvit Rd, T02-709 1644, www.ancientcity.com, ฿400, ฿200 children. Take the Skytrain to Bearing station and catch a taxi from there. Alternatively, take city bus No511 to the end of the line, then catch minibus No36, which passes the entrance.*

The Ancient City lies 25 km southeast of Bangkok in the province of Samut Prakarn and is billed as the world's largest outdoor museum. It houses scaled-down constructions of Thailand's most famous wats and palaces (some of which can no longer be visited in their original locations) along with a handful of originals relocated here. Artisans maintain the buildings while helping to keep alive traditional crafts. The 50-ha site corresponds in shape to the map of Thailand, with the wats and palaces appropriately sited. Allocate a full day for a trip out to the Ancient City. Bikes are available for rent for ฿50.

Samut Prakarn Crocodile Farm and Zoo

ⓘ *T02-703 4891, www.worldcrocodile.com. 0800-1800, ฿300, ฿200 children. Croc combat and elephant show-time is every hour Mon-Fri 0900-1600 (no show at 1200), Sat, Sun and holidays every hour 0900-1700. Take the Skytrain to Bearing station and catch a taxi from there.*

The Samut Prakarn Crocodile Farm and Zoo claims to be the world's oldest crocodile farm. Founded in 1950 by a certain Mr Utai Young-prapakorn, it contains over 50,000 crocs of 28 species. Thailand has become, in recent years, one of the world's largest exporters of farmed crocodile skins and meat. Never slow in seeing a new market niche, Thai entrepreneurs have invested in the farming of the beasts – in some cases in association with chicken farms (the old battery chickens are simply fed to the crocs – no waste, no trouble). The irony is that the wild crocodile is now, to all intents and purposes, extinct in Thailand. (Although a number of captive crocodiles escaped from some of the less well-designed farms during the 2011 floods, most, if not all, escapees were eventually captured or killed.) The show includes the 'world famous' crocodile wrestling. The farm also has a small zoo, train and playground.

Damnoen Saduak Floating Market

ⓘ *Catch an early morning bus (No78) from the Southern bus terminal in Thonburi. Damnoen Saduak opens early, from pre-dawn, aim to get there as early as possible, as the market winds down after 0900, leaving only trinket stalls. The trip takes about 1½ hrs. A/c and non-a/c buses leave every 40 mins from 0600 (a/c ฿80) (T02-435 5031 for booking). The bus travels via Nakhon Pathom (where it is possible to stop on the way back and see the Great Chedi). Ask the conductor to drop you at Thanarat Bridge in Damnoen Saduak. Then either walk down the lane (1.5 km) that leads to the market and follows the canal, or take a river taxi for a small fee. Alternatively, take a taxi: a round trip should cost between ฿1200-1500. Most tour companies also visit the Floating Market.*

Damnoen Saduak Floating Market, in Ratchaburi Province, 109 km west of Bangkok, is an exaggerated and very hokey approximation of the real thing. Still, it is one of the most popular day trips from the capital for a reason, namely the clichéed sight of bamboo-hatted elderly ladies paddling along in their long-tails. Much of it is geared towards tourists these days but, if you take time to explore the further-flung *khlongs*, you should stumble across something more authentic. There are a number of floating markets in the maze of khlongs – Ton Khem, Hia Kui and Khun Phithak – and it is best to hire a long-tailed boat to explore the backwaters and roam around the markets; this should cost about ฿300 per hour (agree the price before setting out).

Most visitors arrive and depart on a tour bus, stopping only for a photo opportunity and the chance to buy overpriced fruit from the canny market sellers. Avoid the crowds and long-tail bottlenecks by arriving around sunrise.

Rose Garden

ⓘ *Km 32, Pet Kasem Rd, Nakorn Pathom province, T034-322 544, www.rosegardenriverside. com. Daily 0800-1800; cultural show 1330 and 1445. Entry to the grounds ฿50, ฿20 children; cultural show ฿500.*

What began in 1964 as a business supplying roses to Bangkok's flower markets has grown to become a Thai 'cultural village', spread over 15 ha of landscaped tropical grounds, 32 km west of Bangkok. It's one of the best places near the capital to learn about local wisdom. Most people go for the contrived but enjoyable cultural shows, but there are also arts and crafts workshops (1000-1200) and an elephant show. Other activities require advance booking and include alms giving by the river, a botanical walk, traditional cooking classes, herbal product workshops, Thai massage workshop, river cruises, bicycle and paddle boat rental and elephant rides. The resort also has a hotel, restaurants, a swimming pool and tennis courts, as well as a golf course close by.

Nonthaburi

① Take an express river taxi (45 mins) to Tha Nonthaburi or a Bangkok city bus (Nos 32, 64 and 97). It is also possible to stay here; see Where to stay, page 82.

Nonthaburi is both a province and a provincial capital immediately to the north of Bangkok. Accessible by express river taxi from the city, the town has a provincial air that contrasts sharply with the overpowering capital: there are *saamlors* in the streets (now banished from Bangkok), plenty of temples, and the pace of life is tangibly less frenetic. About half an hour's walk away are rice fields and rural Thailand. A street market runs inland from the pier, past the *sala klang* (provincial offices), selling clothes, sarong lengths and dried fish. The buildings of the *sala klang* are early 19th century: wooden and decayed and rather lovely. Note the lamp posts with their durian accessories – Nonthaburi's durians are renowned across the kingdom. Walk through the *sala klang* compound (downriver 100 m) to reach an excellent riverside restaurant, **Rim Fung**. Across the river and upstream (five minutes by long-tailed boat) is **Wat Chalerm Phra Kiat**, a refined wat built by Rama III as a tribute to his mother, who is said to have lived in the vicinity. The gables of the bot are encrusted in ceramic tiles; the *chedi* behind the bot was built during the reign of King Mongkut or Rama IV (1851-1868). It is also possible to take interesting day trips along the canal by boat here and Klong Bang Khu Wiang houses an authentic floating market for early risers. Also see the sweet making demonstrations in traditional houses at Klong Khanom Wan and the large public and botanical park, Suan Somdet Phra Sinakarin, off Nonthaburi Pathum Thani Rd.

Koh Kret

① Catch the express river boat to Nonthaburi then get a long-tailed boat to the island. Alternatively, catch a taxi from Nonthaburi to Wat Sanam Neua temple in Pak Kret district. From there you can catch a cross-river ferry for ฿2.

An island in the middle of the Chao Phraya River, just past Nonthaburi, Koh Kret has a sleepy village that specializes in pottery production. A small meditation centre **Baan Dvara Prateep** *① T02-373 6457, www.baandvaraprateep.com*, is currently the only place to stay. Often referred to as a 'step back in time', this interesting little island is most famous for its production of traditional earthenware. During the late 16th century, the ancestors of the Mon families who still live here took refuge on the island to escape political instability. More recently it's become a popular weekend destination for Bangkok residents escaping the bustle of city life. Cars are not allowed on the island, only motorbikes and bikes. A walkway rings the island and it is possible to walk around in two or three hours. Old wooden buildings line both sides of the raised walkway and the surrounding forest's verdant foliage provides plenty of shade. Monks in saffron robes stroll in quiet temple courtyards in villages that give way to banana and coconut plantations. It is lined with pottery shops and quaint eateries with small, covered wooden porches jutting over the water.

National Science Museum

① Ministry of Science and Technology, Klong 5 Klong, T02-577 9999 ext 2102, www.nsm. or.th, Tue-Fri 0930-1600, Sat-Sun 0930-1700 (closed Mon) ฿60, free for children and students.
In neighbouring Pathum Thani province, the Thai name for the museum is Ongkaan Phiphitiphan Withayasaat Haeng Chaat (or Or Por Wor Chor), but even if you manage to say that the chances are that the taxi driver will not know where you mean, so get someone from your hotel to make sure. Take the Chaeng Wattana-Bang Pa In expressway north and exit at Chiang Rak (for Thammasat University's new out-of-town campus). Continue west on Khlong Luang Rd, over Phahonyothin Rd, and follow your nose over khlong 1 to khlong 5 (canals)

until the road ends at a T-junction. Turn right and the NSM is 4 km or so down here on the left.
The National Science Museum (NSM), north of town, past the old airport, opened in Pathum Thani province in 2000. It is part of the Technopolis complex which consists of the Science and Natural History Museum as well as an IT museum and Bioworld. The money for the project – a cool one billion baht – was allocated before the economic crisis. Air-conditioned buildings, internet centre, and lots of hands-on exhibits to thrill children (and adults) is the result. The exhibits are labelled in English and Thai and the recorded information is also in both languages. It is very good, well designed and with charming student helpers for that human touch.

Bang Pa-In Palace

ⓘ *www.palaces.thai.net. 0800-1600, ฿100. Regular bus connections from Bangkok's Northern terminal (Mo Chit; journey time: 1 hr) and train connections daily 0420-2340 from Hualamphong station.*
Coach and river day tours to Ayutthaya normally begin at Bang Pa-In, the summer residence of the Ayutthayan kings in the 17th century. King Prasat Thong (1630-1656) started the trend of retiring here during the hot season and he built both a palace and a temple. The palace is located in the middle of a lake that the king had created on the island. It is said that his fondness for Bang Pa-In was because he was born here.

After the Thai capital was moved to Bangkok, Bang Pa-In was abandoned and left to degenerate. It was not until Rama IV stopped here that a restoration programme was begun. The only original buildings that remain are those of Wat Chumphon Nikayaram, outside the palace walls, near the bridge and close to the railway station. Start at the Varophat Phiman Hall, built by Chulalongkorn in 1876 as his private residence, and, from here, take the bridge that leads past the Thewarat Khanlai Gate overlooking the Isawan Thipaya-at Hall in the middle of the lake. Facing the gate and bridge is the Phra Thinang Uthayan Phumisathian; though it was designed to resemble a Swiss chalet, it looks more like a New England country house.

Behind the 'chalet', the Vehat Chamroon Hall, built in 1889, was a gift from Chinese traders to King Chulalongkorn. It is the only building open to the public and contains some interesting Chinese artefacts. In front stands the Hor Vithun Thasna, a tall observation tower. Another bridge leads to a pair of memorials. The second commemorates Queen Sunanda, Rama V's half-sister and favourite wife who drowned here; it is said her servants watched her drown because of the law that forbade a commoner from touching royalty. South of the palace, over the Chao Phraya River, is the Gothic-style Wat Nivet Thamaprawat, built in 1878 and resembling a Christian church.

Bang Sai

ⓘ *Take a bus from the Northern bus terminal or a boat up the Chao Phraya.*
The **Royal Folk Arts and Crafts Centre** ⓘ *T03-536 6666, Tue-Sun 0830-1600, ฿100,* is based north of Bangkok in the riverside workshops of Amphoe (district) Bang Sai, around 24 km from Bang Pa In. Another popular stop for day-trippers heading to or returning from Ayutthaya, it covers an area of nearly 50 ha. Local farmers are trained in traditional arts and crafts such as basketry, weaving and wood carvings. The project is funded by the royal family in an attempt to keep alive Thailand's traditions. Visitors are offered a glimpse of traditional life and technologies. All products – artificial flowers, dolls, silk and cotton cloth, wood carvings, baskets and so on – are for sale. Other attractions at Bang Sai include a freshwater aquarium and a bird park.

Chachoengsao

ⓘ *Trains leaves from Hualamphong station 0555-1825 (journey time 1 hr 40 mins). The train station is to the north of the fruit market, an easy walk to/from the chedi. Buses depart from both the Mo Chit and Ekkamai terminals but it is quickest from Ekkamai – about 2 hrs, depending on the traffic. A/c buses also stop to the north of the fruit market.*

Chachoengsao lies just 1½ hours from Bangkok by train or bus making it a nifty day excursion from the capital – and offering an insight into 'traditional' Thailand. This is the country's mango capital, with thousands of hectares of plantations (March being the best month for mango fans to visit). It is also famous for Irrawaddy and Indo-Pacific dolphin watching, possible between November and February. Two- to three-hour trips are available from Tha Kham, or call the district office for details T038-573 411.

Chachoengsao lies on the Bang Pakong River, to the east of the capital, and has almost been engulfed by fast-expanding Bangkok. Nonetheless, old-style shophouses and restaurants, as well as some evidence of a much more rustic past, remain. The old heart of the town is near the confluence of the Bang Pakong River and Khlong Ban Mai, on Supakit Road. **Ban Mai market** is worth exploring not so much for its wares – the main market has moved into the centre of the new town – as for its traditional wooden shophouse architecture. A concrete footbridge over Khlong Ban Mai links the two halves of the century-old market. A Chinese clan house reveals the largely Chinese origin of the population of the market area; most arrived before the outbreak of the Second World War. **Wat Sothorn Woramahavihan** is the town's best-known monastery and it contains one of the country's most revered images of the Buddha, Luang Por Sothorn. The monastery is a little over 2 km south of Sala Changwat (the Provincial Hall), on the banks of the Bang Prakong. A public park opposite Chach aengsao Fortress on Maruphong Road offers good floating restaurants along the river bank.

Bangkok listings

For hotel and restaurant price codes and other relevant information, see pages 11-14.

🛏 Where to stay

From humble backstreet digs through to opulent extravagance, Bangkok has an incredibly diverse range of hotels, guesthouses and serviced apartments. The best-value bargains are often to be had in the luxury sector; you'll find some of the best hotels in the world here, many of which offer rooms at knock-down prices. The boutique boom has also seen an explosion of stylish independent guesthouses which often offer exceptional style and comfort at reasonable prices. The guesthouses of Khaosan are cheapish but often more expensive than those in many other parts of the country. Possibly the biggest bargains to be had are with long-stay options or serviced apartments. These are lavish flats, most of which come with all the amenities (pool, gym, maid and room service) you'd expect from a 4- or 5-star hotel, but at half the price. Terms of leasing are generally weekly or monthly and a deposit of 1-3 months is usually required. Officially, apartments are required to demand a minimum stay of a week; however, telephone negotiation of these terms is not uncommon and many allow nightly stays. If you are planning a longer stay, the *Bangkok Budget Apartment Guide* by Andrew Ferrett, ฿425 from Asia Books, lists over 400 apartments in Bangkok and is well worth buying.

Many of the more expensive places to stay are on the Chao Phraya River. As well as river transport, the Skytrain provides excellent transport from this part of town. Running eastwards from the river are Silom and Surawong roads, in the heart of Bangkok's business district and with Skytrain and Metro connections. The bars of Patpong link the 2 roads. Not far to the north of Silom and Surawong roads, close to Hualamphong (the central railway station and Metro stop), is Chinatown. There are a handful of hotels and guesthouses here – but it remains very much an alternative location. A well-established accommodation centre is along Sukhumvit Rd. The Skytrain runs along Sukhumvit's length and it is intersected by the Metro at Soi Asoke. The bulk of the accommodation here is in the $$$ range and the *sois* are filled with shops, bars and restaurants of every description. Note, that the profusion of go-go bars in Soi Nana (Sois 3 and 4) and Soi Cowboy (off Soi 23) can be off-putting. In the vicinity of Siam Sq are a handful of de luxe hotels and several 'budget' establishments (especially along Rama 1 Soi Kasemsan Nung).

Siam Sq is central, has a good shopping area and excellent Skytrain connections, easy bus and taxi access to Silom and Sukhumvit roads and the Old City. The main concentration of guesthouses is along and around Khaosan Rd (an area known as Banglamphu). There is a second, smaller and quieter cluster of guesthouses just north of Khaosan Rd, at the northwest end of Sri Ayutthaya Rd. A third concentration of budget accommodation is on Soi Ngam Duphli, off Rama IV Rd.

Advertisements in the *Bangkok Post*, *The Nation* and hotels' own websites may provide some heavily discounted rates in some more upmarket hotels. Also see www.agoda.co.th, www.asiarooms.com and www.latestays.com, or www.sabaai. com and www.bangkok-apartment.com to view and book serviced apartments online.

Airport

Those needing to stay near the new airport can book in at the $$$$ Novotel Suvarnabhumi Airport Hotel (Moo 1 Nongprue Bang Phli, Samutprakarn, 10540 Bangkok, T02-131 1111, www.novotel.com), which has 600-plus rooms, 2 bars, 4 restaurants, a pool, fitness centre and spa.

Old City *p37, map p44*

The *sois* off the main road are often quieter, such as Soi Chana Songkhram or Soi Rambutri. Note that rooms facing on to Khaosan Rd tend to be very noisy.

The reliable **Sawasdee Chain** has several guesthouses in the area all with attractive, clean interiors and large Thai-style communal areas. See www.sawasdee-hotels.com.

Sri Ayutthaya offers an alternative for travellers who want to stay close to the Old City but avoid the chaos of the Khaosan Rd. It's a gradually developing tourist enclave with restaurants, foodstalls, a couple of travel agents/internet shops and even a **7-11**. The area, known as Tewes, is also known for its bustling flower market. The handily located Tewes Pier sits behind the morning market and temple and commuters feed the fish while waiting for the river taxis. One family runs 4 of the guesthouses; this means that if one is full you will probably be moved on to another. One problem is getting here by taxi, Sri Ayutthaya is a long road and the tricky pronunciation of Tewes (try Tay-wet) can complicate matters. Pick up a card with directions from your guesthouse.

$$$$ Arun Residence, 36-38 Soi Pratoo Nok Yoong, Maharat Rd, T02-221-9158, www.arunresidence.com. A lovely 7-room hotel restored from an old house on the Chao Phraya river, with a commanding view of Wat Arun. It's tastefully decorated and very relaxing. There's a small gallery, a library with free internet access and a popular Thai restaurant attached.

$$$$ Aurum River Place, 394/27-29 Soi Pansook, Maharaj Rd, T02-622 2248, www. aurum-bangkok.com. A swish modern hotel a little further afield in a beautiful colonial building overlooking the river and a stone's throw from Wat Pho. The more expensive rooms overlook the river but there are also

some great views from the (rather basic) rooftop garden. Stylish café downstairs that spills out into a small garden. Neat hotel-style rooms with good facilities.

$$$$ The Bhuthorn, 96-98 Phraeng Bhuthorn Rd, T02-622-2270, www.the bhuthorn.com. Gorgeous, sepia-tinted B&B in a quiet, century-old square teeming with cheap shophouse kitchens. Harking back to King Rama V's era, the antique-filled rooms with en-suites ooze old-world romance, as do the cosy public areas. Breakfast is served in a stunning flower-strewn mini-courtyard, and the Grand Palace is only 10 mins' walk away. The very helpful architect owners also have a newer, bigger heritage B&B just around the corner: **The Asadang**, www. theasadang.com. Both are recommended.

$$$$ Old Bangkok Inn, 609 Pra Sumen Rd, T02-629 1787, www.oldbangkokinn.com. A delightful, small B&B run by a friendly Thai family, Old Bangkok Inn is elegant and cosy, and is one of Bangkok's 'green' hotels, with a PC, DVD player and satellite TV in every room.

$$$$-$$$ Baan Chantra Boutique, 120/1 Samsen Rd, T02-628 6988, www. baanchantra.com. Around the corner from the Khaosan there are just 7 rooms in this exquisite boutique guesthouse. A restored antique Thai wooden house with romantically furnished interiors, pretty balconies and a strict no-smoking policy. Homely ambience and excellent service and attention to detail.

$$$$-$$$ Phranakorn Nornlen Hotel, 46 Tewes Soi 1, T02-628 8188, www. phranakorn-nornlen.com. A little gem of an independent hotel with incredible attention to detail. Airy Thai-style rooms with artistic design are as homely as an artfully crafted doll's house. Wooden shutters, a garden café, beautiful rooftop views and an intimate, relaxed atmosphere. The small team of amicable staff includes an informative 'City Guide' who can help with bookings, etc. Daily cookery classes and other creative pursuits. Recommended.

$$$$-$$$ Royal Princess, 269 Lan Luang Rd, T02-281 3088, www.dusit.com/dusit-princess/princess-larn-luang.html. This gorgeous 4-star hotel is part of the quality-stamped Dusit chain, with excellent facilities and a fantastic location. A/c, restaurants, pool, and all rooms have balconies overlooking the Old City.

$$$$-$$$ Trang Hotel, 99/1 Visutkaset Rd, T02-282 2141, www.tranghotelbangkok.com. Friendly, attractive a/c hotel that is well priced and popular with families and return visitors. It's set around a relaxing courtyard, a little away from the action and major sights, and has a restaurant and pool.

$$$$-$$$ Viengtai, 42 Soi Rambutri, Banglamphu, T02-280 5434, www.viengtai.co.th. A/c, restaurant, pool. A perennial favourite in the mid-range category, rooms here are spacious and reliably smart, if a little conservative on the design front. Helpful well-informed management and a slightly more civilized location on the street parallel to the Khaosan.

$$$$-$$ Feung Nakorn Balcony, 125 Feungnakorn Rd, T02-622 1100, www.feungnakorn.com. Hard to find, but very quiet modern boutique hotel in a converted elementary school, tucked off Feung Nakorn Rd. It's about 10-15 mins' walk from Khao San, Wat Pho and the Grand Palace. Pick from 60 sq m Grand Suites, with their own small patios, cosier standard and dorm rooms, and 3 Thai-style suites, with art deco touches. Best features are the central courtyard and the location. Breakfast is included and there's a bar/restaurant. Recommended.

$$$ Buddy Lodge, 265 Khaosan Rd, T02-629 4477, www.buddylodge.com. Still one of the more upmarket options in the Khaosan Rd area, Buddy Lodge's rooms belie its shopping plaza exterior, featuring hardwood floors and faux-vintage fittings as well as home comforts like a fridge and TV. Deluxes have impressively large balconies. There is also 24-hr room service, a coffee shop and a rooftop pool.

$$$-$$ Baan Dinso, 113 Trok Sin, Dinso Rd, T02-622-0560, www.baandinso.com. Tucked down a quiet alley, this immaculately restored King Rama VI-era wooden house has clean and quaint a/c rooms, some with shared bathrooms. Original golden teak floors, shutters, fixtures and fretwork throughout – very charming. A hearty breakfast is included, and cooking classes are available. Helpful owner and staff. Recommended.

$$$-$$ D&D Inn, 68-70 Khaosan Rd, T02-629 0526, www.khaosanby.com. Large, very popular and well-priced but fairly characterless purpose-built hotel with lift, neat if slightly soulless a/c rooms, and hot showers. The small swimming pool and bar on the roof offers a fine view. Very centrally located. Due to the rapid turnover of guests use of the hotel's safety deposit boxes is recommended.

$$$-$$ Diamond House, 4 Samsen Rd, T02-629 4008, www.thaidiamondhouse.com. Twin rooms have bunk beds which make them feel like a ship's cabin. Fridge, TV, a/c in all rooms and very nice bathrooms. Call ahead to avoid paying inflated walk-in rates.

$$$-$$ Mango Lagoon, 30 Soi Rambutri, T02-281 4783, www.mangolagoonplace.com. A relative newcomer with more than a modicum of charm and comfort. Light and airy rooms look out over the garden café in the courtyard out front.

$$$-$$ New World City Hotel, 2 Samsen Rd, T02-281 5596, www.newworldlodge.com. Popular with long-stay guests and with a cute community feel. A good location for the Old City yet away from the hurly-burly of Khaosan Rd. Rooms have fan or a/c, some are fairly spacious and have satellite TV for a higher price. Some overlook the canal. Safety boxes are free for guests, as is the use of a small gym.

$$$-$ Shanti Lodge, 37 Sri Ayutthaya Rd, Soi 16, Si Tewet, T02-281 2497, www.shantilodge.com. Double rooms with a/c or fan and a dorm. The obvious pick of the budget bunch in a picturesque old wooden house with a pretty garden restaurant complete with resident turtle. The food (mostly vegetarian) is excellent, atmospheric rooms are beautifully decorated and the bohemian atmosphere harks back to halcyon days of the hippy era. There's a breezy space for yoga and Thai massage and a small shop selling crafts and clothing. The all-female staff offer a wealth of no-nonsense information on Bangkok pursuits. Travel agent and internet café.

$$ Sawasdee Bangkok Inn, 126/2 Khaosan Rd, T02-280 1251, www.sawasdee-hotels.com. Good value, clean, fair-sized rooms with wooden floors and some with a/c right at the centre of the action. A vibrant, popular bar and friendly staff. Free safety deposit and left luggage.

$$ Sawasdee Khaosan, 18 Chakrapong Rd, T02-256 0890. Probably the pick of the Sawasdee bunch due to its modern style and location just around the corner from the Khaosarn towards Sanaam Luang. This one has its own bakery and popular cocktail bar looking out onto the street.

$$-$ Lamphu House, 75 Soi Rambutri, T02-629 5861, www.lamphuhouse.com. Undoubtedly one of the best budget options on offer. Situated down a very quiet *soi*. Clean, modern, pleasantly decorated rooms with a/c and very comfy beds, the superior rooms have a large balcony and are the best value. Great restaurant downstairs and an extremely professional spa on the roof terrace. Highly recommended.

$$-$ Sam Sen Sam Place, 48 Samsen Soi 3, T02-6287067, www.samsensam.com. 10 mins' walk from Khao San Rd, down the *soi* that leads to riverside restaurant **Kin Lom Chom Saphan** (see Restaurants), this colourful old teak house radiates a relaxed, homely atmosphere. The cute rooms in pastel shades are spotless; all except the standard rooms have private bathrooms. Charming, quiet and friendly. Decent breakfast too.

$$-$ Sawasdee Smile Inn, 35 Soi Rongmai, T02-629 2340, www.sawasdee-hotels.com. Large, spacious sitting area at the front under a gaudy looking green Thai-style roof. Restaurant and 24-hr bar, so ask for a room at the back if you want an early night. Rooms are clean and simple, all with cable TV. Free safety boxes available.

$$-$ Siam Oriental, 190 Khaosan Rd, T02-629 0312, www.siamorientalgroup.com. Fine, clean rooms (some a/c), smart tiled corridors, and very friendly staff. Internet facilities downstairs, along with a very popular restaurant. Free safety deposit box.

$$-$ Taewaz Guesthouse, 23/12 Sri Ayutthaya Rd. T02-280 8856, www.taewez.com. Relaxed place with wooden floors and cosy but very clean rooms – a/c rooms are a bargain. Internet access, friendly staff.

$$-$ Tavee, 83 Sri Ayutthaya Rd, Soi 14, T02-282 5983. The friendly Tavee family keep their rooms and shared bathrooms immaculately clean and are a good source of information. It's a quiet, relaxed and respectable guesthouse, with a restaurant, a small garden and a number of fish tanks – a world away from the chaos of Khaosan. This place has been operating since 1985 and has managed to maintain a very high standard.

$$-$ Tuptim Bed and Breakfast, 82 Soi Rambutri, T02-629 1535, www.tuptimb-b.com. Recommended budget option with some a/c and en suite shower, but even the shared facilities are exceptionally clean, breakfast included. Very friendly staff.

Phra Arthit Rd *p46*

$$$$-$$$ Navalai River Resort, 45/1 Phra Athit Rd, T02-280 9955, www.navalai.com. Sparkling riverside hotel right next to the Phra Athit pier (the nearest one to Khao San Rd). The pricier rooms come with balconies overlooking the river but be prepared for the noisy boats. Everything is done out in stylish contemporary Thai style, with a/c, en-suite bathrooms and flat-screen TVs throughout. Restaurant and bar.

$$$ New Siam Riverside, 21 Phra Athit Rd, T02-629 3535, www.newsiam.net. This upscale backpacker lodge would be indistinguishable from all the others were it not for two things: a swimming pool and riverside terrace. It also offers TV, a/c and snug beds. Riverview rooms cost almost twice as much. Breakfast buffet is pretty good for the money. Staff are a mixed bunch, though. Recommended.

$$ Bhiman Inn, 55 Phra Arthit Rd, T02-282 6171, www.bhimaninn.com. Another of the boutique boomer crowd but again a stylish title-holder with lots of character. Small pool, a/c rooms with fairly thin mattresses raised on platforms, chic interior design and small plant-filled balconies. Minibar and TV. Restaurant attached. Recommended.

$$-$ Baan Sabai, 12 Soi Rongmai, T02-629 1599. A large, colonial-style building with a green pillared entrance in front. Although not very expensive, it is not the typical backpacker scene. Rooms are simple but large and airy. Storage is available at 10 per bag/suitcase.

$$-$ New My House, 37 Phra Arthit Soi Chana Songkram, T02-282 9263. Another reliable budget option with helpful and friendly management. Rooms are basic but exceptionally clean and comfortable, the attractive traditional-style entrance leads to a spacious lounge and restaurant.

$$-$ Pra Arthit Mansion, 22 Phra Arthit Rd, T02-280 0744, www.phraarthitmansion. com. Leafy though slightly dated hotel, popular with German tour operators. Rooms are huge, carpeted and good value with vast comfy beds and all the trimmings including a/c, fridge, TV and even bath tubs. Quite a bargain in this price range, discounts for over 3 nights stay. Well run with helpful management.

Thonburi, Wat Arun and the khlongs
p51, map p52

There's presently very little accommodation on the Thonburi side of the river. This is a shame as the *khlongs*, particularly to the

north, make it one of the most beautiful parts of the city. However, this may be set to change with the recent extension of the Skytrain route over the river at Saphan Taksin.

$$$$ Anantara Bangkok Riverside Resort & Spa, 257/1-3 Charoen Nakorn Rd, T02-476 0022, bangkok-riverside.anantara. com. Formerly the **Marriott Bangkok Resort & Spa**, this luxury hotel is set beside a canal in spacious surroundings with more than 4 ha of grounds. It's a little downstream from the main action, but free shuttle-boat services run every 30 mins between the hotel and River City piers. Attractive, low-rise design with Thai-style ambience. A good place to escape from the fumes and frenzy after a day sightseeing or shopping – the soothing Mandara garden spa is here too. Recommended.

$$$$ Ibrik Resort, 256 Soi Wat Rakang, Arun-Amarin Rd, Thonburi, T02-848 9220, www.ibrikresort.com. Just 3 beautifully designed rooms in this bijou little resort. A hidden gem worth seeking out for its romantic location, river views and chic oriental interiors. No pool, though.

$$$$ Peninsula, 333 Charoen Nakorn Rd, Klongsan, T02-2861 2888, www.peninsula. com/bangkok. Sited just across the river from Taksin Bridge, the 39-storey **Peninsula** has a commanding riverfront position providing spectacular city views. The large rooms are luxurious and a full range of leisure facilities are on offer, while 4 restaurants provide a variety of (mostly Asian) cuisine. Recommended.

$$$$ Praya Palazzo, 757/1 Somdej Prapinklao Soi 2, T028-832 998, www.praya palazzo.com. Of significant historical interest, this pricey riverside boutique hotel is located in an old Italian-style nobleman's mansion that had been left to ruin. Lovingly restored, it's now a gorgeous sight to behold: 17 palatial rooms with luxe amenities and polished teak floors inside, neat terracotta paintwork, grand opposing staircases and a stately riverside garden with pool outside. Perfect for couples.

Elegant Thai restaurant. It's only accessible by private ferry, which adds to the romance and sense of privileged detachment. Recommended.

$$$$ Resort Bangphlat, 2 Charansanit-wong Rd 77/1, T02-885 5737, www.resort bangphlat.com. Well out of tourist town, this mini-resort will appeal to travellers wanting a Thai nostalgia fix over and above a central location. Features neat rows of 1- or 2-bedroom a/c wooden houses, each with a living room and bathroom downstairs, and a bedroom, balcony and office upstairs. Fridge, cable TV, free wireless and a pretty courtyard area. Staff are friendly enough but don't speak much English. Recommended.

$$$ Ramada Menam Riverside, 2074 Charoenkrung Rd, T02-688 1000, www.menamriverside-hotel.com. Decent enough 5-star high-rise pile beside the river. Rooms are standard contemporary Thai, with silks and soft lighting but nothing too fabulous. Nice location in a rootsy part of the city. Caters to a lot of hi-end Chinese guests and, consequently, is home to one of the best Chinese restaurants in town, the **Ah Yat Abalone**.

Chinatown p48, map p44

$$$$ Royal Orchid Sheraton, 2 Charoen Krung Rd Soi 30 (Captain Bush Lane), T02-266 0123, www.royalorchidsheraton. com. Sited beside the river just outside the steamy narrow lanes of Chinatown, this hotel, while offering some of the best accommodation in this part of town, is not a patch on its sister **Sheraton** on Sukhumvit Rd. Having said that, the Tower Suites offer excellent value, and the gardens are a great spot to laze. Most of the restaurants have al fresco terraces perched above the river.

$$$$ Shanghai Mansion, 479-481 Yaowarat Rd, T022-212 121, www.shanghai mansion.com. Chinatown's only boutique hotel is pure 1930s-in-Shanghai chic – as colourful as an old Shaw Brothers movie set. Dark wood four-poster beds, peony

pattern wallpaper, vibrant silks and lamps. Amenities include TV and Wi-Fi. The pricier Mu Dan Suites up the ante with DVD players and free-standing bathtubs big enough for two. Restaurant and jazz club.

$$$$-$$$ Grand China Princess, 215 Yaowarat Rd, T02-224 9977, www.grand china.com. Centrally located, with balconies over the river and a revolving restaurant up top, this dramatic high-rise, with its magical views over the city, mainly caters to the Asian market, with choice of Asian cuisine, business facilities, fitness centre and pool. The interior grandeur is a bit faded but still holds a certain chaotic charm.

$$$$-$$ Loy la Long, Wat Patumkongka, 1620/2 Song Wat Rd, T026-391-390, www. loylalong.com. The quirkiest guesthouse in town: a converted two-storey teak structure perched over the river, hidden at the back of a Buddhist temple complex. 7 a/c rooms (including 1 dorm) feature recycled wood, gorgeous bathrooms, bold colour schemes, TV and DVD players. There's also a decent breakfast and Wi-Fi. Wake to the sound of waves sloshing beneath the structure, as commuter boats whizz pass. The highlight for most is the communal living room with terrace – a chill-out spot where guests lean back on flowery floor cushions, eyes glued to the wide-screen river views. Great Chinatown location. Recommended.

$$$-$ River View Guesthouse, 768 Songwad Rd, Soi Panurangsri, T02-234 5429, www.riverviewbkk.com. Some rooms have balconies overlooking the river (as the name suggests). It receives mixed reviews, perhaps due to the prioritizing of character over cleanliness, but is worth considering for its location away from the bulk of hotels, close to the Harbour Department boat pier and Chinatown. Some rooms have a/c. The restaurant/bar is on the top floor and overlooks the river; the food is average but the view spectacular. Recommended.

Siam Sq and Ploenchit Rd *p56, map p57*

$$$$ Amari Watergate, 847 Phetburi Rd, T02-653 9000, www.amari.com. Lots of marble and plastic trees, uninspired block, good facilities and good value, great views from the upper floors on the south side of the building. Restaurants include the excellent **Thai on 4**, fitness centre, squash court and pool.

$$$$ Cape House, 43 Soi Langsuan, T02-658 7444, www.capehouse.com. Excellent serviced apartments in a great location. Each apartment comes with DVD, stereo, free Wi-Fi, cable TV, a/c and kitchenette. Has a rooftop pool, library, decent Italian and Thai restaurant, sauna and gym. Recommended.

$$$$ Chateau de Bangkok 29 Ruamrudee Soi 1, T02-651 4400. Owned by the **Accor** hotel chain, these serviced apartments have great amenities, including private jacuzzis, and are centrally located sharing a lovely rooftop pool and gym. Excellent value monthly rates. Restaurant and room service available.

$$$$ Four Seasons Bangkok, 155 Rachdamri Rd, T02-126-8866, www.fourseasons.com. Show-stoppingly stylish and post-modern in atmosphere, with arguably the best range of cuisine (and Sun brunch) in Bangkok, as well as a lavish spa. The restaurants (including **Spice Market** and the well-known **Biscotti** for fine Italian cuisine, see Restaurants, page 86) have excellent reputations and ambience. Recommended.

$$$$ Grand Hyatt Erawan, 494 Rachdamri Rd, T02-254 1234, www.bangkok.grand. hyatt.com. A towering structure with grandiose entrance and an artificial tree-filled atrium plus sumptuous rooms and every facility. The **Spasso Restaurant/Club** here is very popular and very pricey. On the other hand, the bakery, which has a fantastic range of really sinful and delicious cakes, and the noodle shop, **You and Mee** – which are both also on the lower ground floor – are

reasonably priced. Service is excellent and friendly, and this hotel does not charge for drinking water! Makes a great escape from the traffic and pollution for lunch or afternoon tea, even if you're not staying here.

$$$$ Hotel Muse, 55/555 Langsuan Rd, T02-630 4000, www.hotelmusebangkok. com. Upscale 174-room hotel on the very upmarket Langsuan Rd. Has a very over-the-top, fin de siècle Europe meets King Rama V-era theme: think wrought-iron balustrades, framed oil paintings, chandeliers and cow skin rugs. A bold break from the off-the-peg norm; you'll either love it or loathe it. Rooms and suites have 41-in flat screen TVs, movies on demand and iPod docking stations. Pool, spa, two impressive restaurants and a prohibition-era style al fresco rooftop bar. Recommended.

$$$$ Intercontinental Bangkok, 973 Ploenchit, T02-656 0444, www.ichotel group.com. In its former incarnation as **Le Meridien**, the hotel held the title of one of the more distinguished luxury hotels in Bangkok (it opened in 1966). Not much has changed since the takeover however, with the tranquil atmosphere, excellent service and opulent, high-ceilinged surrounds still in place. Lovely rooftop pool and gardens, spa, gym, stylish modern rooms, a chic Italian restaurant and picture-perfect views.

$$$$ St Regis Bangkok, 159 Rajadamri Rd, T02-207 7777, www.starwoodhotels.com/ stregis. This luxury hotel overlooking the Royal Bangkok Sports Club is super-opulent yet soulless, lacking warmth. However, the facilities and service are hard to beat. The clean-lined modern Thai rooms with marble bathrooms are lavishly appointed: signature King bed with 300-thread count linens, 42-in LCD TV and the famous 24-hr butler service are just three of the many high-end amenities. Other highlights include the futuristic Elemis spa, modern Japanese restaurant **Zuma**, plus a bizarre champagne ritual on the hotel bar's terrace at 1830 each evening.

$$$$ Siam@Siam Design Hotel and Spa, 865 Rama 1 Rd, T02-217 3000, www.siam atsiam.com. Noteworthy interior design, mixing industrial with post-modernism. Textures and materials compliment each other superbly, the rooms are as far removed from the commonplace, boring hotel room design as possible. Facilities include restaurant, swimming pool. Recommended.

$$$$ Siam Kempinski, 991/9 Rama 1 Rd, T021-629 000, www.kempinski.com/en/ bangkok. If you want to shop till you flop, this grand luxury hotel is unbeatable: just a few paces from Siam Sq's malls. Swish (but slightly soulless) rooms feature oversized bathtubs, balconies and all-in-one flat-screen entertainment systems with internet, TV, infrared keyboards and movies on demand. Other highlights: the resort-style pool area and molecular Thai restaurant, **Sra Bua by Kiin Kiin**. Any sour taste left by the slightly aloof staff disappears on seeing the buffet breakfast, one of the most decadent in town.

$$$$ Swissotel Nailert Park, 2 Witthayu Rd, T02-253 0123, www.swissotel.com. An excellent hotel and vast tropical oasis bang in the centre of the city. Set in lush canal-side gardens with running track and a stunningly designed tropical lagoon-like pool. Good service, excellent restaurants, attractive rooms all with beautiful views. Also the site of the much-visited phallic Chao Mae Tubtim shrine.

$$$$-$$$ Asia Hotel, 296 Phayathai Rd, T02-217 0808, www.asiahotel.co.th. A package deal and travel agent's favourite due to its handy location, excellent internet deals and impressively ostentatious lobby. However, although the entrance implies a certain degree of grandeur, rooms, aside from the recently upgraded superior suites, are fairly frills-free and tired. The walkway straight to the Skytrain station makes for easy access to the city sights. Good jeweller's on site, several restaurants and 2 pools. It's also the home of the popular ladyboy cabaret show **Calypso**.

$$$ Aphrodite Inn, 5961-65 Ratchadamri Rd, T02-254 5999, www.aphroditeinn.com. The 30 rooms in this hotel are comfortably decorated with colourful touches such as throws and wall hangings. A/c, TV, safety box, spotlessly clean. Recommended for the location at this price.

$$$-$$ A1 Inn, 25/13 Soi Kasemsan Nung (1), Rama I Rd, T02-215 3029, www.aoneinn. com. This, well-run, intimate hotel is, very popular so book ahead. Recommended.

$$ Wendy House, 36/2 Soi Kasemsan 1, Rama I Rd, T02-214 1149. Friendly budget outfit offering spotless but small, boxy rooms, with hot water, and buffet breakfast in the eating area downstairs. Only a short walk from the Skytrain and Siam Sq malls.

$$-$ Lub D Siam Square, 925/9 Rama 1 Rd, T02-6124999, www.siamsquare.lubd. com. Compact raw concrete rooms and dorms with licks of bright colour and fun Bangkok-themed wall art, plus shared bathrooms and a superb location next to the Skytrain and Siam Sq. A big hit with the flashpackers, you'll also find optional 'ladies-only' dorms and a friendly welcome in the reception/lounge area with free internet. Breakfast not included. Recommended.

$$-$ White Lodge, 36/8 Soi Kasemsan Nung (1), Rama I Rd, T02-216 8867. Another brilliantly located crash pad near the malls. Airy, light reasonably sized rooms, with a/c and hot water, and an outdoor patio.

Silom area *p59, map p60*

Of all Bangkok, this area most resembles a Western city, with its international banks, skyscrapers, first-class hotels, shopping malls, pizza parlours and pubs. It is also home to one of the world's best-known red-light districts – **Patpong**.

   Soi Ngam Duphli to the east was the pre-Khaosan backpacker area and now mostly caters for long-stay guests on a tight budget. The rather racy after-hours' scene here is a draw for some and an unwanted distraction for others.

$$$$ Banyan Tree, 21/100 South Sathorn Rd, T02-679 1200, www.banyantree.com. A good location, set back from busy Sathorn Rd. Glittering, sumptuous surroundings immediately relax the soul here. Famous for its divine luxury spa and literally breathtaking rooftop **Moon Bar**. All rooms are suites.

$$$$ Dusit Thani, 946 Rama IV Rd, T02-200 9000, www.dusit.com. The holiday home of royalty, rock stars and other visiting dignitaries and one of the top of the luxury crop, what the **Dusit** lacks in unique design it more than makes up for in comfort and facilities. Ideally located adjacent to Lumpini park. A/c, 9 restaurants, 3 bars, pool, gym, excellent service and attention to detail. Its **Deverana Spa** is one of the finest in the city. Recommended.

$$$$ Furamaxclusive Sathorn, 59 Silom Soi 3 (Piphat 2), Silom Rd, T02-2668030, www.furamaxclusive.com. Stylish, contemporary boutique hotel, tucked away between Silom and Sathorn rds. There's a pool, gym sauna and restaurant, and each room comes equipped with giant flat-screen TV, Wi-Fi, plump bed, a/c and huge bathroom.

$$$$ Mandarin Oriental, 48 Soi Oriental, Charoen Krung, T02-659 9000, www.mandarinoriental.com. At over 100 years old and host to some of history's most infamous literary figures, the **Oriental** is both a Bangkok legend and one of the finest hotels in the world. A fairy-tale like interior of grandiose proportions, beautiful position overlooking the river and incomparable individual service (despite its 400 rooms). The older Author's wing is the place for high tea, with each room named after a famous guest/author from Somerset Maughan to Barbara Cartland. The Garden wing offers similar levels of nostalgic luxury. The modern River wing and Tower feature more contemporary design and river terraces. Recommended.

$$$$ Metropolitan, 27 South Sathorn Rd, T02-625 3333, www.metropolitan.como.bz. Designer chic at its most extravagantly stylish. From its fashionable members/guest-only bar, through to the beautiful contemporary rooms and the much-hyped Thai restaurant, **Nahm** (see Restaurants, page 88), this is one of Bangkok's hippest hotels. Suites come complete with kitchenette and excellent views, while terrace rooms have enticing outdoor showers. Recommended.

$$$$ Shangri-La, 89 Soi Wat Suan Plu, Charoen Krung, T02-236 7777, www.shangri-la.com. Another of the top-end luxury hotels commanding excellent riverside views, the **Shangri-La** is preferred by some to the **Oriental** probably due to its more modern aesthetics and facilities, picturesque verdant grounds and first-class service. A frequent award winner it also houses one of the city's most celebrated spas, **Chi** (see page 113). Recommended.

$$$$ Siri Sathorn Executive Residence, 27 Sala Daeng Soi 1, T02-266 2345, www.sirisathorn.com. Gleaming minimalist tower block with dozens of serviced apartments bang in the centre of Silom. Rooms are large, the upper floors have great views, amenities are top rate and it has a superb location. Recommended.

$$$$ Sofitel Silom, 188 Silom Rd, T02-238 1991, www.sofitel.com. Stark and gleaming hi-tech high-rise with excellent facilities, including the **Scarlett** wine bar on the 37th floor (formerly V9). Rooms are elegantly designed but vast comfy beds dominate the standard rooms, so opt for a more spacious suite. Sunbathers take note; the bijou pool is a little pokey and mostly shaded. Good seasonal promotions.

$$$$ Sofitel So, 2 North Sathorn Rd, T02-624 0000, www.sofitel.com. Hulking new 30-storey city hotel, almost within touching distance of Lumpini Park, on the corner of Sathorn and Rama IV rds (50-m walk from MRT Lumpini). Thai architect Smith Obayawat designed the sleek, dark tower, and five Thai interior designers created the rooms, inspired by the 5 elements. Superior rooms look out over the city; luxury rooms have memorable, Manhattan-esque views over the tree tops, not to mention divine 'MyBeds', Apple mini-media systems and complimentary Wi-Fi. Five restaurants, fitness centre, spa, pool.

$$$$ The Sukhothai, 13/3 South Sathorn Rd, T02-344 8888, www.sukhothai.com. Stunning, reliable modern oriental hotel set in 6 acres of landscaped gardens, complete with decadent pool area and ponds with Sukothai-style brick *chedi* rising out of them. Superior rooms were recently refurbished by the original designer Ed Tuttle, and the service is second to none. Several celebrated restaurants include **Celadon** (Thai) and **La Scala** (Italian), and the Sun brunch is a contender for best in town. Recommended.

$$$$-$$$ Heritage Baan Silom, 639 Silom Rd (near Soi 19), T02-236 8388, www.theheritagebaansilom.com. Charming, neo-colonial style rooms exude comfort; all are finished to a very high standard but they're not exactly spacious (the biggest is 30 sq m). Facilities include mini-bar, plasma TV and a/c. Recommended for the design appeal.

$$$$-$$$ Pinnacle Hotel, 17 Soi Ngam Duphli, T02-287 0111, www.pinnaclehotels.com. A small, clean hotel that is part of a large chain and a pleasant surprise in this rather down-at-heel area. Rooms with all mod cons (including complimentary Wi-Fi), helpful staff, pool, restaurant, gym and rooftop spa.

$$$-$$ Malaysia Hotel, 54 Soi Ngam Duphli, Rama IV Rd, www.malaysiahotelbkk.com, T02-679 7127. The centrepoint of the Soi Ngam Duphli gay cruising scene, this hulking hotel offers good value for money with pool, a/c, restaurants, travel service and all-night coffeeshop that is popular with after-hours' party goers. Superior rooms also come fully equipped with fridge, TV and DVD.

$$ Ibis Bangkok Sathorn, Soi Ngam Duphli, T02-659 2888, www.ibishotel.com. Bog standard but good value chain hotel on a louche bar- and restaurant-lined *soi*

popular with expats and long-stayers. Standard rooms with double or twin beds, safe, Wi-Fi. No room service; mediocre buffet breakfast.

$$-$ Charlie's House, 1034/36-37 Soi Saphan Khu, T02-679 8330, www.charliehousethailand.com. Helpful owners create a friendly atmosphere, and the rooms are carpeted and very clean, with a/c and TV. This is probably the best of the area's budget bunch. There is a restaurant and coffee corner downstairs, with good food at reasonable prices. Recommended.

$ New Road Guest House, 1216/1 Charoen Krung Rd, T02-237 1094. This Danish-owned riverside place provides a range of accommodation from decent budget rooms to hammocks on the roof. A restaurant serves inexpensive Thai dishes, a bar provides a pool table, and there's a small outdoor sitting area.

$ Sala Thai Guesthouse, 15 Soi Saphan Khu, off Soi Sri Bamphen, Rama IV, T02-287 1436. At the end of a peaceful, almost leafy *soi*. The clean rooms have seen better days, but it's family-run and has a cute roof garden. Shared bathrooms. Popular with teachers and long-stay guests. Recommended.

Sukhumvit Road *p61, map p62*

Sukhumvit is one of Bangkok's premier centres of tourist accommodation and is a great place for restaurants and nightlife with several world-class bars and clubs and, it has to be said, no small amount of sleaze. This is also a good area for shopping for furniture: antique and reproduction. Note also that the profusion of expatriate condominiums and hotels in the area between Sukhumvit Soi 18 and Sukhumvit Soi 24 attracts swindlers and petty thieves, particularly purse/bag snatchers and sex tourist-savvy tuk-tuk drivers.

$$$$ The Davis, 88 Sukhumvit, Soi 24, T02-260 8000, www.davisbangkok.net. A pioneer in the boutique market and a total treat of a hotel, **Davis** offers the ultimate in chic and unique interiors with a pool, gym, restaurants and a spa. Luxury traditional Thai accommodation is also available in the neighbouring Baan Davis compound, tucked away in a quiet garden surrounding a small pool. Recommended.

$$$$ The Eugenia, 267 Sukhumvit Soi 31, T022-599 011, www.theeugenia.com. Small 12-room boutique, with a French colonial theme and swimming pool. Antique furniture and fittings and superb attention to detail lull you into thinking this is an old building (it's not). High ceilinged rooms have plump beds and a fresh, classic feel. Some have four posters and aluminium bathtubs. Restaurant **DB Bradley** serves excellent fusion cuisine and is a popular brunch spot.

$$$$ JW Marriott, 4 Sukhumvit Soi 2, T02-656 7700, www.marriott.com. More business-like than the **Marriott** hotel on the river but still luxuriously comfortable and elegant. Pool, health club and spa, and 4 restaurants, including sophisticated modern Japanese at the highly regarded Tsu-Nami.

$$$$ The Landmark, 138 Sukhumvit Rd, T02-254 0404, www.landmarkbangkok.com. Used to be one of the most glamorous hotels in the area now aimed at the travelling family market (despite the sleazy location). Excellent facilities, 12 restaurants, pool, health centre, smart shopping plaza and business facilities. Terrific views from the 31st floor.

$$$$ Rembrandt, 19 Sukhumvit Soi 18, T02-261 7100, www.rembrandtbkk.com. Lots of marble but limited ambience for this ageing business-like hotel, the usual top-end facilities including a pool and restaurants. The Indian **Rang Mahal** restaurant is recommended (as you might expect, given that the hotel is Indian-owned) although it is quite pricey.

$$$$ S15, 217 Sukhumvit Rd, T02-651 2000, www.S15hotel.com. From the moment you enter, welcoming and professional staff signify that this hotel is something special. Plush, richly decorated

hallways in shades of brown and beige lead to extremely comfortable rooms, which come complete with free Wi-Fi, a/c, fridge, minibar, flat screen TV and DVD player. The bathrooms have walk-in showers and bathtubs. Its one minor shortcoming is that there isn't a pool, but there is a spa and gym. Recommended.

$$$$ Sheraton Grande Sukhumvit, 250 Sukhumvit Rd, T02-649 8888, http://www.sheratongrandesukhumvit.com. A superbly managed business and leisure hotel well known for its impeccable service, food and facilities. The rooftop garden is an exotic oasis and the spa offers some of the best massage in town. **Basil** (Thai) and **Rossini** (Italian) see Restaurants, pages 89 and 90) are also top class and **The Living Room** is renowned for its classy jazz brunches. Great location and, if you can afford it, the best place to stay on Sukhumvit. Recommended.

$$$$-$$$ Adelphi Suites, 6 Sukhumvit Soi 8, T02-617 5100, www.adelphisuites.com. These swish rooms represent incredible value, coming equipped with stereo, flat screen TV, DVD player, a/c which can be enjoyed from the room's lounge area. There's also a pantry-style kitchen with fridge freezer and hob. For the facilities and price, recommended.

$$$$-$$$ Aloft Bangkok, 35 Sukhumvit Soi 11, T02-207 7061, www.alofthotels.com/bangkoksukhumvit11. Trendy, cookie-cutter city hotel by the Starwood group. Perfect for party animals, it's on Sukhumvit Soi 11, opposite **Bed Supperclub**. Room and suites are 'tech savvy', with free Wi-FI, 42-in flat-screen TV, which links to your laptop, and iPod docking stations. The colourful decor beams brightest in the neon-drenched **W XYX** bar, which serves smoking potion-like molecular cocktails. Pool, gym, friendly staff, 24-hr snack bar, free entry to **Bed Supperclub**.

$$$$-$$$ Amari Boulevard, 2 Sukhumvit Rd, Soi 5, T02-255 2930, www.amari.com. Great location in the heart of Sukhumvit, good rooms, adequate fitness centre, small pool with terraced Thai restaurant. Popular with European visitors.

$$$$-$$$ Ariyasom Villa, 65 Sukhumvit Soi 1 (far end of Soi), T02-254 8880, www.ariyasom.com. A leafy haven in the concrete jungle – an aristocratic family home turned upmarket mini-resort. Rooms are sumptuous modern Thai, there's a lovely pool and the welcome is friendly. The elegant restaurant, **Na Aroon**, has tall wooden shutters that open on to the garden and serves superb vegetarian food. Patients from the nearby Bumrungrad International Hospital sometimes convalesce here, and we can see why. Recommended.

$$$$-$$$ Davinci Suites, 3/8-10 Soi 31, T02-260 3939, www.davincilespa.com. Faux-European boutique hotel down a very quiet *soi*, but still centrally located. Stylish black and white decor. Very comfortable rooms all with a/c, fridge, flat screen TV. Restaurant.

$$$$-$$$ Park Avenue Grand Mecure Hotel, 30 Sukhumvit Soi 22, www.accor hotels.com. Modern, clean rooms all with a/c, TV, minibar and bathtub. The rooms are on the small side and feel a little cramped. Swimming pool, gym and restaurant. There's also a couple of rooms adapted for wheelchair users. Rates depend on occupancy and can be discounted by up to 50%. Professional staff.

$$$ Baan Sukhumvit, 392/38-39 Soi 20, T02-258 5622, www.baansukhumvit.com. Small rooms with imitation dark teak furniture. Good facilities including a/c, TVs and DVD players in all the rooms. Free Wi-Fi and breakfast for 2. Restaurant downstairs. Weekly rates available. Friendly staff. Recommended.

$$$ Grand Inn Hotel, 2/7-8 Sukhumvit Soi 3, T02-254 9021, www.grandinnthailand.com. Recently renovated hotel in the gritty Nana area. The rooms have a slightly hip, modern feel and are comfortable and clean. Wood floors, TV, fridge and bathtub. Wi-Fi extra.

$$$-$$ Sam's Lodge, 28-28/1 Sukhumvit 19 (upstairs), T02-253 6069, www.sams lodge. com. Budget accommodation with modern facilities and roof terrace. English-speaking staff. Close to Asok Skytrain station.

$$ Bangkok Inn, 155/12-13 Sukhumvit Soi 11/1, T02-254 4834, www.bangkok-inn.com. Friendly and informative German management, clean, basic rooms, with a/c, TV and attached shower.

$$ Bourbon Street, 9/39-40 Soi Tana Arcade, Sukhumvit Soi 63 (Ekamai), T02-381 6801, www.bourbonstbkk.com. Now in a new location. A handful of comfortable, modern rooms, with a/c and TV, attached to a good Cajun restaurant.

$$ City Lodge, Sukhumvit Soi 9, T02-253 7710, www.oamhotels.com/citylodge19. Impressively smart small hotel, with bright rooms and a personal feel. Good discounts available for internet bookings.

$$ Suk 11, 1/33 Sukhumvit Soi 11, T02-253 5927, www.suk11.com. Resembling a rural Thai home, this quirky backpacker favourite is a world unto itself on Sukhumvit. On the same sub-soi as **Cheap Charlie's**, with a façade drowning in potted plants, its wood-plank corridors resemble old Siamese alleyways, and the a/c rooms are simple but clean. Good sister spa opposite. Recommended.

$$ World Inn, 131 Sukhumvit Soi 7/1, T02-253 5391. Basic rooms with the standard TV, mini-bar and en suite bathroom. Coffee shop with Thai and Western food.

$$-$ The Atlanta, 78 Sukhumvit Soi 2, T02-252 1650, www.theatlantahotelbangkok.com. With personality in abundance the **Atlanta**'s rooms are at best basic, although a/c and family rooms are available. The amazing art deco interior is often used by Thai filmmakers and there's a large pool surrounded by hammocks and sunbeds – a real treat for this price range. A sign above the door requests that "Oiks, lager louts and sex tourists" go elsewhere and staff can be sniffy with late-nighters and rule breakers (there is a long list at reception). Excellent restaurant (see Restaurants, page 92). Entertaining staff and a magical days-of-yore travellers ambience. Book early.

Bangkok suburbs *p62*

$$$$ Bangkok Treehouse, Bang Namphueng, Bang Krachao, Samut Prakarn, T08-2995 1150, www.bangkoktreehouse. com. There's nothing else like this secluded riverside eco-resort. Not accessible by car or Skytrain, it has an ambitious A-Z of environmental principles and is truly at one with nature. Guests must catch a long-tail boat to Bang Krachao. The 12 modern bungalows, or 'Nests', have 3 storeys and private rooftops for eyeballing the scenery. There's a chlorine-free pool, an organic restaurant and Ewok-village like walkways tying it all together. Freebies include à la carte breakfast, Wi-Fi, bicycles, mobile-phone rental and, believe it or not, ice cream. It's not cheap, or for everyone, especially mosquito-phobes, but nature-buffs will be beside themselves.

$$$ Mystic Place, 244/11-18 Pradipat Rd, T02-270 3344, www.mysticbangkokhotel. com. Travellers seeking out an off-beat but truly hip boutique boudoir need look no further. Words can not really do justice to this über-kitsch creation in a northern suburb bereft of tourists, so see the website for full glorious details. Each of the 30 quirky rooms was designed independently by 30 guest artists. Themes range from a maharajah's palace to a huge post-industrial loft space. Excellent on-site restaurant serving Thai and Japanese food, cute pool, garden and spa. Ideally located on the Skytrain line and one stop from Chatuchak. Downsides include some paper-thin walls and a lack of room service but otherwise service is good. Book early. Recommended.

$$$ Royal View Rangnam, Soi Ratchawithi 3, Rangnam Rd, T02-642-4447, www.royal viewrangnam.com. Small apartment and hotel block overlooking a cute little park down a quiet soi near the busy Victory Monument transport hub. Some of the adequately furnished, though uninspired, spotless rooms have balconies overlooking the park, and all have a/c, en-suite facilities and TV. Nearby Rangnam Rd is filled with nice bars and coffeeshops. Recommended for the excellent location.

$$$-$ Greenery House, 260 Soi Ladprao 62 (64), Ladprao Rd, T02-530 6097, www.greeneryhouse.com. Brilliant serviced apartment complex buried deep in a quiet residential suburb only a 5-min taxi ride from the Suthisan metro station. Apartments/ rooms can be rented nightly or monthly. There's Wi-Fi, a/c, full cable, swimming pool and a gym. It's very friendly and management speak German, French and English. Due to **Greenery**'s location you'll get an authentic slice of Thai life if you stay here – the *sois* in this area are filled with shophouses, great street food and a friendly vibe. Highly recommended.

Around Bangkok *p65*
Damnoen Saduak Floating Marke
$$ Ban Suchoke, T032-254 301. The one guesthouse of note here, **Ban Suchoke** offers simple but comfortable bungalows with wooden verandas overlooking the canal.

Nonthaburi
$$$ Thai House, 32/4 Moo 8, Tambon Bang Meuang, Bang Yai, T02-903 9611, www.thaihouse.co.th. The area's most attractive accommodation option, this traditional Thai house by the river provides a picturesque pastoral escape from Bangkok's urban jungle. Rooms are cosy and attractively decorated and prices include breakfast.

Bangkok is one of the greatest food cities on earth. You could spend an entire lifetime finding the best places to eat in this city that seems totally obsessed with its tastebuds. The locals will often eat 4 or 5 times a day, each and every one of them able to pinpoint their favourite rice, noodles, *kai yang* (grilled chicken), *moo yang* (grilled pork), *som tam* (spicy papaya salad), *tom yam* (sour, spicy soup) and Chinese eateries. Endless runs of streetfood, steak houses, ice cream parlours, Italian diners, seafood specialists and trendy nouvelle cuisine restaurants vie for your attention. In fact, if you really want to see life as the Thais do, then spend your every waking moment in Bangkok thinking about, finding and eating every conceivable gourmet delight the city has to offer. The Thai capital is fanatical about and infatuated with eating.

Many restaurants (especially Thai ones) close early (between 2200 and 2230). most of the more expensive restaurants listed here accept credit cards. Hotels and upmarket restaurants often offer excellent lunchtime buffets. Note that while there are some old timers among Bangkok's hundreds of restaurants, many more have a short life.

Bangkok has a large selection of fine **bakeries**, many attached to hotels like the Landmark, Dusit Thani and Oriental. There are also the generic 'donut' fast-food places although few lovers of bread and pastries would want to lump them together. The bakeries often double as cafés serving coffee, sandwiches and such like. There are also increasing numbers of **coffee bars** such as Starbucks and its local equivalent, Black Canyon Coffee.

Streetfood can be found across the city and a rice or noodle dish will cost ฿25-40 instead of a minimum of ฿50 in the restaurants. Service is rough and ready and there are unlikely to be menus as most stalls specialize in 1 or 2 dishes only. Judge quality by popularity and don't be afraid to point out what you want if your Thai is lacking. All in all, the experience is quintessential Bangkok and the street is where the majority of locals eat. Some of the best in downtown Bangkok can be found on the roads between Silom and Surawong Rd, on Soi Suanphlu off South Sathorn Rd, or on Sukhumvit Soi 38. In the Old City, the close-knit shophouse kitchens along Tanao and Dinso rds, a short stroll from the Democracy Monument, are highly recommended for a cheap Thai food odyssey. Most whip up authentic dishes made from generations-old recipes for next to nothing. The same goes for the stalls that pop up each evening in Chinatown.

Old City *p37, map p44*

Travellers' food, such as banana pancakes and muesli, is available in the guesthouse/travellers' hotel areas (see Where to stay, above). The Thai food along Khaosan Rd is some of the worst and least authentic in town, watered down to suit the tastebuds of unadventurous backpackers. However, head down nearby **Soi Rambutri** and on to **Phra Arthit** and you've suddenly stumbled on a gourmet oasis, one that also stays open a little later than most others in town.
$$$ Teketei, 146 Rambutee Rd, T02-629 0173. Open 1130-2330. Stakes its own claim as the only authentic Japanese restaurant on the Khaosan. Good sushi, sashimi and vegetarian dishes, but fairly pricey.
$$ The Deck, Arun Residence (see page 71). A view of Thonburi's Wat Arun temple glowing in the distance is the main attraction, but this elegant riverside perch also serves decent modern Thai and Western dishes. Good for couples. To snag the best seats on the 2nd-floor decking, make a reservation.
$$ Khin Lom Chom Saphan, 11/6 Samsen Soi 3, T02-628-8382, www.khinlomchom saphan.com. Big, bonhomie-filled open-air riverside eatery serving boldly spiced

Food courts

If you want a cheap meal with lots of choice, then a food court is a good place to start. They are often found along with supermarkets and in shopping malls.

Buy coupons and then use these to purchase your food from one of the many stalls – any unused coupons can be redeemed. A single-dish Thai meal like fried rice or noodles should cost around ฿25-30. The more sophisticated shopping malls will have stalls servings a wider geographical range of cuisines including, for example, Japanese and Korean.

There are food courts in the following (and many more) places:

Mah Boon Krong (MBK), Phaya Thai Rd (west of Siam Square, BTS Siam station).
Panthip Plaza, Phetburi Rd.
United Centre Building, 323 Silom Rd (near intersection with Convent Rd, BTS Sala Daeng station).
Central Chitlom Food Loft , Ploenchit Rd (access from Chit Lom BTS station).

Elsewhere you will find more upmarket food courts:
The Emporium, 622 Sukhumvit Rd (corner of Soi 24).
Siam Discovery Centre, Rama 1 Rd (BTS Siam station).
Siam Paragon Rama 1 Rd (access from Siam BTS station).

Thai-Chinese style seafood and ice-cold beer towers. Live music in the evenings. The food is excellent, but its most memorable feature are the river views, framed by the monolithic Rama VIII suspension bridge. Bring your camera.
$$-$ Coconut Palm Restaurant, 394/3-5 Maharaj Rd, T02-6222246, daily 1100-2200. This medium-sized popular Thai restaurant provides welcome a/c relief just behind Wat Pho and is rammed full of locals at the weekend. Good range of authentic Thai dishes, English-restaurant menu; try the iced lemon tea if the heat is getting to you. Recommended.
$$-$ Rub-ar-roon Cafe, 310-312 Maharaj Rd, T02-6222312, daily 0800-1800. Arty café in a restored, vintage shophouse. Sells decent-enough Thai and Western food and good coffee. Recommended.
$ Hemlock, 56 Phra Athit Rd, Phra Nakorn, T02-282 7507. Our pick of all the cool boutique Thai restaurants on this strip, this bohemian little Thai joint feels more Mediterranean than Siamese, thanks to its stippled cream walls, white tablecloths, jazz CDs and wine list. Attracts off-beat literati

as well as tourists. Good value, with some unusual dishes.
$ Hippie de Bar, Khao San Road (down alley opposite), T02-629 3508. Not as hippyish as it sounds, this rambling house-of-retro serves authentic Thai food and beer snacks. With its outdoor area strewn with fairy lights, Britpop and Thai indie music selection, and young hip Thai crowd, it's Khao San's coolest eatery/hang-out.
$ Madame Musur, 41 Soi Rambuttri. Surprisingly good Northern Thai food in a bamboo and tarpaulin, semi-outdoor setting.
$ May Kaidee, 111 Tanao Rd, Banglamphu, www.maykaidee.com. Open 0800-2300. This tiny, simple vegetarian restaurant is a Khaosan institution. Take the *soi* down by Burger King and it's the 1st on the left. Delicious, cheap Thai vegetarian dishes served at tables on the street. Super-cheap cooking classes also held. They have another branch nearby, at 59 Samsen Rd, and one up in Chiang Mai.
$ Mont Nom Sod, 160/1-3 Dinsor Rd (near Giant Swing), T02-224 1147. Legendary for its fresh sweet milk and thick hot toast slathered in *sankaya*

(Thai-style custard). A delicious late-morning or early evening pitstop.

$ Ricky's Coffee Shop, 22 Phra Arthit Rd. Daily 0800-2400. A civilized spot for breakfast, good coffee or a quick, typically Thai, 1-dish meal. Excellent Thai and Western snack food from cheese and olives to yellow curry. The charming wooden interior and small pavement seating area offer plenty of ambience. Sit upstairs for a view of the efficient chefs and spotless tiny kitchen and take in the framed pictures of Peking in the 1920s.

$ Roti Mataba, 136 Phra Arthit Rd. Mon-Sat 0700-2100. Unmissable for curry fans, **Roti Mataba**'s tiled chip-shop-style interior is piled high with the circular pancake-type breads, which come stuffed with meat or egg and vegetables or dipped into a range of point-and-choose curry pots. Sweet tooths can finish with a condensed milk or honey topping.

$ Royal India, 95 Soi Rambutri. Open 1130-2400. Sister branch of the infamous Pahurat branch (see page 89). For some reason the standards aren't quite up to scratch here but the excellent service, presentation and sweet leafy surrounds set back off the street almost make up for it.

$ Thip Samai, 313 Mahachai Rd, T02-221 6280, www.thipsamai.com. Of Mahachai's many excellent street kitchens, this one is the most famous. Spatula-rattling cooks stationed outside this humble old-school shophouse rustle up what is regarded by many as the best pad thai in town, if not the universe. There are dissenters of course, but you can't argue with them until you've tried it.

Chinatown *p48, map p44*

The street food in Chinatown is some of the best in Thailand. You'll find everything from fresh lobster through to what can only be described as grilled pig's face. Everything is very cheap so just look for the more popular places and dive in.

There are also plenty of restaurants selling highly expensive bird's-nest soup or, more controversially, shark fin soup. Both of these specialities might be – in both budgetary and culinary terms – out of many visitors' reach. The best time to go is early evening, when the food stalls are out in force.

$$ Hua Seng Hong Restaurant, 371-372 Yaowarat Rd, T02-222 0635. The grimy exterior belies the fantastic restaurant within. Dim sum, noodles, duck and grilled pork are all awesome, staff brisk yet efficient. Perfect spot. Highly Recommended.

$ The Canton House, 530 Yaowarat Rd, T02-221 3335. Hugely popular dim sum canteen set on the main drag. The prices – ฿15 – for a plate of dim sum are legendary and this has to be one of the best value places to eat in town. The food is OK but nothing exceptional while the frenetic, friendly atmosphere is 100% Chinatown. Recommended.

$ Samsara, Songwat Rd (in alley behind Wat Patumkongka), T02-639 6853. Khao San would kill for a joint like this: an art-strewn café housed in a rustic wood-plank shack right at the river's edge. Best in the late afternoon when the sun wanes slowly behind Thonburi on the far bank. Solid Thai and western snacks, plus a good selection of local and Belgian beers. It's near **Loy La Long Hotel** (see Where to stay); head to Wat Patumkongka and duck down the alleyway to the right of the entrance. Recommended.

$ T&K Seafood, Corner of Yaowarat and Phadung Dao Rd. Scoff scintillating seafood at this hectic streetside kitchen. Dishes are prepared at street level or lowered down on ropes from the upstairs kitchen. There is inside seating but most patrons sit on plastic chairs at fold-up tables on the corner, amid the noise, traffic and heat. You can't go wrong with the river prawns, steamed fish or stir-fried cockles with basil and chilli.

Siam Sq and Ploenchit Rd *p56,*
map p57

Like Chinatown, Siam Sq has a shark's fin soup specialists. Those who are horrified by the manner in which the fins are removed and the way fishing boats are decimating the shark populations of the world should stay clear. Siam Sq is also dotted with Asian noodle shops, refreshment stalls, sushi bars and the odd cakeshop/café, most of them geared towards the taste-maker teens that roam here.

$$$ Biscotti, Four Seasons, 155 Rachdamri Rd, T02-126 8866. Italian 'fusion' is served at one of 3 superb restaurants at this top-class hotel (the others being **Spice Market** and the steakhouse, **Madison**). Very popular, book ahead.

$$$ Gianni's, Soi Tonson. An excellent Italian restaurant in the area, with light, airy decor and excellent pasta and main courses, not to mention very polished service and a good wine list.

$$$ L'Espace de l'Oriental, main floor, Paragon Centre, T02-610 9840, www. mandarinoriental.com. Only in Bangkok can opulent dining take place in a shopping mall. Despite its location, **L'Espace** serves fine international and Thai cuisine.

$$$ Oishi Grand, 2nd Floor, Siam Discovery Center. Yes, it's a chain, but this is the best Japanese buffet blow-out going. ฿699 buys you 3 hrs of non-stop sushi, sashimi, tepanyaki, soups, desserts, drinks – you name it. Its popularity with locals is testimony to the quality and value on offer.

$$$ Once Upon a Time, 32 Phetburi Soi 17 (opposite Panthip Plaza), T02-252 8629. Traditional Thai tuned to foreign tastebuds, served in a lush setting with an old house in one corner. Retreat here after slogging around IT mall Panthip Plaza.

$$$ Spice Market, Four Seasons, 155 Rachdamri Rd, T02-126 8866, www.four seasons.com/bangkok. Open daily for lunch and dinner. Westernized Thai, typical hotel decoration, some of the city's best Thai food and an excellent set menu.

$$$ Witch's Oyster Bar, 20-21 Ruamrudee Village, T02-255 5354, www.witch-tavern. com. Open 1100-0100. Bangkok's first oyster bar is run by an eccentric Thai. A good place to eat late on good crab cakes and international cuisine.

$$ Ban Khun Mae, 458/6-9 Siam Sq Soi 8, T02-658 4112. Good Thai food and friendly service in quaint, faux-vintage Thai surroundings that are slightly at odds with this funky shopping area.

$$-$ Central Chitlom Food Loft, Central shopping Centre Chitlom. Don't be put off by the shopping centre location, for a 1-stop food centre/shopping stop **Central Food Loft** is as stylish as they come. Wonderful view, chic ambience and fine food from all over the globe in the multiple concessions, from sushi to pie and mash.

$$ Din Tai Fung, 7th Floor, Central World, Rajdamri Road, T02-646 1282. Thailand's first branch of Taipei's legendary xiao long bao (steamed pork dumpling) restaurant. The supple bundles arrive sagging under the weight of their fillings and hot broth. Yummy and addictive. Packed at lunch and dinnertimes, but worth a short queue.

$$ Neil's Tavern, 58/4 Soi Ruanrudee, Ploenchit Rd, T02-256 6875. Open 1130-1345, 1730-2230. Very popular international food, including great steaks. It's named after Neil Armstrong and opened the year he set foot on the moon. There's another branch at 24 Sukhumvit Soi 21.

$$ Taksura, 334/1 Soi Thammasaroj, Phayathai Rd, T02-215 8870, www.taksura. com. Old wooden house with an outdoor terrace, a straightforward menu of Thai beer snacks and mains, and a fun, young vibe. Part of a popular Bangkok pub chain. Much more character than the Siam Sq norm, but you do have to trudge north, over Hua Chang bridge, to find it.

$ Hong Kong Noodles, Siam Sq Soi. Usually packed with university students and serves stupendously good *bamii muu deang kio kung sai naam* (noodle soup with red pork and stuffed pasta with shrimp).

$ Mango Tango, Siam Sq Soi 5 (next to the Novotel Siam Square), T08-1619 5504. As the name suggests, this funky dessert café is mango-mad. All the desserts and smoothies are made with the extra sweet nam doc mai variety. A refreshing pit-stop.

$ Sanguan Sri, 59/1 Wireless Rd, T02-252 7637. This old bunker like building on the right, about 200 m before the Ploenchit Rd junction, serves exquisite Thai food but is open only during the day. It's swarming with office workers at lunchtime, so go just before midday to ensure you get a table.

Cafés and bakeries
Café de Tartine, front of Athenee Residence, Soi Ruamrudee, 65 Wireless Rd, T02-168 5464, www.cafetartine.net. Simple French baked fare: croissants, quiches, salads, soups, assertively flavoured baguettes. The area's most popular lunch stop for expats, especially homesick Gallic ones. Pleasant old world-style interior and a very friendly owner. Recommended.

La Brioche, ground floor, Novotel Bangkok on Siam Square, Siam Sq Soi 6. Good range of French patisseries.

Starbucks, centre of Soi Langsuan. This large branch in a faux-Thai teak house, with its own garden, small library and free Wi-Fi, attracts the creative all-day-on-a-coffee crowd and makes for a great city escape.

Silom area *p59, map p60*
$$$ Angelini, Shangri-La Hotel, 89 Soi Wat Suan Plu, T02-236 7777. Open 1830-late. One of the most popular Italian restaurants in town – a lively place with open kitchens, pizza oven and the usual range of dishes. Menu could be more imaginative.

$$$ The Anna Restaurant, 27 Soi Piphat, T02-237 2788, www.theannarestaurant. com. Great Thai-cum-fusion restaurant in a century-old, colonial-style residence named after Anna of *King & I* fame. Some classic Thai dishes like *larb, nua yaang* and *som tam*, along with fusion dishes and Western

desserts, such as apple crumble and banoffee pie. Nice outdoor eating area.

$$$ The Dome at State Tower, 1055 Silom Rd, T02-624 9555, www.lebua.com. Dine in ultimate style on top of the city in one of its highest skyscrapers. An array of restaurants to try but the super-stylish Sirocco has views, an ambience and a price list that all take the breath away. Well worth splashing out on for a special occasion.

$$$ Eat Me, 1/6 Phipat Soi 2 (off Convent Rd), T02-238 0931. Open 1500-0100. Join Bangkok's creative gourmet crowd at this super-chic art café and restaurant. The stylish interior borrows art from various Bangkok galleries and the fabulous Pacific Rim-inspired fusion food is about as far from the 'spicy spaghetti' set as you can get. A lot pricier than your average cool café but worth every mouthwatering baht, the desserts especially so. Small, leafy outdoor area.

$$$ Gaggan, 68/1 Soi Langsuan, T02-652-1700. Progressive Indian cuisine by a passionate chef who trained at Spain's famous (and now defunct) school of molecular gastronomy, El Bulli. The 10-course tasting menu, 1600, is the way to go, pairing mains off the à la carte menu with inventive starters and other curry house game-changers (chutney foams, etc). Gorgeous setting: a big, nook-filled Thai townhouse, with a colonial summer house feel and an upstairs terrace. Recommended.

$$$ Issaya Siamese Club, 4 Soi Sri Aksorn, Chua Ploeng Rd, Sathorn, T02-672 9040, www.issaya.com. Thai celebrity chef Ian Kittichai has restaurants in the Middle East and New York but resisted opening a restaurant in his homeland until he found the right location. His patience paid off; this stately 1920s house is really something special. As well as the dining room, there's an evocative lounge bar and lawn with bean bags to kick back on. Don't miss the desserts; these are where Ian's modern cooking techniques really shine.

$$$ La Table de Tee, 69/5 Sala Daeng Rd, www.latabledetee.com. The titular 'Tee', a young chef from the northeast who trained at London's Michelin-starred **Roussilon**, serves a surprise 6-course tasting menu for ฿900 nightly. Expect lip-smacking Asian or Western dishes made with classical French techniques and local produce. It's down a blink-and-you'll-miss it alley; call if you get lost.

$$$ Le Bouchon, 37/17 Patpong Soi 2, T02-234 9109. Daily 1100-0200. Tiny family-run hole-in-the-wall serving classic French country cuisine (Provence) for reasonable prices. Its popularity with Bangkok's French expat community is such that reservations are a must in spite of the sleazy location.

$$$ Le Normandie, Oriental Hotel, see Where to stay, page 78. Mon-Sat open for lunch and dinner and Sun for dinner. La Normandie maintains extremely high standards of French cuisine and service (with guest chefs from around the world), jacket and tie required in the evening but the service is still not overbearing – set lunch and dinner menus are the best value.

$$$ Lord Jim's, Oriental Hotel, see Where to stay, page 78. A fine restaurant, offering great views and stunning international food.

$$$ Nahm, Metropolitan, 27 South Sathorn Rd, T02-625-3388, www.metropolitan. bangkok.como.bz. Some locals won't dine at this upscale Thai restaurant on principle – an Australian claiming to cook authentic Thai is anathema, even borderline offensive, to them. But they're missing out: Nahm is the most exciting Thai fine-dining experience currently on offer in the capital. David Thompson, the chef behind London's formerly Michelin-starred restaurant of the same name, sources his recipes from old books and reverentially reworks long-lost dishes. Spicings can be fierce, and it's not cheap, but ultimately it's worth the splurge. The huge tasting menu, 1500, offers the best value. Recommended.

$$$ Vertigo, 61st floor, Banyan Tree Hotel, 21/100 South Sathorn Rd, T02-679 1200. Open 1800-2300. As the name suggests, this stunningly located restaurant commands some dizzying views, which are best seen at sunset. The excellent service and elegantly presented food can occasionally be a bit 'style over substance' for these prices. Also see the **Moon Bar**, in Bars and clubs, page 94.

$$$ Zanotti, 21/2 Sala Daeng, Soi 2 (off Silom Rd), T02-636 0002. Open daily for lunch and dinner. Extremely popular, sophisticated restaurant serving authentic Italian cuisine, including wonderful Italian breads and salads, pizzas, risotto and exceptional pasta dishes.

$$ The Barbican, 9/4-5 Soi Thaniya, Thaniya Plaza, Silom Rd, T02-234 3590. Open 1100-0200. Chic café-bistro in a stylish expat pub, serving duck, steaks, sophisticated sandwiches and fish.

$$ Bua Restaurant, Convent Rd (off Silom Rd). Reliable and reasonably priced Thai restaurant. A good place to road test more obscure dishes. Our pick of the picture-based menu: the wing bean salad.

$$ Celadon, Sukhothai Hotel, 13/3 South Sathorn Rd, T02-344 8888. Exceptional contemporary Thai cuisine in stunning classical surrounds. Booking highly recommended.

$$ Gallery Café, 86-100 Charoen Krung Soi 30, T02-234 0053. Reasonable Thai food in an artistic environment extending over 4 floors.

$$ Himali Cha Cha, 1229/11 Charoen Krung, T02-235 1569, www.himalichacha. com. Good choice of Indian cuisine in mountainous portions for the very hungry. Originally set up by Cha Cha and now run by his son – "from generation to generation" as it is quaintly put. Another branch on Sukhumvit Soi 31.

$$ Indian Hut, 311-2-5 Surawong Rd (opposite the **Manohra Hotel**), T02-237 8812, www.indianhut-bangkok.com. Long-standing and resolutely popular north Indian restaurant; well priced, good service.

$$ Just One, 58 Soi Ngam Duphli, T02-679 7932. Outside seating under a huge tree lit with fairy lights. Mix of Thai and *farang* customers nibble on Thai dishes. Raw prawns 'cooked' in lime and garlic is a speciality.

$$ Ruen Urai, Rose Hotel, 118 Surawong Rd, T02-266 8268, www.ruen-urai.com. Faithfully updated Thai food in traditionally elegant, Jim Thompson-esque surrounds: a 100-year-old Thai teak house, tucked away in the grounds of sleazy Suriwong Rd's Rose Hotel. The downstairs dining room has modern touches; upstairs is an intimate teak-panelled room filled with old Buddhist artefacts and family heirlooms. Worth seeking out.

$$ Sara Jane's, 55/21 Narathiwat Ratchanakharin Rd, Sathorn, T02-679 3338. Great Thai salad and good duck. The Isaan food is yummy and excellent value. Very foreigner friendly, this is a fine place for finding your Thai-food 'feet' before heading out to sample the street food.

$$ Silom Village, 286 Silom Rd (north side, opposite Pan Rd). There are several excellent Thai restaurants in this shopping mall. Pick from hundreds of stalls, all cooking in front of you, and dine in an enjoyable village atmosphere.

$$ Tongue Thai, 18-20 Charoen Krung 38, T02-630 9918. Tucked in an unassuming alley just behind the Mandarin Oriental is this quaint 2-floor shophouse restaurant, decorated with rustic Siam objets d'art. Decent-sized portions of Thai food; watch out for a few unapologetically spicy dishes

$ Hai Somtum, 2/4-5 Soi Convent, off Silom Rd, T02-631 0216. With efficient service and a tourist-proof picture menu, this is a great spot to sample different kinds of somtum (spicy papapa salad), among other classic northeastern dishes. Manic at weekday lunch and dinnertimes, when famished office workers invade the place.

$ Krua Aroy Aroy, Pan Rd (opposite the Indian temple), T02-635 2365. Open 0800-2030. Cheap hole-in-the-wall kitchen just across from Silom's Wat Khaek. Head here at lunchtime to feast on rich regional curries spooned over silk-smooth kanom jeen (rice noodles), including a superlative chicken massaman. They also serve a contender for the city's best kao soi (northern-style chicken curry topped with crispy egg noodles).

$ Royal India, 392/1 Chakraphet Rd, Pahurat, T02-221 6565. A little off the beaten track in Little India (Pahurat) but this infamous restaurant is well worth seeking out. A favourite haunt of Thai politicians and expats, Royal India serves delicious Indian dishes and thalis in simple red-brick surrounds.

$ Soi Polo Fried Chicken, 3 Soi Polo, Wireless Rd, T02-251 2772. A smidge overrated, but still a good (but zero-frills). spot to feast on northeastern mainstays like papaya salad, laab (minced meat salad) and, most famously of all, half or whole fried chicken. Here it comes smothered in crispy deep-fried garlic. Don't forget a pouch of sticky rice to go with it.

$ Tamil Nadu, 5/1 Silom Soi (Tambisa) 11, T02-235 6336. Good, but limited South Indian menu, cheap and filling. The *dosas* are recommended.

Cafés and bakeries

The Authors' Lounge, Oriental Hotel, see Where to stay, page 78. Classy and relaxed atmosphere with impeccable service. For an extravagant treat, the high tea is unmissable.

Folies, 309/3 Soi Nang Linchee (off south end of Soi Ngam Duphli), T02-286 9786, www.folies.net. French expats and bake-o-philes maintain this bakery makes the most authentic pastries and breads in town. Coffee available; a great place to sit, eat and read.

Harmonique, 22 Charoen Krung, T02-237 8175 Small, elegant coffee shop with good music, fruit drinks and coffee. Great atmosphere.

Sukhumvit Road *p61, map p62*
Nana is also known as 'Little Arabia' for its plethora of Middle Eastern and Muslim eateries. Only a few of these places sell alcohol but sheesha cafés (often in upstairs lounges) are plentiful and generally welcoming. For vegetarian food, see Atlanta Hotel, page 81 and Govinda, page 92.

$$$ Bacco, 35/1 Sukhumvit Soi 53, T02-6624538, www.bacco-bkk.com. Daily 1100-1500 and 1800-2400. Probably the best Italian food in town and, considering the location and quality of the food, very reasonably priced. Homemade pastas, the best ingredients and awesome breads and hams await the diner. Highly recommended.

$$$ Basil, Sheraton Grande Sukhumvit, 250 Sukhumvit Rd, T02-649 8366. One of the best Thai fine-dining experiences in town. In a woody, evocatively-styled space, waiting staff serve creative dishes with steaming portions of plain, organic brown or jasmine rice. Excellent desserts include sungkaya fakthong: 2 slivers of pumpkin half filled with custard and served with coconut ice cream.

$$$ Bed Supperclub, 26 Sukhumvit Soi 11, T02-651 3537, www.bedsupperclub.com. Daily 2000-0200. Fabulous futuristic inter-national dining at its most upliftingly laid back. Recline and dine on comfy padded platforms filled with plump cushions, funky beats and beautiful people. The food is exceptional, too, and prices reflect this. An à la carte menu is served Sun-Thu (restaurant closed Mon); a surprise 4-course menu Fri-Sat. Make early bookings for weekends/holidays and be on time. Bring a passport as ID for entry.

$$$ Bo.lan, 42 Soi Pichai Ronnarong, Sukhumvit Soi 26, T02-260 2962, www.bolan.co.th. Chefs Bo and Dylan trained with David Thompson, the chef behind **Nahm** (see page 88) but their Thai restaurant has arguably been a bigger success. Like Thompson, they pluck forgotten recipes from old cookbooks, recreate them using scrupulously sourced local products and serve them in fine-dining surrounds. Some complain about the prices (the set menu costs a whopping ฿1,680) but on the flip side, some of these dishes are likely to be the most unusual you'll ever taste.

$$$ Curries & More by Baan Khanitha, 31 Sukhumvit Soi 53, T02-259 8530, www.curriesandmore.com. Excellent modern

Thai food in a swish converted 80-year-old house. Also in the tree-filled compound is a 2-storey wine bar and a dessert café. Draws the Thonglor professional set.

$$$ Kuppa, 39 Sukhumvit Soi 16, T02-663 0450. Coffee house with pale-wood interior and an upstairs art gallery. An eclectic but well-done range of Thai and 'inter' dishes, from fresh crab and prawn cakes to pumpkin ravioli and Australian rib-eye. Attracts a distinctly fashionable Thai crowd. Popular for brunch.

$$$ La Colombe d'Or (formerly Le Banyan), 59 Sukhumvit Soi 8, T02-253 5556. Open 1800-0000. Classic French food from foie gras to crêpes suzette and pressed duck. Highly regarded food, but a bit stuffy.

$$$ L'Opera, 53 Sukhumvit Soi 39, T02-258 5606, www.lopera-bangkok.com. Long-standing Italian restaurant with Italian manager, conservatory, good food (excellent salted baked fish), professional service, lively atmosphere. Popular, so booking recommended.

$$$ Rang Mahal, Rembrandt Hotel, 19 Sukhumvit Soi 18, T02-261 7100. Some of the finest Indian food in town, award-winning and very popular with the Indian community. Spectacular views from the rooftop position, sophisticated, elegant and expensive.

$$$ Rossini, Sheraton Grande Sukhumvit, 250 Sukhumvit Rd, T02-649 8364. This hotel-based Italian restaurant is open for lunch and dinner. A tantalizing array of dishes and excellent bread. Still one of the best Italian places in town. Consistently excellent.

$$$ Seafood Market, Sukhumvit Soi 24, www.seafood.co.th. A deservedly famous restaurant that serves a huge range of seafood: "if it swims, we have it". Choose your seafood and have it cooked to your own specifications.

$$ Baan Khanittha, 36/1 Sukhumvit Soi 23, T02-258 4181, www.baan-khanitha.com. The original branch of this popular Thai restaurant is a rambling house with tastefully decorated rooms. Recently renovated, it attracts clients of all nationalities – the food is of a consistently high standard and service is excellent.

$$ Bei Otto, 1 Sukhumvit Soi 20, T02-262 0892. Thailand's best-known German restaurant. Sausages made on the premises, good provincial atmosphere and large helpings. There's an attached deli next door for takeaway. Also makes very good pastries, breads and cakes.

$$ Bourbon Street, 9/39-40 Soi Tana Arcade, Sukhumvit Soi 63 (Ekamai), T02-381 6801, www.bourbonstbkk.com. Open 0700-0100. Venerable New Orleans-themed restaurant now in a new Ekamai location. Cajun specialities, including gumbo, jambalaya and red fish, along with steaks, Mexican dishes (buffet every Tue) and pecan pie.

$$ Crêpes and Co, 18/1 Sukhumvit Soi 12, T02-653 3990, www.crepesnco.com. Open 0900-2400. The name says it al:, a really popular place that specializes in crêpes but also serves good salads. Mostly Mediterranean but some local culinary touches, such as the *crêpe mussaman* (a Thai-Muslim curry). Also have another swisher branch at the Eight Thonglor mall, near Thonglor Soi 8.

$$ Firehouse Pub & Restaurant, 3/26 Sukhumvit Soi 11, T02-651 3643, www.firehousethailand.com. This tiny, fireman-themed fast food joint turned heads when it picked up the 'Best New Burger 2011' award from the excellent Bangkok Burger Blog. As well as these towering beasts made with Thai-French rib-eye, they also serve decent spicy buffalo wings, fish and chips, and tacos. Just across from Q Bar, to which it delivers.

$$ Gedhawa, 24 Sukhumvit Soi 35, T02-662 0501. One of the homeliest, cosiest Thai restaurants in town. Serves mostly Northern food – from sai aour (sausage) to nam prik ong (spicy dip) – in a slightly kitsch, pastel-pink setting bedecked in Lanna-style lanterns, textiles and trinkets. Recommended.

$$ Le Dalat, 57 Sukhumvit Soi 23, T02-664 0670. Open daily for lunch and dinner. Open since 1985, this classy Vietnamese restaurant recently relocated but remains on the same soi. Not only is the food good, but the ambience – think aristocratic French-Vietnamese – is satisfying too.

$$ Lemon Grass, 5/1 Sukhumvit Soi 24, T02-258 8637. Open daily for lunch and dinner. Thai food in a rustic Thai-style house. Recommended and popular, if a little long in the tooth.

$$ Mellow, Penny's Balcony, Thonglor (Sukhumvit Soi 55), T02-382 0065. Hip Thonglor joint done just right. The food is American-Italian comfort with a Thai twist (think chicken wings in Sriracha sauce or calzone with baby clams) and not spectacular. However, they have an excellent cocktail and wine list, long happy hours and a very cool semi-industrial, red-brick setting that overlooks the street.

$$ Mrs Balbir's, 155/1-2 Sukhumvit Soi 11, T02-651 6498, www.mrsbalbir.com. North Indian food, including succulent chicken dishes, orchestrated by Mrs Balbir, a Malay-Indian. Also runs cookery classes.

$$ Nasir al-Masri, 4-6 Sukhumvit Soi 3/1, T02-253 5582. Reputedly the best Arabic food in Bangkok: falafel, tabhouleh, hummus, and it's frequented by large numbers of Arabs who come for a taste of home. No alcohol served.

$$ Snapper, 22 Sukhumvit Soi 11, T02-651 1098. More upmarket than a normal fish and chip shop, and it uses sustainably sourced New Zealand fish only. Good for a hearty meal before a night out on this popular party *soi*.

$$ Soul Food Mahanakorn, 56/10 Sukhumvit Soi 55 (Thong Lor), T08-5904 2691, www.soulfoodmahanakorn.com. American food critic Jarett Wrisley's casual, Thai-style izakaya serves a fluid menu of snacky regional street food and signature cocktails in stylish wood-panelled shophouse surrounds.

$$ Tapas Café, 1/25 Sukhumvit Soi 11, T02-651 2947, www.tapasiarestaurants. com. Daily until 1900. Stylishly converted townhouse serving excellent tapas. Attentive staff, very drinkable sangria, happy hours.

$ Cabbages and Condoms, 6 Sukhumvit Soi 12, T02-229 4611, www.cabbagesand condoms.com. This is a Population and Community Development Association (PDA) restaurant, so all proceeds go to this condom-obsessed charity. Eat rice in the Condom Room, drink in the Vasectomy Room. Good *tom yam khung* and honey-roast chicken; curries all rather similar but good value. Very attractive courtyard area decorated with fairy lights.

$ Govinda, 6/5 Sukhumvit Soi 22, T02-663 4970. Vegetarian restaurant serving a range of excellent pizzas, risottos and salads created by an Italian chef serving up plenty of 'fake' meat substitutes. Attractive outdoor seating area.

$ Isao, 5 Sukhumvit Soi 31, T02-258-0645. No-frills Japanese eatery with chic modern decor: bench seating, bamboo slats adorning the walls, an open kitchen. Excellent sushi and new-fangled dishes, and great value set dishes. Recommended.

$ Phuket Town, 160/8 Thong Lo, Soi 6, Sukhumvit 55, T02-714 9402. Converted shophouse with a distinctive Sino-Portuguese-style frontage that reflects the owner's Phuket origins. The kitchen is also rooted in the island's heritage, rustling up southern Thai specialities made with ingredients they have shipped up regularly. Don't miss the signature steamed fish balls. Recommended.

$ The Restaurant, Atlanta Hotel, see Where to stay, page 81. Excellent Thai food in fantastically quirky surrounds. The highlight is the 1930s art deco interior, but don't expect tablecloths and candelabra – it's more about rickety tables and lively entertainment from the Fawlty Towers-style staff. Still, the food is great, with some excellent vegetarian options.

$ Sabai Jai Gai Yang, Ekamai Soi 1, Sukhumvit Soi 63. Feast on finger-lickin' grilled chicken with fried garlic, among untold other top-notch Isaan and Thai dishes, at this perpetually packed favourite. The downmarket open-air setting oozes beer-fuelled bonhomie. Open late.

$ Wannakarm, 98 Sukhumvit Soi 23, T02-259 6499. Well-established, very Thai restaurant. Dowdy decor and little English spoken, but many rate the food.

$ Zanzibar, 139 Sukhumvit Soi 11, T02-651 2700. Open 1730-0200. Bistro-style bar/ restaurant serving Thai and Western food. Plenty of glass walls, plants and trees give it that half-inside, half-outside feeling. Comfortable armchairs and a relaxing atmosphere. Music is usually chilled jazz and blues, and it regularly has live Thai bands.

Cafés and bakeries

Cheesecake House, 69/2 Thonglor Soi 22, Sukhumvit Soi 55, T02-711 4149. Rather out of the way for most tourists but patronized enthusiastically by the city's large Sukhumvit-based expat population. As the name suggests, cheesecakes of all descriptions are the speciality.

Bangkok suburbs *p62*

$$ Smile (English signage), 302/38 Suthisan Vinijchai Rd (just around the corner from Suthisan metro station; leave from exit 3), T02-693 2561. Daily 1100-2300. The Yunnan family that run this unpretentious a/c restaurant create fresh handmade noodles for each individual dish. The result is one of the best places to sup noodles in town – the braised beef with noodles is completely unforgettable. Highly recommended.

$$-$ Café de Norasingha, Phaya Thai Palace, Phramongkutklao Hospital, 315 Rachawithi Rd. Come for the tasty Thai dishes, coffee and cheesecake; stay for the setting. A dead-ringer for a Viennese coffeehouse, this stunning high-ceilinged room dominates the entrance to the rarely visited Phaya Thai Palace and used to serve as a waiting room during King Rama VI's reign (1910-1925).

$$-$ Reflection Again, 21 Ari Soi 3, T02-270 3341, www.reflectionagain.com. Feisty Thai food in a minimalist white townhouse, hidden on a quiet backstreet in a hip old-money suburb. Live music and a lovely garden bar atmosphere in the evening. Recommended.

$ Isaan Rot Det, 3/5-6 Rangnam Rd, T02-246 4579. One of the best places for northeastern, or Isaan, food in this neighbourhood, if not the city. The atmosphere is non-existent but the gritty staples – grilled chicken, papapa salad, minced meat laab salads – are done very well. English menu.

☊ Bars and clubs

Bangkok's raunchy nightlife took a plunge in the early noughties, when former PM Thaksin Shinawatra introduced earlier closing times; extended-licence clubs now adhere to a 0200 or 0300 curfew. Couple this with the (admittedly infrequent) urine testing that goes on at some nightspots – special police units arrive and take urine tests from all guests in the search for drug use – and Bangkok is losing its reputation as Asia's hottest, wildest nightlife destination.

Don't let this put you off. Thais still love to party and have just adapted their love of food and fun accordingly, with earlier nights out and more subdued after-hours' drinking. The city also has plenty of fantastic venues – everything from boozy pubs through to über-trendy clubs. You can listen to decent jazz and blues, or get into the achingly hip Thai indie scene, or even hear local and international DJs spinning the hippest beats. There are also a clutch of rather seedy after-hours clubs for those truly determined not to arrive home before sunrise (just ask your nearest over eager tuk-tuk or taxi driver).

Currently, the best source for Bangkok nightlife listings is www.siam2nite.com,

though there is a lot of online competition. Also check the Bangkok listing magazines and newspapers (especially on Fri) for the latest information on who's spinning and what's opening. These days most of the city's nightlife clans and club nights have a presence on Facebook, using it to relay news of upcoming events to their party faithful live. Search the following sites and you'll be a clued-up clubber in no time: Dudesweet (indie), Bangkok Invaders (hip-hop), Club Soma (Britpop), BIG organization (DJ parties, Silom/Sukhumvit club crawls), Trasher (pop) Zudrangma Records (Thai folk).

Away from the tourist-orientated nightlife areas (Khao San, Silom and lower Sukhumvit), Royal City Av (or RCA) is where most of Bangkok's middle-class 20-somethings come to party for a pittance. The huge strip of glam, fashionable, banging megaclubs stretches as far as the eye can see and is packed every night of the week with a young and sassily attired crowd. Buy your bottle and mixers Thai style and settle in for prime people-watching opportunities. A similar, albeit more cliquey, scene buzzes in the bars and clubs along Ekamai (Sukhumvit Soi 63) and Thonglor (Sukhumvit Soi 55).

Note ID is required for entry into all official nightclubs; carry a photocopy of your passport (preferably colour and laminated) at all times.

Old City and around *p37, map p44*
Ad-Here, 13 Samsen Rd. Turn right at the temple end of Khaosan, walk for 10 mins and eventually you'll stumble across one of Bangkok's worst-kept secrets with saxophone sounds drifting out onto the pavement. This tiny place packs in magical live blues bands and a lively crowd of all ages and nationalities. Open from 1700 but the bands don't arrive until around 2200. **Amorosa**, Arun Residence, see Where to stay page 71. This rooftop bar down a tiny back soi, behind Wat Pho, provides one of the best places for a sun-downer in

Bangkok. Sup cocktails, beer, decent fresh coffee and iced-teas in a riverside location directly opposite Wat Arun. It's low-key but all the better for it – highly recommended

Brick Bar, 265 Khaosan Rd (at Buddy Lodge), T02-629 4477. A dark, cavernous red-brick vault, where fresh-faced twentysomethings jump around to live ska and rock. Boisterous, boozy fun; expect to spend half the night clinking glasses with new friends.

Brown Sugar, 469 Phrasumen Rd, www. brownsugarbangkok.com. A venerable blues and jazz bar that recently relocated from its Sarasin Rd location. Regular bands play excellent jazz in swinging surrounds. Upstairs, they stage art exhibitions, film screening, plays, poetry reading, concerts and "whatever you can think of".

Café Democ, 78 Rachdamnern Klang. A happy hop and a skip from the Khaosan and sitting right under the shadow of the Democracy monument is this trendy little bijou bar with its fun, fashionable clientele. The turntables turn one corner into an impromptu dance floor but look out for special events featuring familiar guest DJs.

The Club, 123 Khao San Rd, www.theclub khaosan.com. Strut down the long, shady-looking blue neon entranceway and you'll find yourself in a loud, banging techno castle bathed in trippy UV light. A friendly, inebriated mix of Thais and backpackers shake their tooshes to the DJs here each night. Raucous fun, but your eardrums might not thank you for it.

Gazebo, 44 Chakrapong Rd, T02-629 0705. Open 2000-very late. Popular with Thais and farangs, this Moroccan-themed rooftop terrace hosts so-so live bands, while the indoor area plays more full-on dance music. Shisha pipes available. Friendly, relatively relaxed and hugely popular, mainly due to the fact that it's often the last club standing.

Lava Club, 249 Khaosan Rd, T02-281 6565. Daily 2000-0100. Playing the ubiquitous mainstream hip-hop, this cavernous subterreanean venue resembles a heavy

metal club, decked out in black, with red lava running down the walls and floors. Lots of skimpily attired women, baggy-clothed boys and badly attired travellers.

Phranakorn Bar, 58/2 Soi Damnoen Klang Tai, Rachdamnern Rd, T02-622 0282. Daily 1800-0100. Head to the mellow white rooftop of this funky 3-storey art bar for views of the Old City, including the Golden Mount. Tasty beer snacks draw an artsy crowd.

Silk Bar, 129-131 Khaosan Rd, T02-281 9981. The wide decked terrace is a great place to sit and people watch. Live DJs in the evenings.

999 West, turn right between **Lava Club** and **Lek GH**. Open 2000-0200. Formerly the legendary Susie Pub, this is still the place for an alternative Thai experience of clubbing down Khaosan, attracting way more locals than travellers. Thumping local tunes and bright neon signage announces its presence. On weekends it's a seething mass of bodies from early on right up until closing.

Silom and Lumpini Park area *p59, map p60*

One of the greatest concentrations of bars is to be found in the red-light districts of Patpong (between Silom and Surawong roads). Dancing queens of every gender and sexual preference should head to Silom Soi 4. For more hi-energy beats, the slick pick-up joints and cabaret bars on Silom Soi 2 offer glam surrounds and heaving crowds (See below).

Bamboo Bar, Oriental Hotel, see Where to stay, page 78, T02-236 0400. Sun-Thu 1100-0100, Fri-Sat 1100-0200. One of the best jazz venues in Bangkok, classy and cosy with good food and pricey drinks – but worth it if you like your jazz and can take the hit.

Hyde & Seek, 65/1 Athenee Residence, Soi Ruamrudee, T02-167 5152, www.hydeand seek.com. Daily 11000-0100. A designer Georgian-influenced gastrobar with a spacious outdoors area, upscale pub grub and fancy artisanal cocktails by local mixologists, 'Flow'. Rammed with slick, iPhone clutching yuppie types every Thu, Fri and Sat.

Molly Malone's, 1/5-6 Convent Rd (opposite Patpong), T02-266 7160. Daily 1100-0200. Irish pub serving draft Guinness and a predictable but satisfying menu – beef and Guinness pie, etc. Well-patronized by Bangkok expats, it has a good atmosphere, friendly staff and sofas for lounging and reading (upstairs). Big screens show live sports, too.

Moon Bar at Vertigo, 61st floor of the **Banyan Tree Hotel**, 21/100 South Sathorn Rd, T02-679 1200. Super-sophisticated roof-top bar with a breathtaking view of Bangkok. The best place for swanky sundown cocktails in the city. See Restaurants, page 88.

O'Reilly's, corner of Silom and Thaniya, 62/1-4 Silom Rd (right next to Silom Skytrain station), T02-632 7515, www.oreillyspubbangkok.com. Open 0800-0200. Another themed Irish pub, with all the usual cultural accoutrements: Guinness and Kilkenney, rugby on the satellite, etc.

Oriental Hotel, see Where to stay, page 78. A particularly civilized place to have a beer and watch the sun go down is on the veranda, by the banks of the Chao Phraya River. Expensive, but romantic (strict dress code of no backpacks, flip-flops or T-shirts).

Scarlett, 37th floor, **Pullman Bangkok Hotel G**, 188 Silom Rd, T02-238 1991, www.accorhotels.com. The replacement for the much loved V9 wine bar is so new that we hadn't time to scope it out, but expect magnificent views, stunning design and a startlingly affordable wine list with bites to match.

Tapas, 114/17 Silom Soi 4, T02-234 4737, www.tapasroom.net. This decade-old bar, with its sophisticated Moroccan feel, is filled with flickering candles and contagious house beats. Attracts a friendly mix of expats and locals. The bar upstairs caters for the dancing crowds at the weekends with live drumming sessions and guest DJs; the terrace is good for people watching.

Viva Aviv, Unit 118 River City, Charoen Krung Soi 30, T02-639 6305, www.vivaaviv.com. Slick, maritime-themed riverside bar, where the Scandinavian mixologists that brought the city **Hyde & Seek** (see above) conjure up fancy new cocktails, most made with rum and local ingredients. Hosts packed Sun afternoon DJ parties about once a month.

Gay and lesbian

See also the Gay and lesbian section in Planning your trip, page 21. The hub of Bangkok's gay cruiser scene can be found on Silom sois 2 and 4, with clubs, bars and restaurants.

Balcony, 86-8 Silom Soi 4, T02-235 5891, www.balconypub.com. Daily 1700-0200. Cute bar where you can hang out on the terraces watching the action below.

DJ Station, Silom Soi 2, www.dj-station.com. Daily 2200-0200, 100 admission. This is the busiest and largest club on a busy *soi*. 3 floors of pumping beats and flamboyant disco. Essential and recommended.

G.O.D., Silom Soi 2/1. A few years back, the site of the funny Freeman katoey cabaret was reborn as 'Guys on Display', a pumping 3-storey afterhours club.

Sphinx and Pharoah's, 100 Silom Soi 4, T02-234 7249, www.sphinxbangkok.com. Daily 1800-0200. Sited at the end of the *soi*, this comfy little restaurant was recently overhauled and serves excellent food, including great *larb*. There's a karaoke bar upstairs.

Telephone, 114/11-13 Silom Soi 4, www.telephonepub.com. Daily 1800-0200. Flirty, European-style bar where phones at the tables allow you to call other guests.

Sukhumvit Road *p61, map p62*

The strip of bars that run the length of Sukhumvit Rd are mostly populated by bar girls and their admirers. These watering holes generally pump out bad music and serve awful German food and tepid lager. Delve a bit further into Sukhumvit's *sois* and backstreets and you'll find a happening, urban nightclub scene, the equal of anything in Asia. If you want to indulge in more than just alcohol, take note of the notorious urine tests (see page 93); the nightclubs in this area are particular targets.

Bed Supperclub, 26 Sukhumvit Soi 11, T02-651 3537, www.bedsupperclub.com. Daily 2000-0300. Still Bangkok's hottest designer nightspot a decade after it opened. A futuristic white pod filled with funky beats, awesome cocktails, superb food, pillow-soft designer sofa beds and hordes of beautiful people. Big name international DJs tend to spin on Thu; check the website for the changing nightly music policy and guest DJs.

Cheap Charlie's, 1 Sukhumvit Soi 11. Open 1500 until very late. Very popular with expats, backpackers and locals. Lively, cheap and unpretentious open-air bar in kitsch faux-tropical surrounds.

Iron Fairies, 394 Thonglor (Sukhumvit Soi 55), T08-4520 2301 (mob), www.theiron fairies.com. Daily 1800-0200. Vials of fairy dust, steam-punk machinery, projections of black-and-white silent movies, and live jazz are just a few highlights at this most whimsical of wine bars, based on a series of children's fairytales penned by the owner, Ash Sutton. Recommended.

Nest, Le Fenix 33/33 Sukhumvit Soi 11, T02-305-4000, www.thenestbangkok. com. Attracting a cosmopolitan and well-dressed cross-section of nightowls, this sleek rooftop bar is a good spot for early evening Bellinis. Open to the elements, it has retractable canopies in case of storms, funky seating (including bird's nest-shaped beds perfect for couples) and often hosts packed DJ parties at weekends.

WTF, 7 Sukhumvit Soi 51, T02-662-6246, www.wtfbangkok.com. This intimate shophouse bar, lined with old movie posters, hosts live music, art exhibitions and other hip left-field happenings across its 3 levels. One-off parties heave with local journos, creatives, NGO workers

and self-styled artistes. Good tapas-style snacks, too.

Bangkok suburbs *p62*

Motorcycle Emptiness, 394/1 Ladprao Soi 94, T08-9780 9946. This tin-roof venue done out in wrought iron touts itself as 'Bangkok's venue for live original underground music' and many indie hipsters rate it as such. As well as gigs by all-sorts, it also hosts open jams.

Parking Toys, 17/22 Soi Maiyalap, Kaset Nawarmin, T02-907 2228. Keeping a low profile on a long party strip of Thai pubs, bars and clubs offering endless authentic Thai-style entertainment, is this bijou hidden gem. With a low-key interior filled with retro collectibles and artfully crafted slapdash design, **PTs** attracts an almost exclusively hip suburban crowd of cultural creative types. The secret is in the music, with some of Bangkok's best bands playing everything from electronic dance to rockabilly, ska and metal.

Raintree Pub, 116/63-34 Soi Ruamjit, Rangnam Rd, T022-457 230, www.raintree pub.com. 1700-0100. The grizzled musicians who step up in this driftwood time capsule strum a dying form of folk protest music called Pleng Pua Chiwit, or Songs for Live. Good beer snacks; friendly, authentic.

Route 66, Royal City Av, 29/33-48 Rama 3 Rd, T02-203 0936. This hi-tech super-club, with 3 zones and a large outdoor area, is packed most nights with dolled-up students and office types. Live bands play Thai hits and DJs mainly spin hip-hop. Always evolving, it's the oldest club on Royal City Av, a nightlife strip to the east that taxi drivers know simply as 'RCA'.

Saxophone, 3/8 Victory Monument, Phayathai Rd, Golden Mount. Daily 1800-0300. **Saxophone** has a long-standing and well-deserved reputation for delivering live music, great food and low-ceilinged ambience. Get there early for decent seats. The nightly alternating house bands include jazz, blues, reggae and soul players, along with occasional performances by local ska sweethearts (and Glastonbury aficionados) T-Bone.

Tawandaeng German Brewery, 462/61 Narathiwat Rama 3 Rd, T02-678-1114, www.tawandang.co.th. This giant barrel-shaped beer hall is a Bangkok institution that drips bonhomie. Locals flock here for the micro-brewed beer, deep-fried pork knuckle, chintzy cabaret shows and live Thai folk music. Gets more raucous as the night wears on. Great fun.

Viva Bar, Section 26, Chatuchak Weekend Market. Sat and Sun only. An unmissable Bangkok institution. Thirsty shoppers stop at Viva for a smoothie in the intimate, wood-lined surrounds, but, by night (1900-2100), the bar becomes a heaving mass of tambourine-banging bodies downing bottled beers and icy jugs of Margaritas. Consistently brilliant bands play to a friendly mixed crowd. Not far from the MRT station.

⊕ Entertainment

Bangkok *p36,*
maps p38, p44, p57, p60 and p62
Art galleries and cultural centres
There's no distinct art neighbourhood to gravitate towards here; most art galleries are spread scattershot through the city, alone or clustered together in small groups. The best way to keep track of what's hanging where is by picking up a copy of the *Bangkok Art Map*, www.bangkokartmap.com, a free monthly fold-out map with excellent listings. The **Silom Galleria** (aka Jewelry Trade Center), next door to the **Holiday Inn Silom**, has a few decent galleries tucked away in its eerily quiet bowels; Sukhumvit Soi 31 is home to an interesting trio (**Koi**, **La Lanta** and **Attic Studios**); and Section 7 of the **Chatuchak Weekend Market** is surely the city's biggest and most fertile art incubator, with 100 plus gallery stalls. For films, books and other Anglo-centric entertainment, check the local press,

especially *The Bangkok Post* and *The Nation*. Probably the best source of information about Thai artists is www.rama9art.org.

Alliance Française, 29 South Sathorn Rd, T02-670 4200, www.alliance-francaise.or.th. Great place for showcasing French culture and movies, it also stages annual French-Thai cultural festival, **La Fête** (www.lafete-bangkok.com) with the French embassy.

Bangkok Art and Culture Centre, 939 Rama 1 Rd, Pathumwan, T02-214 6630, www.bacc.or.th. Bangkok's very own Guggenheim is an 11-storey behemoth directly opposite MBK mall, right next to the National Stadium BTS station (to which it's linked via a walkway). The lower floors feature art-related shops and temporary gallery guest spaces; the upper ones 3000 sq m of state-sanitized exhibitions from local and foreign artists, all of them free. Nothing edgy but worth a look.

Bangkok Sculpture Centre, 4/18-19 Nuanchan Rd, T02-791 9400, www. bangkoksculpturecenter.org. Mon-Sat 1000-1600. Private 4000 sq m facility displaying 200-plus Thai sculptures dating from the 15th century through to the present day. They recommend foreigners get in touch in advance.

Bangkok University Art Gallery, Kluaynam Thai Campus, Rama IV Rd, T02-350 3626, http://fab.bu.ac.th/buggallery. Daily 1000-1900. Showcasing rising local talents, this 2-storey facility is one of Bangkok's most important spaces.

Chulalongkorn Art Centre, Centre of Academic Resources, Chulalongkorn University, Phaya Thai Rd, T02-218 2965, www.car.chula.ac.th/art. Mon-Fri 0900-1900, Sat 0900-1600. Another important university space, though you'll find more than just student work here, with international artists regularly exhibiting.

Goethe Institute, 18/1 Soi Goethe, Sathorn Soi 1, T02-287 0942, www.goethe.de/bangkok. Everything from classical music recitals to film screenings and art exhibitions. International and Thai.

Kathmandu Photo Gallery, 87 Soi Pan, Silom Rd, T02-234 6700, www.kathmandu-bkk.com. Homely shophouse gallery run by Manit Sriwanichpoom, a respected Thai photographer renowned for his caustic critiques of Thai society, most notably his Pink Man series. Bi-monthly exhibitions range from the socio-political to the comedic to retrospectives of forgotten talent. Recommended.

The Reading Room, 2 Silom Soi 19, T02-635 3674, www.readingroombkk.org. A non-profit contemporary art library and archive that also hosts talks, screenings and workshops covering a range of fields, from art, literature and film to socio-political issues.

Siam Society, 131 Asok Rd (Sukhumvit Soi 21), T02-661 6470, www.siam-society. org. Open Tue-Sat. Stages performances of music, dance, and drama; and hosts lectures and exhibitions.

Thavibu Gallery, Suite 308, Silom Galleria F3, 919/1 Silom Rd (near Soi 19), T02-266 5454, www.thavibu.com. One of the only spaces to hang Burmese and Vietnamese pieces.

Cinemas

Remember to stand for the national anthem, which is played before every performance.

Bangkok cinemas are on the whole hi-tech, ultra luxurious and a great escape from the heat of the city. Prices can range from 100 to 300 for incredibly sumptuous reclining VIP seats, complete with pillows and blankets. Find details of showings from English-language newspapers and at www.movieseer.com. In the past there have been 2 international film festivals held here every year, though, in recent years, successors to the famous **Bangkok International Film Festival**, which was tainted by a corruption scandal, have not come to fruition. Bangkok is also a popular location for many Asian and Hollywood film makers; the American comedy sequel *The Hangover Part 2* was shot here.

Easily accessible cinemas with English soundtracks include **Siam Paragon Cineplex**, Rama I Rd, T02-515 5555; **EGV**, 6th floor, Siam Discovery Centre (Siam Tower), Rama I Rd (opposite Siam Sq), T02-812 9999; **SFX Emporium**, Sukhumvit Soi 24, T02-268 8888; and **SFX Mahboonkrong** (MBK shopping centre), T02-268 8888. Two Siam Sq cinemas built in the late '60s – the grand, art deco **Scala**, Siam Sq Soi 1, T02-251 2861, and the less impressive **Lido Multiplex**, 256 Rama I Rd, Siam Sq, T02-252 6498, screen blockbusters and world cinema respectively. Bangkok's only independent art house cinema is **House**, 31/8 RCA Plaza, RCA, T02-641 5177, www.houserama.com.

Kite flying

Sanam Luang, a huge oval field opposite the Grand Palace, has long been a haven for kite lovers during the strong breezes of the hot season (Feb-mid Apr). The tradition dates back to the Sukothai period and has been practised here for centuries due to its wide open spaces. There used to be an international kite festival here each Mar, the highlight being competitive kite battles, but for the past couple of years this has been held a couple of hours' drive south, in the seaside town of Cha-am.

Muay boxing (Thai boxing)

First developed during the Ayutthaya period (1351-1767), Thai boxing is both a sport and a means of self-defence. Brutal and often bloody, it differs from Western boxing in that contestants are allowed to use almost any part of their body (although head butts and throws are forbidden). To placate spirits and show respect to their teachers, a graceful ritual dance, the ram muay, is performed before bouts. Traditional music plays during them. In addition to Bangkok's 2 main boxing stadiums (below), bouts can also be seen occasionally at the **National Stadium**, Rama I Rd (Pathumwan), and at **Hua Mark Stadium**, Khlong Ton Rd, near

Ramkhamhaeng University. Alternatively, you can just turn on the television; bouts are often televised live (see www.muay thai2000.com). If you want to learn more about the sport see the **World Muay Thai Council** website, www.mcmuaythai.org.
Lumpini, Rama 1V Rd, near Lumpini Park, T02-251 4303, www.muaythailumpini. com. Boxing nights are Tue, Fri (1830) and Sat (1700, 2030). Tickets for foreigners cost ฿2000 for a ringside seat; cheaper seats cost about 1000-1500. (Thais only pay 200.)
Rachdamnern Stadium, Rachdamnern Nok Av, T02-281 4205. Boxing nights are Mon, Wed and Thu (1830) and Sun (1700 and 2030). Seats 1000-2000.

Thai performing arts

Most tourists encounter classical Thai dancing and music during a 'traditional' Thai meal at some dowdy restaurant that the locals wouldn't been seen dead at. Many tour companies or travel agents organize these hokey 'cultural evenings'. Much more interesting are the troupes putting modern twists on the occasionally beguiling, often rather stuffy tradition.
18 Monkeys Dance Theatre, www.18 monkeysdancetheatre.com. Contemporary dance group founded by classically trained choreographer, Jitti Chompee. Specializing in fresh, topical takes on old Thai art forms (folk opera likay, etc), they've dazzled and confounded at venues city-wide, including **Bed Supperclub**.
Joe Louis Puppet Theatre, 2194 Charoenkrung Rd, www.thaiasiatique.com. Details were scant at the time of writing but, with any luck, displays of traditional Thai puppetry are once again thrilling tourists at this much-loved troupe's new home: riverfront shopping and entertainment complex, **Asiatique**. Manipulated using levers and sticks, the ornate masked puppets re-enact classic tales from the Ramakien, Thailand's national epic.
National Theatre, 2 Rachini Rd, T02-224 1342. Performances of khon (classical Thai masked dance) are staged on the last Fri of each month at 1700.
Pichet Klunchun Dance Company, www.pklifework.com. Another modern dance company that puts on singular shows, this one helmed by a dancer who trained in khon and had successful runs in New York.
Sala Chalermkrung, 66 Charoen Krung Rd, T02-623 8148, www.salachalermkrung.com. This former cinema dating from the 1930s is the de facto home of expressive Thai masked dance khon. Shows at 1930 every Thu and Fri. Tickets ฿800-1200 through www.thaiticketmajor.com.
Thailand Cultural Centre, Thiam Ruam Mit Rd, T02-247 0028 (ext 8 for English). Run down and a hassle to get to but often worth the schlepp. Performances from visiting ballet and theatre groups as well as the **Bangkok Symphony Orchestra** and special Thai Productions. Tickets for most are sold via www.thaiticketmajor.com.

✿ Festivals

Bangkok *p36,*
maps p38, p44, p57, p60 and p62
See www.tourismthailand.org for a full calendar of exact dates.

Jan-Feb

Chinese New Year (movable) Chinatown's businesses close down, but Chinese temples are packed, and dragons roam the streets to the sound of a million firecrackers.
La Fête (runs until Apr) An exuberantly eclectic French-Thai cultural festival that stretches its creative tentacles all over town, www.lafete-bangkok.com.

Mar-Apr

Red Cross Fair (movable) Held in Amporn Gardens next to the Parliament. Stalls, classical dancing, folk performances, etc.
Kite Flying (movable, for 1 month) Every afternoon and evening at Sanaam Luang.

Tattoo Festival (movable, Sat near the last full moon before Songkran) Annual tattoo festival at the Wat Bang Phra temple just outside Nakhon Chaisi. Thousands of devotees come to be tattooed by the monks or to have the their existing tattoos 're-empowered'. A day trip from Bangkok.

Songkran (13-15 Apr) Prepare for a drenching as the city heat gets washed away by a constant flow of water and sacred paste. The Khaosan Rd and Patpong/Silom are the places to head to or avoid depending on your chaos-tolerance levels.

May

Royal Ploughing Ceremony (movable) An ancient Brahman farming ritual featuring sacred white oxen and celebrating the start of the rice-growing season. Held at Sanam Luang.

Sep

Swan-boat races (movable) Races on the Chao Phraya River.

Oct

Vegetarian Festival (movable) Look out for the yellow flags on foodstalls and in restaurants. Not as colourfully gruesome as the celebrations down south, but just as tasty. Chinatown offers some of the best gourmet opportunities, as well as lively street theatre.

Nov

Loy Krathong A beautiful spectacle as the city's waterways are set alight by a flotilla of magical *krathong's* (floating miniature caskets of candles, flowers and incense) to honour the water spirits. Firework displays also take place along the Chao Phraya River.

Golden Mount Fair (movable) Stalls and theatres set up all around the Golden Mount and Wat Saket. Candles are carried in procession to the top of the mount.

Marathon Fortunately this road race takes place at one of the coolest times of year, www.bkkmarathon.com.

World Film Festival Excellent, punter-focussed film festival with a yen for fresh arthouse fare and distaste for the usual red-carpet pageantry, www.worldfilmbkk.com.

Bangkok Design Festival A short burst of design-led exhibitons, film screenings and installations, www.bangkokdesignfestival.com

Fat Festival Bangkok's biggest independent music festival held by FAT104.5 radio station. This is where the city's hip creatives gather to take in the latest sounds from the region.

Dec

The King's Birthday (5 Dec) A public holiday and Father's Day. Crowds dressed in yellow, the King's colour, head to Sanam Luang in the Old City to celebrate their beloved monarch and, if they're lucky, catch a glimpse of him.

Trooping of the Colour (movable) The elite Royal Guards swear allegiance to the king and march past members of the royal family. It is held in the Royal Plaza near the equestrian statue of King Chulalongkorn.

Beer Gardens When cooler temperatures arrive for a few weeks each Dec, so do pop-up al fresco beer gardens, hosted by the local lager brands.

Concerts in the Park During the cooler months, the Bangkok Symphony Orchestra puts on free late-afternoon Sun sessions at Lumpini Park's pavilion. Bring a mat and picnic, www.bangkoksymphony.org.

New Year Celebrations (31 Dec) Fireworks at Sanaam Luang and hotels along the river and a mass countdown at Central World Plaza.

O Shopping

Bangkok *p36,*
maps p38, p44, p57, p60 and p62
After eating, the next big love for many
Bangkok residents is shopping. From
energetic all-night flower and fruit markets
through to original (and fake) Louis Vuitton,
Bangkok has the lot, though branded,
Western goods are often cheaper back
home. It is also wise to do your shopping
at the end of your trip rather than the
beginning. That way you'll have had a
chance to gauge the real value of things
and avoid being overcharged. Most
street stalls will try and fleece you, so be
prepared to shop around and bargain
hard. The traditional street market is now
supplemented by other types of shopping.
Some arcades target the wealthier shopper,
and are dominated by brand-name goods
and designer wear. Others are not much
more than street side stalls transplanted to
an arcade environment. Most department
stores are fixed price, though you can still
ask for a discount. Shops do not generally
open until 1000 or 1100.

Sukhumvit Rd and the *sois* to the north
are lined with shops and stalls, especially
around the **Ambassador** and **Landmark**
hotels. Many tailors are to be found in
this area. Higher up on Sukhumvit Rd
particularly around Soi 49 are various
antique and furniture shops.

Nancy Chandler's *Map of Bangkok* is the
best shopping guide. See Planning your trip,
page 15, for further shopping information.

Antiques
Permission to take antiques out of the
country must be obtained from the **Fine
Arts Department** on Na Phrathat Rd, T02-
224 4702. Shops will often arrange export
licences for their customers. Buddha images
may not be taken out of the country –
although many are.

In Bangkok you will find Chinese
porcelain, old Thai paintings, Burmese
tapestries, wooden figures, hilltribe textiles,
Thai ceramics and Buddhist art. Be careful
of fakes – go to the well-known shops only.
Even they, however, have been known to
sell fake Khmer sculpture which even the
experts find difficult to tell apart from the
real thing.

More pricey antique shops can be found
at **OP Place**, a classical white European
building on Charoen Krung Soi 38, just
around the corner from the **Mandarin
Oriental**; and the upper floors of jewellry
mall **Silom Galleria**, 919/1 Silom Rd
(near Soi 19), www.silomgalleria.net.

Serious shoppers should consult
Robin Brown's *Guide to buying antiques
and arts and crafts in Thailand* (1989,
Times Books: Singapore).

Books & Collectibles, 3rd Floor Silom
Galleria, 919/9 Silom Rd, T02-630 2890.
Paper ephemera: from complete sets of
Siamese cigarette cards and brochures
filled with beaming Miss Thailand beauty
queens to rare 1st editions of steamship-
era travelogues.

Old Maps and Prints, 4th floor, River City
Complex, T02-237 0077, www.classicmaps.
com. Has a wide range of historical maps
and engravings, mostly of Asia.

Paul's Antiques, 50 Sukhumvit Soi 13,
T02-253 9025, www.paulsantiques.com.
Mostly high-quality furniture from
Thailand and Burma (Myanmar). They
make pieces from reclaimed teak and
fix up antiques, and so appeal to home-
owners as well as collectors.

River City, a 4-storey shopping complex
next to the **Royal Orchid Sheraton Hotel**,
www.rivercity.co.th, houses a large number
of the more expensive antique shops and
holds monthly auctions, an excellent place
to start. Reputable shops here include
Verandah (414) and **Acala Room** (312)
for Tibetan and Nepalese art.

Rod's, Kamphangphet Rd (near Chatuchak
Market), T08-7978 0578, www.rodsantique.
com. Warehouse of 20th-century treasures –
from classic imported cars to vinyl

furniture – on the same site as Rotfai Market (see Markets). Unlike the market, it's open daily 1000-1800. Recommended.

Books and maps

Look out for books on Southeast Asia and reprints of historical volumes by **White Lotus**, www.whitelotuspress.com. They are stocked in many bookshops around town.
Asia Books, www.asiabooks.com. Excellent for books on Asia and sells a wide range of street maps and A-Zs but less comprehensive than **Kinokuniya Books**. There are 27 branches, including: 221 Sukhumvit Rd, between Sois 15 and 17; 4th floor, Siam Discovery, Rama 1 Rd; 2nd floor Siam Paragon, Rama 1 Rd; 3rd floor, Thaniya Plaza, Silom Rd; 2nd floor, Times Sq, Sukhumvit Rd; and 3rd floor, Central World, Rachdamri Rd.
Chatuchak Weekend Market (see pages 64 and 107). Second-hand books are available in sections 22 and 25, 1 and 27.
Chulalongkorn University Book Centre, Witthayakit Building, Soi Chulalongkorn 64, T02-218 9881, www.chulabook.com. Not on campus but in a more convenient location in Siam Sq, next to the British Council. Good for academic, business and travel books.
Dasa Book Café, 714/4 Sukhumvit (between Sois 26 and 28), T02-661 2993, www.dasabookcafe.com. Daily 1000-2000. A bookworm's browsing dream, **Dasa** offers 2 floors of high-quality new and second-hand books, a lovely quiet interior and a coffee shop with some of the best chocolate cake in Bangkok.
Elite Used Books, 593/5 Sukhumvit Rd, near Soi 33/1 and Villa Supermarket. Good range of second-hand books in several languages.
Kinokuniya Books, www.kinokuniya. com/th. Has the best selection of English and Thai books in town at its three mall branches. The biggest is on the 3rd floor of Siam Paragon, Rama I Rd. Also on the 3rd floor of the Emporium Shopping Centre, Sukhumvit Soi 24 (BTS Phrom

Phong Station), and on the 6th floor of the **Isetan Department Store**, Central World, Rachdamri Rd.
River Books, 396 Maharat Rd (100 m south of Wat Pho), T02-222 1290, www.riverbooks bk.com. Mon-Fri 0845-1700. Small bookstore owned by the imprint behind many of the best books on Thai and regional culture, history and art.
Shaman, 46/1 Khao San Rd. Piled high with second-hand best-sellers, mildewed classics and travel guides. Also surprisingly good for those interested in boffing up about the region, with sections devoted to Southeast Asian history, travel, politics, religion, etc.

Department stores and shopping malls

Visitors to Bangkok no longer have to suffer the heat of the market stall – the city is fast becoming another Singapore or Hong Kong with shopping malls springing up all over the place. The huge number of department stores and shopping centres feature endless retail, eating and entertainment opportunities. Where else in the world could you find a 'knowledge park' (**Central World Plaza**), aquarium (**Siam Paragon**), 'cultural design centre' (**Emporium**) or water park (**Central Bang Na**) atop a shopping mall?
Central Department Store, www.central. co.th, linked to the **CentralWorld** (see below), formerly known as the World Trade Centre, by the Skytrain station at Chitlom. Other outlets are on Silom Rd, Bang Na (north off the Northern bus station), Ladphrao (1691 Phahonyothin Rd), Pinklao (close to the southern bus station) and Rama 3 Rd. This is the largest chain of department stores in Bangkok, with an enormous range of top-end Thai and imported goods at fixed prices; credit cards are accepted.
CentralWorld, corner of Ratchadamri and Rama 1 Rds, www.centralworld.co.th. The city's (and debatably Asia's) biggest mall: a gargantuan and spacious

multi-zoned complex, with hundreds of international and local brand stores; there are restaurants, a cinema, food court and supermarket on its top floors, and an expansive plaza where events (not all of them welcome) are staged out front. Latched on to its northern end is Japanese department store Isetan, and to its southern end, Zen (see below).

The Emporium, Sukhumvit Soi 24 (directly accessible from BTS Phrom Phong Station). An enormous place, dominated by the **Emporium Department Store** but with many other clothes outlets as well as record and bookshops, designer shops and more. The ground and 1st floors are monopolized by the big names in fashion – **Kenzo**, **Louis Vuitton**, **Gucci**, **Versace**, are all there – along with some expensive-looking watch and jewellery shops. For the slightly less extravagant, there are a number of trendy clothes shops on the 2nd floor, many of them home-grown Thai labels like **Greyhound**, **Jaspal** and **Soda**. The 3rd and 4th floors have the more prosaic shops, including **Boots the Chemist**. **Exotique Thai** occupies the space between the escalators on the 5th floor; here you can find a nice selection of decorative items for the home, while the rest of the floor is dedicated to household goods, along with a large food hall. On the top is a cinema and the **Thailand Creative and Design Center (TCDC)**, a slick facility staging free design exhibitions and with a state-of-the-art library.

Mah Boonkhrong Centre (MBK), corner of Phayathai and Rama 1. Long-established, downmarket and packed full of bargains with countless small shops/stalls. Especially good for clothes, cameras, mobile phones and paraphernalia.

Peninsula Plaza, between the Hyatt Erawan and Regent hotels. Overshadowed by the newer, sleeker competition, but still considered one of the smarter shopping plazas in Bangkok, carrying high-end imported and local labels.

Pratunam Market, north along Rachprasong Rd, crossing over Khlong Saensap, at the intersection with Phetburi Rd. Good for fabrics and clothing.

Robinson's, Sukhumvit Rd (corner of Soi 19 and Rachadapisek Rd). A smaller, slightly less upmarket department store than **Central**.

Siam Center, Rama 1, opposite Siam Sq. Mostly fairly young and funky fashion stores, including the highest concentration of innovative Thai boutiques in town and surf/sportswear specialists on the top floor. Plenty of restaurants from fast food to 'boutique' bakeries.

Siam Discovery Centre (Siam Tower), Experimental Thai furniture and funky homeware stores, international fashion brands, Southeast Asia's first **Madame Tussauds** and an ice rink are the draws at this gleaming 6-storey complex next door to Siam Centre.

Siam Paragon, Rama 1 Rd, next to Siam Centre, www.siamparagon.co.th. The undisputed holder of the title of most ostentatious/palatial shopping experience in town. This multi-billion-baht project houses exclusive and high-end retail, dining and entertainment opportunities beyond the dreams even the most die-hard shopaholic. Its endless designer wares from couture to cars could bust a billionaire. A constant calendar of events and entertainment includes an ocean world in the basement, theatre and exhibition halls.

Siam Square, at the intersection of Phayathai and Rama I rds. Partly destroyed during the 2010 riots, this maze of *sois* cut through with pedestrian-only alleys teems with trendy clothing, bags, belts, jewellery, bookshops and local fast-food chains. The hundreds of boutiques scattered every which way hoard local up-and-comers.

Terminal 21, 2/88 Sukhumvit Rd (by Soi 19 and Asok BTS station), www.terminal21.co.th. With its kitsch floors themed after famous capitals and hundreds of home-grown Thai boutiques, the latest mall addition has quickly captured the imagination of the shopping-mad locals. The ground and middle floors host the same big names you see in every mall here, but the 1st (Tokyo – ladies' wear), 2nd (London – menswear) and 3rd (Istanbul – accessories) are more interesting, each a maze of narrow little stores helmed by resourceful locals. The prices are very reasonable, similar to what you pay at Chatuchak market, but the temperatures are much more favourable to long browsing sessions. Includes restaurants and a cinema.

Tokyu, MBK Tower on Rama I Rd. Department store with a Japanese slant.

Zen, Central World Plaza, corner of Rama I and Rachdamri rds. A trendy 'lifestyle megastore' aimed at the young, moneyed and hip; mostly clothing with some housewares. Destroyed by arsonists in the May 2010 riots but has since risen from the ashes.

Fashion

Bangkok has set its sights on becoming the fashion capital of Southeast Asia and is certainly a bustling centre of creativity when it comes to both cutting-edge home-grown couture and smaller independent labels. Former Prime Minister Thaksin Shinawatra's **Fashion City Project** and **Elle Fashion Week**, now held twice yearly, have raised the bar for major-league labels **Greyhound**, **Fly Now** and **Stretsis**, while Siam Square, Chatuchack Weekend Market and even the once-hippy/fake-label haven of the Khaosan Rd all rock with young designers' more daring wares. Also visit shopping malls such as **Siam Paragon**, **Siam Discovery**, **Siam Centre**, **Central**, **Zen** and **Emporium** as well as **Siam Square** for branches of these boutiques alongside numerous other emerging labels.

Cheap designer wear with meaningless slogans and a surfeit of labels (on the outside) are available just about everywhere and anywhere, and especially in tourist areas like Patpong and Sukhumvit. Imitation **Lacoste** and other garments are less obviously on display now that the US is pressurizing Thailand to respect intellectual copyright laws but they are still available. Note that the less you pay, the more likely that the dyes will run, shirts will shrink after washing, and buttons will eject themselves at will.

Disaya, 1st floor, Gaysorn Plaza, T02-656 1388, www.disaya.com. Playful ready-to-wear clothes inspired by a range of whimsical influences. The label's biggest claim to fame: the late Amy Winehouse wore a Disaya printed chiffon strapless dress on the cover for her smash sophomore album, Back to Black.

Fly Now, 2nd floor, Gaysorn, 999 Ploenchit Rd, www.flynowbangkok.com. Directional but wearable ladies' wear, blending Thai-style femininity and flair with current Western influences. As seen at London Fashion Week.

Greyhound, www.greyhound.com. Chic streetwear for the modern, style-savvy urban casual ("basic with a twist" they call it), a look the Thais carry off with aplomb. Stores at **Emporium** (2nd floor); **Siam Center** (3rd floor) and **Siam Paragon** (1st floor). Sub-labels Playhound and Hound & Friends are also stocked here.

Issue, 266/10 Siam Sq, Soi 3, T02-658 4416, www.issue.co.th. A small boutique making big waves on the international fashion circuit with its cool casual blend of fabulous fabrics, ethnic influences and modern shapes. Also at **Siam Paragon** (2nd floor) and **Gaysorn** (2nd floor).

Kai Boutique, 187/1 Bangkok Cable Building, Thanon Rachdamri, T02-251 0728, www.kaiboutique.com. One of Bangkok's longest-standing high-fashion outlets, **Kai Boutique** sells its own effortlessly stylish creations alongside other newer names on the design scene. This flagship store also offers evening wear and cutting-edge bridal creations.

Mob.F, 4th floor Siam Center, Rama 1 Rd, T02-658 1115, www.mob-f.com. Hip, multi-brand Thai fashion store with a particular emphasis on new sartorial talent.

Sretsis, 2nd floor, Gaysorn Plaza, Ploenchit, T02-656 1125, www.sretsis.com. A much-loved local label created by a trio of Thai sisters who are the darlings of the design scene. The influences of one of the trio's internship at Marc Jacobs is apparent in these exquisitely feminine yet fantastically funky creations. Also at **Emporium** (1st floor).
Urface, 430/29 Siam Square Soi 10, T08-1458 6778, www.urfacestore.com. One-off hipster shoulder and handbags made from recycled materials by local artists. Thai celebrity-approved.

Furniture and interior design
Alexander Lamont, Shop 8 & 23, 3rd floor, Gaysorn Plaza, 999 Ploenchit Rd, T02-656 1392, www.alexanderlamont.com. British furniture and household object designer Alexander Lamont employs almost 200 Thais at his atelier in the northern suburbs. Specializes in unusual materials (stingray skin, parchment, etc) to lend his finely wrought pieces an antique-like finish.
Ayodhya, 4th floor, Gaysorn Plaza, 999 Ploenchit Rd, T02-656 1089, www.ayodhya trade.com. One of the best known Thai eco-furniture labels, employing hemp, cotton and water hyacinth. Available at **Siam Paragon** (4th floor), **Emporium** (5th floor) and the **Panta Showroom** (4th floor, Siam Discovery).
Corner 43 Décor, 61/2 Sukhumvit Soi 53, T02-260 1124, www.corner43.com. Beguiling designer furniture made from versatile rattan and other locally sourced organic materials.
Crystal Design Centre, 1420/1 Praditmanutham Rd, T02-101 5999, www.crystaldesigncenter.com. A dauntingly big mall-style complex, located on a main thoroughfare in the far north of the city. Its 8 low-rise buildings teem with home decor and furniture brands. Building C is the one to head to for affordable Thai-made pieces, showcasing the likes of **Anyroom**, **Deesawat** and **Hygge**.

Jim Thompson's Factory Outlet, 153 Sukhumvit Soi 93, T02-332 6530, www.jimthompson.com. Daily 0900-1800. Sells Jim Thompson's famous brand of home furnishings at slightly more affordable prices. A short taxi ride from On Nut Skytrain station.
Papaya, Ladphrao Soi 55, T08-6994 4445, http://design-athome.com. Huge, thrift store-style warehouse loaded with kitsch/retro furniture, lamps and tchotchkes. A great space, but not everything's for sale (they hire out props to the TV/film industry) or as cheap as you might hope.
P. Tendercool, 48-58 Charoenkrung Soi 30, T02-266 4344, www.ptendercool.com. Belgian designers Pieter Compernol and Stephanie Grusenmeyer craft monumental handmade tables out of bronze and reclaimed wood. Their atelier/showroom is a 400 sq m Art Deco-style warehouse near the river.
Siam Discovery Centre (Siam Tower) has some great interior design shops, including **Habitat**, **Panta** and **Anyroom**, on the 4th floor.

Gold and bronzeware
Gold is considerably cheaper than in the USA or Europe; there is a concentration of shops along Yaowarat Rd (Chinatown), mostly selling the yellow 'Asian' gold. Price is determined by weight (its so-called 'baht weight').

Thai bronzeware, or the less elaborate Western designs, are available in Bangkok. There are a number of shops along Charoen Krung, north from Silom Rd, eg **Siam Bronze Factory**, 1250 Charoenkrung Rd (between Sois 36-38), T02-234 9436, www.siambronze.com. The cutlery has become particularly popular and is now even available at the big department stores.

Handicrafts
Most of the city's malls and department stores have impressive handicraft sections, albeit pricey ones. With a little bit of

effort, you can pick up similar carvings, wall hangings, woven baskets, fabrics and other Thai-made trinkets at the Chatuchak Weekend market for quite a lot less.

Chitralada Shop, Suan Chitralada, Dusit Palace (Ratchawithi Gate), T02-282 8435, www.chitraladashop.com. This shop sells products produced under the auspices of 'The Support Foundation of Her Majesty Queen Sirikit', an initiative that encourages rural people to produce original handicrafts indigenous to their region. Silks, basketware, crocheted tablecloths, fashion accessories and toys. The rather strict dress codes of the palace grounds apply (see page 37).

The Chonabod, 131 Samsen Rd (near Soi 3), http://the-chonabod.blogspot.com. As well as notebooks, T-shirts and other items inspired by old Thai graphic design, this bijou shophouse stocks quaint old-fashioned toys made by villagers in the north.

Narai Phand, Ground floor, President Tower, 973 Ploenchit Rd, 27 Rachdamri Rd, just east of Gaysorn, T02-656 0398, www. naraiphand.com. A good place to view the range of goods that are made around the country: celadon, ceramics, lacquerware, Benjarong tea sets, etc. Cheap but generally poor quality.

Sop Moei Arts, 8 Rm 104, Sukhumvit 49 Rd, T02-714 7269, www.sopmoeiarts.com. Tue-Sat 0930-1700. Baskets and textiles made by the Pwo Karen, an ethnic minority from the north's Mae Hong Son province, fill this modest retail outlet located on the ground floor of a tennis club.

Thai Craft Fair, 3rd floor, Jasmine City Building, Sukhumvit Rd (near entrance to Soi 23), T02-676-0636, www.thaicraft.org. Monthly fair-trade fair packed full of quality pieces sourced directly from artisans nationwide, especially hilltribes in the north. Now includes organic produce as well as crafts. Usually open 1000-1500.

Health and beauty

Over the past decade, local entrepreneurs have been converting Thailand's samun phrai (herbs) and spa know-how into high-end beauty and health products that are great for gifts or self-pampering. All the top department stores have sections devoted to them, while many have their own flagship stores.

Karmakamet, 2nd floor, CentralWorld, T02-613 1397, www.karmakamet.co.th. Their luscious range of smellies comes in opulent, old-world packaging. Also at Chatuchak, Section 2, Soi 3.

Panpuri, Lobby level, Gaysorn Plaza, T02-656 1199, http://panpuri.com. From perfume diffusers and candles to skincare. Also at 5th floor, Central Chidlom.

Thann, 2nd floor CentralWorld, www. thann.info. One of the best known chic Thai spa brands. Also at: Ground floor, **Siam Paragon**; 4th floor, **Siam Discovery**; 5th floor, **Emporium**; 3rd floor, **Gaysorn Plaza**, and 1st floor, **Isetan** (CentralWorld).

Urban Tree, 934 Samsaen Soi 24, T02-243 2989, www.urbantreeorganics.com. Herbal soaps, body scrubs, aromatherapy oils and other homemade organic products fill this charming little shophouse.

Jewellery

Thailand has become the world's largest gem-cutting centre and it is an excellent place to buy both gems and jewellery, although not for the uninitiated (see box, page 124). The best buy of the native precious stones is the sapphire. Modern jewellery is well designed and of a high quality. Always insist on a certificate of authenticity and a receipt.

  Ban Mo, on Pahurat Rd, north of Memorial Bridge, is the centre of the gem business although there are shops in all the tourist areas particularly on Silom Rd near the intersection with Surasak Rd, eg **Rama Gems**, 987 Silom Rd. **Uthai Gems**, 28/7 Soi Ruam Rudi, off Ploenchit Rd, just east of Witthayu Rd, is recommended, as is **P Jewellery** (Chantaburi), 9/292 Ramindra Rd, Anusawaree Bangkhan, T02-522 1857.

Buying gems and jewellery

More people lose their money through gem and jewellery scams in Thailand than in any other way – 60% of complaints to the Tourism Authority Thailand (TAT) involve gem scams.

DO NOT fall for any story about gem sales, special holidays, tax breaks – no matter how convincing.

NEVER buy gems from people on the street (or beach) and try not to be taken to a shop by an intermediary. Any unsolicited approach is likely to be a scam. The problem is perceived to be so serious that in some countries Thai embassies are handing out warning leaflets with visas.

Rules of thumb to avoid being cheated: Choose a specialist shop in a relatively prestigious part of town (the TAT will recommend shops).

Note that no shop is authorized by the TAT or by the Thai government; if they claim as much they are lying.

It is advisable to buy from shops which are members of the Thai Gem and Jewellery Traders Association. Avoid touts.

Never be rushed into a purchase. Do not believe stories about vast profits from reselling gems at home.

Do not agree to have items mailed ('for safety').

If buying a valuable gem, a certificate of identification is a good insurance policy. The Department of Mineral Resources (Rama VI Rd, T02-2461694) and the Asian Institute of Gemological Sciences (919/1 Silom Rd, T02-6743257, www.aigs laboratory.com) will both examine stones and give such certificates.

Compare prices; competition is stiff among the reputable shops; be suspicious of 'bargain' prices.

Ask for a receipt detailing the stone and recording the price.

For more information (and background reading on Thailand) the Buyer's Guide to Thai Gems and Jewellery, by John Hoskin can be bought at Asia Books (see page 102). For up-to-date information on all scams in Thailand, visit www.bangkokscams.com.

For Western designs, try **Matina Amanita**, on the lobby level of Gaysorn Plaza, 999 Ploenchit Rd, or **Yves Joaillier** on the 3rd floor of the Charn Issara Tower, 942 Rama IV Rd. The **Jewellery Trade Centre** (aka the Silom Galleria), next door to the Holiday Inn Silom on the corner of Silom Rd and Surasak Rd, contains a number of gem dealers and jewellery shops on the ground floor.

Markets

The markets in Bangkok are an excellent place to get a real taste of the city: browse, take photographs and pick up bargains. Part of the lifeblood of Bangkok, the encroachment of more organized shops and the effects of the redeveloper's demolition ball are inimical to one of Bangkok's finest traditions, though such is their stronghold that impromptu markets still thrive and multiply on every bare piece of land in the city, however temporary. Below are some of the more established pick of the bunch. Nancy Chandler's Map of Bangkok, available from most bookshops, is the most useful guide to the markets of the capital.

Banglamphu Market, Chakrapong and Phra Sumen roads, close to the backpackers' haven of Khaosan Rd. Stalls here sell cheap clothing, shoes, food and household goods.

Chatuchak Weekend Market is the largest and is by Chatuchak Park (see page 64). Nearest Skytrain station: Mo Chit.

Khlong Thom Market, Chinatown, between Luang and Charoen Krung rds, off Mahachak Rd. Part of the charm of this Sat dusk-till-dawn flea market is its after-dark ambience, enhanced by the fact that shoppers bring their own flashlights as many stalls can't afford lighting. (It's also known as Talat Fai Chai, literally the 'flashlight market'.) Great for bargain-hunters, the market offers everything second hand imaginable, from vintage clothes to unwanted furnishings.

Khaosan Rd Market, close to Banglamphu Market on the infamous backpackers' strip. Much more geared to the needs and desires of the foreign tourist: counterfeit CDs, DVDs designer clothing and footwear, cheap noodles and falafel, rucksacks, leather goods, jewellery, souvenirs and so on. After sunset it steps up a gear in the fashion stakes with students and young designers touting their creative wares. Not necessarily as cheap as other markets but open late (1100-0000) and very convenient.

Nakhon Kasem, known as the **Thieves' Market**, is in the heart of Chinatown (see page 50). It's not what it used to be but aside from the mainstay of hardware items, the market houses a few 'antique' shops selling brassware, old electric fans and woodcarvings (tough bargaining is needed and don't expect everything to be genuine). Fun and fairly frantic.

Or Tor Kor, Kampaengphet Rd, opposite the Weekend Market. One for the foodies, run by the **Agricultural Market Organisation (OTK)**. Offers quality produce including takeaway delights such as locally produced curry pastes, jams and coffee, alongside a gourmet's dream of prepared sweets and savouries to sample. Come hungry.

Pahurat Indian Market (see page 48). A small slice of India in Thailand, with mounds of sarongs, batiks, buttons and bows; venture deep inside the maze of stalls to get a real taste of this market's treasures.

Pak Khlong Market, near the Memorial Bridge. A wholesale market selling fresh produce, orchids and cut flowers. It's an exciting place to visit at night when the place is a hive of activity (see page 48).

Patpong Night Market, arranged down the middle of Patpong Rd, linking Silom and Surawong rds. From 1700. Geared to tourists: selling counterfeit CDs and DVDs, handicrafts, T-shirts, leather goods, fake watches. Bargain hard.

Pratunam Market, spread over a large area around Rachprarop and Phetburi roads. Famous for cut-price clothing and fabrics. Both indoor and outdoor stalls are a bit soulless but many of the mass-produced tourist items can be found here at much lower prices. Venture behind the outdoor stalls to find a maze of tailors whipping up everything from school uniforms to sequined showgirl/boy creations.

Ratchada Night market, on Ratchadapisek Rd, near MRT Lad Phrao. A Sat night flea market where hip locals flog second-hand and retro gear out of the backs of cars and VW convertibles. Note: the replacement for the Suan Lum night bazaar will be here.

Rotfai Market (Talad Rotfai), Kampaengpetch Rd, a 10-min walk from the Weekend Market. A retro fetishist's dream, this hip Sat and Sun evening flea market flogs its wares (antiques, vintage clothing, household collectibles) beside disused old railway carriages. Recommended.

Sampeng Lane (see page 50), close to the Thieves' Market. A particularly busy market packed with stalls specializing in bulk buys of everything from fabric, ceramics, hair accessories and Chinese lanterns, to stationery, arts and crafts materials, clothes and household goods. The atmosphere is chaotic and exciting with plenty of steaming foodstalls. You can also buy individual items.

Tewes Market, near the National Library. There are great photo opportunities at this daily wet market, selling flowers, food, fish and plants.

Music

CDs and music DVDs can be bought from many stalls in tourist areas, although the choice is fairly limited.

Do Re Me, 2422/6 Siam Sq, Soi 11. This hip little music store is a Bangkok institution. New and more obscure releases abound in every category (aside from Thai). Browsing the piles is welcome and the owner is a renowned fount of all musical knowledge.

Zudrangma Records, 7/1 Sukhumvit 51, T08-8891-1314, www.zudrangmarecords.com. In the same alley as beatnik bar restaurant **WTF**, this shophouse stocks the tunes (be it the rare vinyl originals or CD compilations) driving the old Thai folk music revival.

Pottery and celadon (ceramics)

There are several pottery 'factories' on the left-hand side of the road on the way to the Rose Garden, near Samut Sakhon (see page 66). Also see Koh Kret (page 67). Distinctive green-hued ceramics, originally produced during the Sukhothai period (from the late 13th century), have recently been revived. Try **Thai Celadon House**, 83 Rachdapisek Rd (near Soi 16), which also sells seconds, or **Narai Phand** (see above).

Silk

Beware of 'bargains', as the silk may have been interwoven with rayon. It is best to stick to the well-known shops unless you know what you are doing. Silk varies greatly in quality. Generally, the heavier the weight the more expensive the fabric. 1-ply is the lightest and cheapest; 4-ply the heaviest and most expensive. Silk also comes in 3 grades: grade 1 is the finest and smoothest and comes from the inner part of the cocoon. Finally, there is also 'hard' and 'soft' silk, soft being rather more expensive. Handmade patterned silk, especially *matmii* from the northeast, can be much more expensive than simple, single-coloured industrial silk – well over ฿10,000 per piece. There are several specialist silk shops at the top of Surawong Rd (near Rama IV) and a number of shops along the bottom half of Silom Rd (towards Charoen Krung) and in the Siam Centre on Rama I Rd.

Anita's Thai Silk, 298/2 Silom Rd, T02-234 2481, www.anitasilk.com. Slightly more expensive than some, but the extensive range makes it worth a visit.

Chatuchak Weekend Market, see page 64, sells lengths from Laos and northeast Thailand.

HM Factory for Thai Silk, 45 Soi Promchai, Sukhumvit Soi 35, T02-258 8766, www.hmfactory-thaisilk.com. Silk is made on the premises, good-quality *matmii* silk.

Jagtar, 153 Ratchadamri Rd, T02-255 7380, www.jagtar.co.th. Some lovely silk curtain fabrics as well as cushion covers in unusual shades and other accessories made from silk. Originality means prices are high.

Jim Thompson's, 9 Surawong Rd, T02-632 8100, www.jimthompson.com. Daily 0900-2100. Famous silk shop which is expensive, but has the best selection. See also Jim Thompson's House, page 57.

Shinawatra, 94 Sukhumvit Soi 23, T02-258 0295, www.tshinawatra.com. Factory (industrial) silk available.

Spectacles

Glasses and contact lenses are a good buy in Bangkok and can be made up in 24 hrs. Opticians can be found throughout the city.

Supermarkets

The city is now littered with the Brit-Thai **Tesco Lotus** supermarket chain, although those familiar with the brand may be surprised to see that the budget 'Basics' range features fish sauce rather than baked beans.

Central Department Store (see Department stores and shopping malls, page 102). Features a well-stocked 'international' supermarket, usually in the basement.

Isetan (Central World Plaza), Rachdamri Rd. Japanese ingredients, has a great bakery.

Villa Supermarket, branches on Sukhumvit Rd (near Soi 49), Sukhumvit Soi 11 and elsewhere in town (www.villamarket.com). Caters for homesick expats and is the best place to go to for imported mainstays such as Marmite or cheese. The branch on Sukhumvit Rd is open 24 hrs and has a wine 'loft' upstairs.

Tailoring services

Bangkok's tailors are skilled at copying anything, either from fashion magazines or from a piece of your own clothing, however, aggressive sales methods and below-par results are also not uncommon. Always request at least 2 fittings, inspect the shop's finished garment for stitching quality, ask for a price in writing and pay as small a deposit as possible. Cheap package deals are best avoided. Tailors are concentrated along Silom, Sukhumvit and Ploenchit roads and Gaysorn Sq.

Ambassador & Smart Fashion, 28-28/1 Sukhumvit Soi 19, T08-1824 2094, www. ambfa.com. Bespoke tailors. Free pick-up available from your hotel, T02-253 2993.

Duly, Sukhumvit Soi 49 (corner with 49/3), T02-662 6647, www.laladuly.com. English-style fine shirtmakers offering both ready-to-wear and made-to-measure services.

Rajawongse, 130 Sukhumvit Rd (near Sukhumvit Soi 4), T02-255 3714, www.dress-for-success.com. Over 30 years in the suit business. Recommended.

Textiles

Khompastr, 56-58 Nares Rd (near Suriwong Road), T02-266 8415, www.khomapastr fabrics.com. Distinctive screen-printed cotton fabrics from Hua Hin.

Woodwork

There are lots of woodworking shops along Boriphat Rd where it crosses Khlong Banglamphu (near Wat Saket). If you want curtain rings or a replica Thai gable, one of the timber merchants here should be able to help you.

⚙ What to do

Bangkok *p36,*
maps p38, p44, p57, p60 and p62
Bowling
Bowling has really taken off in the city, and bowling alleys are available in almost every shopping centre. Most blast loud music, serve towers of beer and dim the lights to create a futuristic nightclub feel that may put you off your game. You may need to book ahead at weekends.

Blu-O is at Siam Paragon, 991 Rama I Rd, and Esplanade, Ratchadapisek Rd. **Major Bowl** are at CentralWorld (Ratchadamri Rd); J Avenue, Thonglor, Sukhumvit Soi 55; Central, Rama 3 Rd. Both are run by the Major Cineplex group and include karaoke rooms, www.majorbowlhit.com.

Strike Bowl, MBK, Siam Sq, and at various suburban malls, www.sfcinemacity.com.

Cookery courses
Hands-on classes have sprung up all over the city, offering the chance to prep pastes, chop meat, dice veg, stir-fry, deep-fry or stew a range of dishes and then gorge on the delicious results.

Amita Thai Cooking Class, 162/17 Soi Wutthakat 14, Thonburi, T02-466 8966, www.amitathaicooking.com. Thu-Tue 0930-1330. ฿3000 (including pick-up and drop-off at your hotel). Handpick ingredients from the herb garden, cook them in a pretty canalside home, then enjoy your 4-course meal in a pavilion overlooking the canal.

Blue Elephant, 233 South Sathorn Rd, T02-673 9353, www.blue elephant.com. One of the most famous cooking schools, with an innovative menu and beautiful, impeccably equipped surrounds in the former Thai-Chinese Chamber of Commerce. A 1-day course is ฿2800.

Helping Hands Thai Cooking School, Klong Toey, T08-4901 8717, www.cooking withpoo.com. Khun Poo, a long-time resident of Bangkok's most notorious slum, runs classes as part of a community self-help program. The price, ฿1200, includes transfers and a market tour. Recommended.

May Kaidee, 33 Samsen Rd, T02-281 7699, www.maykaidee.com. A vegetarian restaurant with its own veggie cooking school. At ฿1200 for 8 dishes, it's one of the best budget options. Children are welcome, ฿600.

Mrs Balbir's Cooking School, 155/1-2 Sukhumvit Soi 11, T02-651 0019, www.mrs balbirs.com. Learn to cook 4 Indian dishes. ฿2220, includes a ฿500 gift voucher for the well-known restaurant (see page 91).

Oriental Hotel, 48 Oriental Av, T02-659 9000 (see Where to stay, page 78), Mon-Sat 0900-1300. ฿4000 per class or ฿20,000 for 6 consecutive classes. Different dishes taught each day in an old teak house on the other bank of the Chao Phraya; student gastronomes are ferried across from the hotel. A 3 days/4 nights or 5 days/6 nights package that includes staying at the hotel, limousine transfers and a jet lag massage is also available.

Cycling

More and more tourists and locals are turning to pedal power, a phenomenon best demonstrated by the emergence of 'fixies', close-nit clans of young Thais who hang out in open corners of the city, usually after dark, to flip tricks on their beloved fixed-gear bikes. Two-wheel adventures around the capital (and beyond) are offered by **Amazing Bike Tours**, **Grasshopper Adventures** and **Spice Roads**, among others (see City tours, below). A recommended half-day trip is to Bang Krachao, a lush peninsula of undeveloped land just across the Chao Phraya River that's crisscrossed with irrigation canals and raised concrete paths (see page 65).

Bangkok Metropolitan Association, T02-225 7612. Under the 'Bangkok Bike Smile' slogan, the BMA offers a free bicycle service along 2 set routes. Bikes are available Mon-Fri 1000-1800 and Sat-Sun 1000-2000 at 5 points in the Old City (Lan Khon Muang near the City Hall, Suan Saranrom Park, the Grand Palace, the BMA tourist office on Phra Athit Rd, and Suan Santi Chaiprakan Park) and at 7 points on the Thon Buri side of the Chao Phraya River (Pin Klao Bridge, Rot Fai pier, Wat Rakhang pier, Wat Arun, Wat Kanlayanamit, Santa Cruz Convent School and the Princess Mother Memorial Park). Officially, you need to show a copy of your passport to borrow one but, in reality, the stations are often unmanned.

Golf

Most courses open at 0600 and play continues till dusk but early booking is imperative. Green fees start at roughly ฿500. Weekday green fees are two-thirds or less of the weekend fees. Most also have clubs for hire (as well as shoes) and players are expected to use caddies. See www.thai golfer.com for advice on local courses and competitions. There are a number of golf practice/driving ranges off New Phetburi and Sukhumvit roads.

Amata Spring Country Club, 700/3-9 Moo 6, Nongmaidaeng Rd, T038-468 888, www.amataspring.co.th. About 1 hr's drive from Bangkok is this testing course that boasts Asia's only floating green and often hosts the **Royal Trophy**, a Ryder Cup-style event between the best golfers in Europe and Asia.

Bangpoo Country Club, Km 37 191 Moo 3, Praksa Muang, T02-324 0320, www.bangpoo golf.com. 18-hole course designed by Arnold Palmer; oddly set within an industrial estate on the outskirts of Bangkok.

Muang-Ake, 52 Moo 7, Phahonyothin Rd, Amphoe Muang, Pathum Thani, T02-535 9335. 40 mins from city centre. Club hire. Phone to check regulations for temporary membership. Its sister course next door offers floodlit night golfing.

Health clubs

Expensive hotels have fitness centres and health clubs; many allow day membership.

Most of the big gyms are members only, though many offer free 1-3 day trial passes. **California Wow**, Liberty Sq, Silom Rd (near corner of Soi Convent), T02-631 1122, www.californiawowx.com. Mon-Sat 0600-0100, Sun 0800-2200. You can't miss this several-storey building with the motivating sounds of its dance and fitness bouncing onto the pavement. It's all about the body beautiful here with everything from glossy hi-tech machines to hot yoga. No pool though. Also at **Siam Paragon**.

Clark Hatch Physical Fitness Centre. 10 outlets throughout the city, www.clark hatchthailand.com. The one on Silom Rd (9th floor, Thaniya Plaza, right by Sala Daeng BTS station) has a 16-m pool and its own website: www.clarkhatchthaniya.com.

The Olympic Club, 8th floor Pathumwan Princess Hotel, MBK Center, 444 Phayathai Rd, T02-216 6700, www.theolympic-club. com. Gym, tennis courts and a 25-m swimming pool. The hotel is linked to the MBK shopping mall. Call for day rates.

Racquet Club @ 49, 6-8 Amara 3, Sukhumvit Soi 49/9, T02-714 7200, http:// rqclub.com. Day rate for full use of its extensive facilities (gym, pool, tennis courts, indoor football, rock climbing wall) is ฿525 Mon-Fri and ฿625 Sat, Sun and hols.

Horse racing

Thailand's yen for horse racing began over a century ago, when King Rama V bestowed land for the first racecourse. Sun races open to the public alternate between this historic track, located within the grounds of the hyper-exclusive **Royal Bangkok Sports Club** on Henri Dunant Road, and the **Royal Turf Club** over in Dusit. Occasionally races our held on Sat. A number of betting options are available for those who fancy a flutter; check the schedule at www.rbsc.org or call T02-652 5000.

Tennis

Many hotels have courts.
Racquet Club @ 49, 6-8 Amara 3, Sukhumvit Soi 49/9, T02-714 7200, http:// rqclub.com. 7 covered tennis courts, 11 badminton courts, 5 squash courts and 1 racquet ball court. Day rate ฿525 Mon-Fri and ฿625 Sat, Sun and hols, includes use of all facities: gym, pool, rock climbing wall, etc.
Santisuk Courts, Sukhumvit Soi 38, T02-391 1830. Daily 0700-2200, ฿80-100 per hr, 6 courts, racket hire, cash only.
The 50 Tennis & Fitness Club, 1050/8 Sukhumvit Soi 50, T02-742 8889, www.the50tennisclubs.com. 6 'Plexipave' outdoor courts. ฿160 per hr 0600-1800; ฿260 1800-2200. Racquets for rent.

Theme parks

For **Safari World** and **Siam Water Park**, see pages 64 and 65.
Dream World, 10 mins' drive from Don Muang Airport, Km 7, Rangsit-Ong Kharak Rd, T02-533 1152, www.dreamworld-th.com. Mon-Fri 1000-1700, Sat and Sun 1000-1900. ฿500. A sprawling fantasy land with rides for all ages, lots of space and a Snow Town (an indoor sleigh riding hall/giant freezer). Not up to American standards but still good family fun. To get there by bus, catch either No 188 from the Northern Bus Terminal (Mor Chit) or No 538 from Victory Monument.

Therapies
Meditation

See the *Bangkok Post* and *Nation* newspaper listings for details of vipassana (insight) courses and meditation events. The website www.dham mathai.org also provides information on meditation centres in Bangkok and beyond.
Ariyasom Villa, 65 Sukhumvit Soi 1 (far end of Soi), T02-254 8880, www.ariyasom.com. This upmarket mini-resort (see Where to stay, page 81) hosts regular meditation and dharma courses and activities led by Thai and Western monks, bhikkunis (female monks) and teachers.

Traditional Thai massage

While a little less arousing than the Patpong-style massage, the traditional Thai massage (nuat boraan) is probably more invigorating, using methods similar to those of Shiatsu, reflexology and osteopathic manipulation. It probably has its origins in India and is a form of yoga. It aims to release blocked channels of energy and soothe tired muscles.

The thumbs are used to apply pressure on the 10 main 'lines' of muscles, so both relaxing and invigorating the muscles. Headaches, ankle and knee pains, neck and back problems can all be alleviated through this ancient art (a European visitor to the Siamese court at Ayutthaya 400 years ago noted the practice of Thai massage). Centres of massage can be found in most Thai towns – wats and tourist offices are the best sources of information. In Bangkok, Wat Pho is the best-known centre and murals on the temple buildings' walls help to guide the student. For Thais, this form of massage is as much a spiritual experience as a physical one – hence its association with monasteries and the Buddha.

Wat Bowonniwet in Banglamphu on Phra Sumen Rd (see map, page 62).
Wat Mahathat, Maharat Rd, T02-222 6011, facing Sanaam Luang, www.mcu. ac.th/IBMC. Bangkok's most renowned meditation centre (see page 43). The Vipassana Meditation Centre located in section 5 of the monastery offers walk-in classes in English daily 0700-1000, 1300-1600 and 1800-2000. Attendance is free but donations are welcome. Simple dorms are available if you want to practise more intensively.
World Fellowship of Buddhists, 616 Benjasiri Park, Sukhumvit Soi 24 (off Soi Medhinivet), T02-661 1284, www.wfb-hq. org. Contact the centre for details on meditation for Westerners. Talks and sitting/walking meditation sessions are held regularly; call for details.

Traditional Thai massage

For further information, see box, above. The city overflows with massage services: everything from top-end spas to the somewhat seedier massage parlours. Competition means that even the swankiest of spas often offer great traditional massage at surprisingly low costs, and you're less likely to be propositioned by your masseuse. Other signals of a non-sexual service include the word 'traditional' or 'health' massage on the sign, or a depiction of meridian lines. Large shopping centres often have reliable traditional massage shops. A tip for the tight-muscled: 'jep' is the polite Thai equivalent of 'ouch!', or try squeaking out a 'bao bao' ('gently'). The following centres offer quality massages by trained practitioners:

The Chi Spa at the Shangri-La Hotel, www.shangri-la.com/bangkok, T02-236 7777. For blow-the-budget pampering, the Shangri-La's Chi Spa is part of the largest and arguably most attractive hotel on the river and houses what is widely considered to be the finest spa in Bangkok. Inspired by the Himalayan healing arts, the interior instantly casts a magical spell over visitors with its candle-lit niches and wooden screens; the multi-therapy 'journeys' also involve an element of Eastern mysticism that enhance the dreamlike ambience.
Healthlands, 96/1 Sukhumvit Soi 63, Ekamai, T02-392 2233, www.healthlandspa. com. Open 0900-2400. A no-nonsense chain of massage specialists offering what Thais refer to as 'real' massage, opposed to the softly-softly spa equivalent. For connoisseurs of Thai massage or those with slight masochistic tendencies this is

the real deal – note the well-developed shoulder muscles of the otherwise tiny masseuses. The 'health' side is taken seriously here but spa treatments are also available. Other branches in Sathorn, Asok, Pinklao and Pattaya.

Ruen Nuad, 42 Soi Convent (off Silom Rd close to the Skytrain exit), T02-632 2662. Highly recommended bijou boutique spa and massage centre inside a beautiful, peaceful wooden house in the centre of the city. Expect to pay a little more than average but the reasonable prices still belie the magical ambience and attention to detail. Thai, aromatherapy and herbal massage.

Wat Pho, T02-221 2974, www.watpo massage.com (see page 37). The centre is located at the back of the wat, on the opposite side from the entrance. The school offers body massage, with or without herbs, and foot massage. The service is available 0800-1700 and costs from ฿260 for a 30-min body massage to ฿520 for a 1-hr body massage with herbal compress. A foot massage is ฿420 for 50 mins. For Westerners wishing to learn the art of traditional Thai massage, special 30-hr courses can be taken for ฿9500, stretching over 5 consecutive days (6 hrs per day). There is also a foot massage course for ฿7500, also 30 hrs over 5 consecutive days.

Yoga

Iyengar Yoga Studio, 3rd floor, Fiftyfifth Plaza, Sukhumvit Soi 55, www.iyengar-yoga-bangkok.com, T02-714 9924. Specialize in Iyengar yoga, a form that employs props to help you perform postures.

Lullaby Yoga, Life Center at Q House Lumpini, 1 South Sathorn Rd (corner of Rama IV and Sathorn rds), T02-677 7261, www.lullaby-yoga.com. Most styles offered: traditional Vinyasa yoga, hot yoga, 1-hr morning yoga and relax yoga, among others. Good reputation. Workshops and free trials for first-timers. There's another branch nearby, on the 3rd floor of All Seasons Place on Wireless Rd.

Rasayana Retreat, 41/1 Soi Prommitr, Soi Sukhumvit 39, T02-662 4803, www.rasayana retreat.com. A detoxification and rejuvenation centre offering detox programmes, colonic irrigation, pilates and yoga classes and an excellent raw food café and spa.

Yoga Elements Studio, 23rd floor, Vanissa Building, Soi Chitlom, T02-655 5671, www.yogaelements.com. Vinyassa and Ashtanga yoga and meditation as well as various workshops and a superb standard of guest teachers and speakers from across the globe. The beautifully designed studio commands stunning sunset views of the city. Packages available.

Tours and travel agents
Boat tours

Either book a tour at your hotel, one of the tour operators recommended below, or go to one of the piers and organize your own long-tail trip. The most frequented piers are located between the Oriental Hotel and the Grand Palace or under Taksin Bridge (which marks the end of the Skytrain line). The pier just to the south of the Royal Orchid Sheraton Hotel is recommended. Organizing your own trip gives greater freedom to stop and start when the mood takes you. It is best to leave in the morning. For the Khlong Tour mentioned above under half-day tours (excluding Wat Rakhang and Wat Suwannaram), the cost for a long-tail which can sit 6-8 people should be about 1000-1500 per hr depending on the stops, distance and duration. 2 hrs for 2000 is a recommended starting point for a decent trip. If visiting Wat Rakhang and Wat Suwannaram as well as the other sights, expect to pay about an extra 200-300. Always agree the route, stops and cost before setting out.

There are around 30 private boats (in addition to long-tails and regular ferries) offering cruises on the Chao Phraya.

Chao Phraya Cruise, T02-541 5599, www.chaophrayacruise.com. Dinner cruises, departing from River City.

Khao San Road Mystery Tours

More than one traveller has been duped by the mystery rogue bus journeys sold by the travel agents along Khao San Road which lure customers with offers of cheap all-nighters to far-flung destinations in the kingdom.

Theft, coercion and painfully slow or cramped services are not uncommon, with the luxurious VIP bus promised when you buy your tickets transforming into a beaten up jalopy when it comes to departure time. The buses often stop at expensive restaurants for a long wait or finish their journey in the middle of the night emptying guests into the 'only available' hotel. Worse still are thefts and scams. Over the years dozens of travellers have had their valuables stolen – sometimes even by the bus crew themselves who have, on occasion, been known to disappear into the night leaving travellers stranded and penniless.

Travellers should opt for the safe, inexpensive and relatively luxurious government-approved VIP buses from the public bus stations. Those cheap packages often to turn out too good to be true and are often more expensive than simply buying the ticket yourself.

For up-to-date information on all scams in Thailand, and especially Bangkok, visit www.bangkokscams.com.

Chao Phraya Express Boat Company, T02-623 6001, www.chaophrayaexpress boat.com. In addition to the express boat service (see page 119), they run tourist boats, which offer unlimited hops between 9 of the most culturally edifying river piers (Sathorn, Oriental, Si Phraya, Ratchawong, Tha Tien, Maharaj, Wang Lang and Phra Arthit) for only 150 per day. Run at half hour intervals 0930-1630. Tickets can be bought at Sathorn or Phra Athit piers or once on board. A range of boats (from long-tails to cruisers) can also be chartered to take you on everything from 1-hr cruises to fully-fledged day trips to Bangsai, Bang Pa-In, Ayutthaya or Koh Kret (see website). **Grand Pearl Cruises**, T02-861 0255, www.grandpearlcruise.com. Operate 3 cruisers. Like other companies, they offer passengers either a bus trip up to Ayutthaya and a cruise down, or vice versa (1900). In the evenings, the company also offers dinner cruises for 1500. **Loy Nava**, T02-437 4932, www.loynava. com. Dinner cruises aboard a charming old rice barge depart from Tha Siphraya pier (by the Royal Orchid Sheraton Hotel) at 1800 and 2000.

Manohra, T02-476 0022, www.manohra cruises.com, is a restored rice barge owned by the **Anantara Bangkok Riverside Resort & Spa**. It offers dinner cruises at 1930 (1400 or 1990 depending on menu) and shorter sunset cocktail cruises (1800-1900, charter only). Luxury 3-day cruises to Ayutthaya, stopping at Ko Kret are also available. A free 10-min river taxi runs from Tha Sathon to the hotel (close to Saphan Thaksin Skytrain station). **Mekhala**, T02-655-6245, www.asian-oasis. com. Overnight journeys to Ayutthaya onboard a luxurious restored teak rice barge. Air-conditioned cabins. **River Sun Cruise**, T02-266 9125, www.river suncruise.co.th. Daily Ayutthaya sightseeing tours depart from River City at 0730, return at 1530. **Wanfah Cruise**, T02-622 7657, www. wanfah.in.th. Offer an afternoon long-tail klong tour and river barge cruise combo. Dinner cruises also available from River City.

City tours

Bangkok has innumerable tour companies that can take visitors virtually anywhere; most run the same range of tours, but if there is not one to fit your bill, many companies will produce a customized itinerary for you, for a price. Most top hotels have their own tour desk, and it is probably easiest to book there (arrange to be picked up from your hotel as part of the deal). Most will also book airline, bus and train tickets and hotel rooms.

The tour itineraries given below are the most popular; prices per person are about 600-1000 for a half day, 1000-2000 for a full day (including lunch).

Half-day tours Grand Palace Tour; Temple Tour to Wat Traimitr, Wat Pho and Wat Benjamabophit; Khlong Tour around the *khlongs* (canals) of Bangkok and Thonburi, to Floating Market, Royal Barges Museum and Wat Arun (mornings only); Old City Tour; Crocodile Farm Tour; Rice Barge and Khlong Tour (afternoons only); Damnoen Saduak Floating Market Tour; Thai Dinner and Classical Dance, eat in traditional Thai surroundings and consume toned-down Thai food.

Full-day tours Damnoen Saduak and Rose Garden; Pattaya, the infamous beach resort; River Kwai, a chance to see the famous bridge and war cemeteries, as well as the Great *Chedi* at Nakhon Pathom; Ayutthaya and Bang Pa In.

Specialist city tours
See also **Smiling Albino**, below.
Amazing Bangkok Cyclist (ABC), T02-665 6364, www.realasia.net. Half-day and full-day cycling and walking tours around the city's 'green belt', including the less-explored riverside areas of Bang Krachao and Phra Padaeng.
Bangkok Food Tours, T08-9126 3657 (mob), www.bangkokfoodtours.com. Neighbourhood food-tasting tours with friendly English-speaking locals who have rooted out all the best local kitchens in the area. Recommended.
Grasshopper Adventures, T2-280 0832, www.grasshopperadventures.com. Offer a handful of city bike tours, including a night ride. Respected outfit since 2004.

Spice Roads, T02-712 5305, www.spice roads.com. Full and half day cycling tours of central Bangkok and surroundings, often with a cultural slant. Offer similar tours all over the country and Southeast Asia.

Thailand tours
For further information on travelling by private bus, see page 118.
Asian Trails, 9th floor SG Tower, 161/1 Soi Mahadlek Luang 3, Rajdamri Rd, Lumpini, Pathumwan, T02-626 2000, www.asiantrails.travel. Specialists in Southeast Asia travel and tours.
Bike and Travel, 802/756 River Park, Moo 12, Kookot, Lamlookka, Prathumthani, 121330, T02-990 0274, www.cycling thailand.com. Thai crew offering multi-day cycle tours across the country.
Buffalo Tours, Lertpanya Building, Suite 707, 41 Soi Lertpanya, Sri-Ayutthaya Rd, Phyathat Rd, Rajathanee, T02-245 6392, www.buffalotours.com. Arrange tours throughout the region.
Cruise Asia Ltd, 133/14 Ratchaprarop Rd, Makkasan, Rajthevi, 10400, T02-640 1400, www.cruiseasia.net. River Kwai cruises on a colonial-style river cruiser.
Traidhos Three Generation Barge Program, T02-879 1032, barge.threegeneration.org. A non-profit organization offering educational 1-5 day trips on an antique rice barge for groups interested in exploring the river's history, arts, ecology and culture.
Smiling Albino, T02-718-9561, www. smilingalbino.com. Prefab and custom-built tours of Southeast Asia's hidden corners (including Bangkok's) led by local insiders. Overnight tours pair gritty grass-roots encounters with upscale sleepovers.
State Railway of Thailand, T1690, www. railway.co.th. Organizes day trips to Nakhon Pathom and the bridge over the River Kwai, and to Ayutthaya. Trips run on weekends and holidays and depart early.
Wild Thailand, T02-901 0480, www. wildthailand.com. Eco and adventure our specialist.

Bangkok *p36,*

maps p38, p44, p57, p60 and p62
Bangkok lies at the heart of Thailand's transport network. Virtually all trains and buses end up here and it is possible to reach anywhere in the country from the capital. Bangkok is also a regional transport hub, and there are flights to most international destinations. See Planning your trip, page 6, for international transport. For Transport in Bangkok, see page 9.

Air

The airport website, www.bangkokairport online.com, offers excellent up-to-date information on transport services.
Suvarnabhumi International Airport, is around 25 km southeast of the city. There are regular connections to many of the provincial capitals on THAI or any of the budget airlines. Tickets can also be bought at most travel agents. Bangkok Airways flies to **Krabi, Koh Samui, Trat, Phuket, Sukhothai, Chiang Mai** and **Lampang**

Don Muang Airport, 25 km north of the city at Don Muang, re-opened to budget airlines in Mar 2007. However, following the late 2010 floods that paralysed central provinces and much of Bangkok, only **Nok Air**, were flying there. This situation may change quickly, especially as Suvarnabhumi is reaching capacity. Assuming it does again find favour with the low-cost carriers, Don Muang is worth considering as your primary choice for domestic routes, as there will be fewer queues, it's easier to transit and connections to the city are just as good. There is a shortage of gates at Suvarnabhumi, which means domestic flights are often stuck miles down the runway, requiring a 10-min bus journey to reach the terminal. Getting between the new and old airports is relatively easy: a taxi transfer should cost ฿250-300 and shouldn't take more than 1 hr, but allow for longer.

Airline offices Air France, Vorawat Building, 20th floor, 849 Silom Rd, T02-635 1199. **Air India**, SS Building, 10/12-13 Convent Rd, Silom, T02-235 0557. **Air Lanka**, Ground floor, Charn Issara Tower, 942 Rama IV Rd, T02-236 9292. **Alitalia**, SSP Tower 3, 15th floor, Unit 15A, 88 Silom Rd, T02-634 1800. **American Airlines**, 518/5 Ploenchit Rd, T02-251 1393. **Asiana Airlines**, 18th floor, Ploenchit Centre, 2 Sukhumvit 2 Rd, T02-656 8610. **Bangkok Airways**, 99 Mu 14, Vibhavadirangsit Rd, Chom Phon, Chatuchak, T02-265 5678 (ext 1771 for reservations centre), www.bangkokair.com. **British Airways**, 14th floor, Abdulrahim Place, 990 Rama 1V Rd, T02-636 1747. **Canadian Airlines**, 6th floor, Maneeya Building, 518/5 Ploenchit Rd, T02-251 4521. **Cathay Pacific**, 11th floor, Ploenchit Tower, 898 Ploenchit Rd, T02-263 0606. **Continental Airlines**, CP Tower, 313 Silom Rd, T02-231 0113. **Delta Airlines**, 7th floor, Patpong Building, Surawong Rd, T02-237 6838. **Eva Airways**, Green Tower, 2nd floor, 425 Rama IV Rd, opposite Esso Head Office. **Finnair**, 6th floor, Vorawat Building, 849 Silom Rd, T02-635 1234. **Gulf Air**, 12th floor, Maneey Building, 518 Ploenchit Rd, T02-254 7931. **Japan Airlines**, 254/1 Ratchadapisek Rd, T02-692 5151. **KLM**, 19th floor, Thai Wah Tower 11, 21/133-134 South Sathorn Rd, T02-679 1100. **Korean Air**, Ground floor, Kong Bunma Building (opposite Narai Hotel), 699 Silom Rd, T02-635 0465. **Lao Airlines**, 491 17 ground floor, Silom Plaza, Silom Rd, T02-236 9822. **Lufthansa**, 18th floor, Q-House (Asoke), Sukhumvit Rd Soi 21, T02-264 2400. **MAS (Malaysian Airlines)**, 20th floor, Ploenchit Tower, 898 Ploenchit Rd, T02-263 0565. **Myanmar Airways**, 23rd floor, Jewellery Trade Centre, Silom Rd, T02-630 0334. **PBAir**, T02-261 0220, www.pbair.com. **Qantas**, 14th floor, Abdulrahim Place, 990 Rama IV Rd, T02-636 1747. **SAS**, 8th floor, Glas Haus I, Sukhumvit Rd Soi 25, T02-260 0444. **Singapore Airlines**, 12th floor, Silom Centre, 2 Silom Rd, T02-236 5295/6. **Swiss**, 21st floor

Abdulrahim Place, 990 Rama 1V Rd, T02-636 2160. **THAI**, 485 Silom Rd, T02-234 3100, and 89 Vibhavadi-Rangsit Rd, T02-513 0121. **Vietnam Airlines**, 7th floor, Ploenchit Centre, 2 Sukhumvit 2 Rd, T02-656 9056.

Bus
Local
Used by an average 3.4 million people each day, public buses are the cheapest way to get around town, although it's worth noting that more people have their belongings stolen on them than almost anywhere else, so beware of pickpockets. There is quite a range, including a/c and non-a/c buses, micro-buses and expressway buses. All run 0500-2300, apart from the limited all-night services that run 2300-0500.

Many numbered buses only have their destination written in Thai, so a route map outlining which ones go where is indispensable. Good maps are available from bookshops, as well as hotels and travel agents or tour companies. Major bus stops have maps of routes in English. Also see the **BMTA (Bangkok Mass Transit Authority)** website, www.bmta.co.th, for detailed information on all bus routes and tourist destinations in English and Thai. Tickets cost ฿7-24.

Long distance
For journeys to other provinces, there are 3 main bus stations in Bangkok.

Northern bus terminal (or Mo Chit Mai – New Mo Chit – aka Mo Chit 2), is at the western side of Chatuchak Park on Kamphaeng Phet 2 Rd, T02-936 3659. It serves all destinations in the north and northeast as well as towns in the central plains.

Southern bus terminal (or Sai Tai Mai) is on Borom Ratchonani Rd, T02-894 6122. Buses for the west (eg **Kanchanaburi**) and the south leave from here.

Eastern bus terminal, Sukhumvit Rd (Soi Ekamai), between Soi 40 and Soi 42, T02-391 2504, serves **Pattaya** and other destinations in the eastern region.

Buses leave for most major destinations throughout the day, and often well into the night. There are overnight buses on the longer routes to **Chiang Mai**, **Hat Yai**, **Chiang Rai**, **Phuket** and **Ubon Ratchathani**, for example.

In addition to the government-operated buses, there are many private companies that run 'tour' buses to most of the major tourist destinations. Tickets bought through travel agents will normally be for these private tour buses, which leave from offices all over the city as well as from the public bus terminals. Shop around as prices may vary. Note that although the private buses may pick up passengers from their hotel/guesthouse, they are generally more expensive, less reliable and less safe than the government services. Many pick up passengers at Khaosan Rd and are notoriously cramped and differ considerably from the 'luxury VIP seating' promised on purchase.

Car hire
Given the driving conditions in Bangkok, it's often advisable (and sometimes cheaper) to hire a car with driver: approx ฿1500-2000 for 8 hrs excluding fuel. Approximate cost for car hire only is ฿900-1500 per day, ฿6000-10000 per week; Hertz, 72/8-9 North Sathorn Rd, T02-266 4666, www.hertz.co.uk, and Avis, 2/12 Witthayu Rd, T02-255 5300, www.avisthailand.com, charge more than the local firms, but have better insurance cover. Both also have branches at the airport. Other companies include **Budget**, 19/23 Royal City Av, New Phetburi Rd, T02-203 9294, www.budget.co.th; **Highway Car Rent**, 1018/5 Rama IV Rd, T02-633 9999, www.highway.co.th, and **Thai Rent A Car**, 1st floor, Petchaburee building, 2371 New Petchaburee Rd, T02-318 8888, www.thairentacar.com.

Metro (MRT) and Skytrain (BTS)
With the opening of the **Metro** (**MRT**) in 2004 and extensions currently ongoing, Bangkok is slowly developing an efficient

transport system. The MRT line, which loops through 18 stations, connecting Hualamphong with Lumpini Park, Sukhumvit Rd and Chatuchak Market, is a shining example of Thai modernity. The entire network is a/c, the comfortable trains run regularly and stations are well lit and airy. Unlike some more extensive underground networks in the west, there is mobile phone reception too. There is a lack of integration with the Skytrain – separate tickets are needed and interchanges (at Chatuchak Park, Sukhumvit and Silom) are awkward and badly planned – but fares are cheap at ฿15-40.

The **Skytrain** (**BTS**) runs on an elevated track through the most developed parts of the city; it is quite a ride, veering between the skyscrapers. There are 2 lines, both of which have been recently extended and which converge at Siam Station (Siam Sq): one runs from Mo Chit on Phahonyothin Rd (close to the Chatuchak Weekend Market, north of the city centre) to Bearing in the east (Samut Prakarn province). The 2nd line runs from the National Stadium on Rama I Rd to Wongwian Yai on the Thonburi side of the river. Further extensions have been proposed from Mo Chit north to Saphan Mai, from Bearing to east Samut Prakan, from Wongwian Yai to Bang Wa and from National Stadium west to Phran Nok. The Skytrain covers a large chunk of the tourist, business and shopping areas, so is very useful. It is also quick and cool – although the tramp up to the stations can be a drag and the open stations themselves are not a/c. Trains run 0600-2400, every 3-5 mins during peak periods and every 10-15 mins out of the rush hour. Fares are steep by Thai standards but worth it for most overseas visitors: ฿15 for one stop, ฿40 for the whole route. Multi-trip tickets can also be purchased, which makes things slightly cheaper. For up to date information, call T02-617 7340, or see www.bts.co.th.

Motorcycle taxi

These are usually used to run up and down the long *sois* that extend out of the main thoroughfares. Riders wear numbered vests and tend to congregate at the end of the busiest *sois*. The short-hop fare down a *soi* is usually ฿10, though there is usually a pricelist (in Thai) at the gathering point. Some riders will agree to take you on longer journeys across town and fares will then need to be negotiated – expect to pay anything from ฿25-100, depending on your negotiation skills and knowledge of Thai. A ride through Bangkok's hectic traffic with a Red Bull-fuelled motorcycle taxi driver is one you are likely never to forget – if you make it back alive.

River transport

River taxi The cheapest way to travel on the river, **Chao Phraya Expressboats** (*rua duan*), www.chaophrayaexpressboat.com, serve 35 piers between Nonthaburi in the north and Rajburana (Big C) in the south. At peak hours they leave every 10-15 mins, off-peak about 15-25 mins. There are 4 types, distinguished by the coloured flags that flutter at the rear. Three of them (the green flag, yellow flag and no flag) run Mon-Fri during morning and afternoon peak hours only. Fares on these routes depend on distance and range from ฿10-32. Orange flag boats run daily 0600-1900 and cost a flat fee of ฿15. Green, yellow and orange flag Express boats do not stop at all piers; boats without a flag (the local line) do. Each pier (known as tha in Thai) is demarked with a sign in Thai and English. Tha Sathorn, or Central Pier, is the only one that is a short walk from the Skytrain at BTS Saphan Taksin station. Note that boats will only stop if passengers wish to board or alight, so make your destination known. Be warned that Thais trying to sell boat tours will tell you Express boats are not running and will try to extort grossly inflated prices. Walk away and find the correct pier.

Ferries These slower, chunkier boats ply back and forth across the river, between Bangkok and **Thonburi**, and cost ฿43.

Khlong or long-tailed boats (*hang yaaw*) can be rented for about ฿1000 per hr, or more (see Tour operators, page 114). See the *khlong* trips outlined on page 71 for information on what to see on the river. A good map, *Rivers and Khlongs*, is available from the TAT office (see page 30).

Taxi

Taxis are usually metered (they must have a/c to register); look for the 'Taxi Meter' illuminated sign on the roof. Hail one down by waving your hand with your palm down (up is considered impolite), and check that the meter is 'zeroed' before setting off.

Fares are ฿35 for the first 2 km, ฿4.50 per km up to 12 km, and ฿5 per km thereafter. Most trips in the city should cost ฿40-100. If the travel speed is less than 6 kph – always a distinct possibility in the traffic-choked capital – a surcharge of ฿1.25 per min is added. Passengers also pay the tolls for using the expressway, ฿15-45. Taxi drivers sometimes refuse to use the meter despite the fact that they are required to do so by law. This is particularly the case in tourist areas like Patpong and Banglamphu. If a driver refuses to use the meter, simply get out and hail another – there are usually scores around. It's also best to make sure you have sufficient 20s and 100s to pay, as drivers rarely have change; tollways make good places to break big notes. Taxi drivers make a poor living on long hours in Bangkok and tipping, though not expected, is much appreciated. It is usual to round fares up or down to the nearest ฿5. Remember that Bangkok's taxis are some of the cheapest in the world and their drivers some of the worst paid. For most tourists the arrival of the metered taxi has actually lowered prices, as it has eliminated the need to bargain.

To call a taxi: **Siam Taxis**, T1661 or **Radio Taxi**, T1681, charge ฿20 plus the fare on the meter. They also offer long-distance/ all-day hire from ฿1500. Note that taxi drivers are not renowned for their knowledge of Bangkok. Many are upcountry boys who speak little English, so it's handy to have a rough idea of where you want to go, as well as a business card, map, telephone number of your location and/or an address written in Thai.

Train

The State Railway of Thailand website, www.railway.co.th, is a good starting point for planning trips, with timetables and fares in English, though, when it comes to procuring your tickets, you're better off going to the station in question or using a travel agent.

Bangkok has 2 main railway stations. Hangar-like **Hualamphong**, Rama IV Rd, T1690, is the primary station, catering for most destinations; condensed railway timetables in English can be picked up from the information counter on the main concourse. The exceptionally enthusiastic staff at the tourist information table at the main entrance offer efficient and reliable advice.

Bangkok Noi (Thonburi station), on the other side of the Chao Phraya River, is where trains to **Nakhon Pathom** and **Kanchanaburi** depart/arrive.

Tuk-tuk

The formerly ubiquitous motorized *saamlor* is rapidly becoming a piece of history in Bangkok, although they can still usually be found near tourist sites. Best for short journeys, they are uncomfortable and, being open to the elements, you are likely to be asphyxiated by car fumes. Bargaining is essential. and the fare should be negotiated before boarding, though most tuk-tuk drivers try to rip tourists off, so taking a metered taxi will be less hassle and cheaper. Expect to pay in the region of ฿30-100 for a short hop across town. Tuk-tuk drivers also have a reputation for hustling in other ways and perpetrate all kinds of scams. The general advice is to try a tuk-tuk once for the novelty value and then avoid.

O Directory

Bangkok p36,
maps p38, p44, p57, p60 and p62
Immigration
For the latest information on visas and tourist visa exemptions see the consular information section of the **Thai Ministry of Foreign Affairs** website, www.mfa.go.th. The immigration department that deals with tourists (visa extensions, etc) is on the northern outskirts of the city: Immigration Bureau, Government Complex Chaeng Wattana, B Building, Floor 2 (South Zone), Chaengwattana Rd Soi 7, Laksi, Bangkok 10210, T02-141-9889, www.immigration. co.th. Tell your taxi driver to take you to 'Thor Mor Chaeng Wattana'. Open Mon-Fri 0830-1200, 1300-1630, closed Sat, Sun, official holidays and for lunch.

Language schools
Bangkok has scores of language schools. The best known is the **AUA** school at 179 Rachdamri, T02-252 8170, www. auathailand.org. Another big one is **Language Express**, 1st floor, Mahatun Plaza Building, Ploenchit Rd, T02-675 3915, www.languageexpress.co.th. See the local English-language press for more.

Libraries
See http://my.bangkoklibrary.com for a comprehensive overview of reading resources in the city.
National Library, Samsen Rd, close to Sri Ayutthaya Rd, T02-281 5212, www.nlt.go.th. Daily 0930-1930. **Neilson Hays Library**, 195

Surawong Rd, T02-2331731, www.neilson hayslibrary.com. Mon-Sat 0930-1600, Sun 0930-1230. A small library of English-language books housed in an elegant Italianate building dating from 1922. It is a private membership library, but welcomes visitors who might want to see the building and browse; occasional exhibitions are held here. **Siam Society Library**, 131 Sukhumvit Soi 21 (Asoke), T02-661 6470, www.siam-society.org. Tue-Sat 0900-1700. Membership library with excellent collection of rare Thai and foreign-language books and periodicals (especially English) on Thailand and mainland Southeast Asia.

Medical services
Bangkok Adventist Hospital, 430 Phitsanulok Rd, Dusit, T02-282 1100, www.mission-hospital.org. Vaccination service and 24-hr emergency unit. **Bangkok Christian Hospital**, 124 Silom Rd, T02-235 1000, www. bkkchristianhosp.th.com. Efficient walk-in service. Good for common ailments. **Bangkok General Hospital**, New Phetburi Soi 47, T02-310 3000, www.bangkokhospital.com. **Bumungrad International**, 33 Sukhumvit Soi 3, T02-667 1000, www.bumrungrad. com. World class in every respect, including the prices. Multilingual. **BNH Hospital**, 9/1 Convent Rd, T02-686 2700, www.bnhhospital. com. Considered, along with Bumungrad, to be one of the top 2. **Dental Hospital**, 88/88 Sukhumvit 49, T02-260 5000, www.dental hospitalbangkok.com. Good but expensive. **St Louis Hospital**, 27 South Sathorn Rd, T02-675 5000, www.saintlouis.or.th.

Tourist police
24-hr hotline T1155, 4 Rachadamnoen Nok Av, Dusit.

Contents

Footnotes

Useful words and phrases

Thai is a tonal language with five tones: mid tone (no mark), high tone (ˊ), low tone (ˋ), falling tone (ˆ), and rising tone (ˇ). Tones are used to distinguish between words which are otherwise the same. For example, 'see' pronounced with a low tone means 'four'; with a rising tone, it means 'colour'. Thai is not written in Roman script but using an alphabet derived from Khmer. The Romanization given below is only intended to help in pronouncing Thai words. There is no accepted method of Romanization and some of the sounds in Thai cannot be accurately reproduced using Roman script.

Polite particles
At the end of sentences males use the polite particle *krúp*, and females, *kâ* or *ká*.

Learning Thai
The list of words and phrases below is only very rudimentary. For anyone serious about learning Thai it is best to buy a dedicated Thai language text book or to enrol on a Thai course. Recommended among the various 'teach yourself Thai' books is Somsong Buasai and David Smyth's *Thai in a Week*, Hodder & Stoughton: London (1990). A useful mini-dictionary is the Hugo *Thai phrase book* (1990). For those interested in learning to read and write Thai, the best 'teach yourself' course is the *Linguaphone* course.

General words and phrases

Yes/no	*chái/mâi chái, or krúp (kâ)/mâi krúp (kâ)*
Thank you/no thank you	*kòrp-kOOn/mâi ao kòrp-kOOn*
Hello, good morning, goodbye	*sa-wùt dee krúp(kâ)*
What is your name? My name is …	*koon chêu a-rai krúp (kâ)? Pom chêu …*
Excuse me, sorry!	*kor-tôht krúp(kâ)*
Can/do you speak English?	*KOON pôot pah-sah ung-grìt*
a little, a bit	*nít-nòy*
Where's the …?	*yòo têe-nai …?*
How much is …?	*tâo-rài …?*
Pardon?	*a-rai ná?*
I don't understand	*pom (chún) mâi kao jái*
How are you?	*mâi sa-bai*
Not very well	*sa-bai dee mái?*

At hotels

What is the charge each night?	*kâh hôrng wun la tâo-rài?*
Is the room air conditioned?	*hôrng dtìt air reu bplào?*
Can I see the room first please?	*kor doo hôrng gòrn dâi mái?*
Does the room have hot water?	*hôrng mii náhm rórn mái?*
Does the room have a bathroom?	*hôrng mii hôrng náhm mái?*
Can I have the bill please?	*kor bin nòy dâi mái?*

Travelling

Where is the train station?	*sa-tahn-nee rót fai yòo têe-nai?*
Where is the bus station?	*sa-tahn-nee rót may yòo têe-nai?*
How much to go to ...?	*bpai ... tâo-rài?*
That's expensive	*pairng bpai nòy*
What time does the bus/train leave for ...?	*rót may/rót fai bpai ...òrk gèe mohng?*
Is it far?	*glai mái?*
Turn left/turn right	*lée-o sái / lée-o kwah*
Go straight on	*ler-ee bpai èek*
It's straight ahead	*yòo dtrong nâh*

At restaurants

Can I see a menu?	*kor doo may-noo nòy?*
Can I have ...?/ I would like ...?	*kor ...*
Is it very (hot) spicy?	*pèt mâhk mái?*
I am hungry	*pom (chún) hew*
breakfast	*ah-hahn cháo*
lunch	*ah-hahn glanhg wun*

Time and days

in the morning	*dtorn cháo*	Monday	*wun jun*
in the afternoon	*dtorn bài*	Tuesday	*wun ung-kahn*
in the evening	*dtorn yen*	Wednesday	*wun pÔOt*
today	*wun née*	Thursday	*wun pá-réu-hùt*
tomorrow	*prÔOng née*	Friday	*wun sÔOk*
yesterday	*mêu-a wahn née*	Saturday	*wun sao*
		Sunday	*wun ah-tít*

Numbers

1	*nèung*	20	*yêe-sìp*
2	*sorng*	21	*yêe-sìp-et*
3	*sahm*	22	*yêe-sìp-sorng... etc*
4	*sèe*	30	*sahm-sìp*
5	*hâa*	100	*(nèung) róy*
6	*hòk*	101	*(nèung) róy-nèung*
7	*jèt*	150	*(nèung) róy-hâh-sìp*
8	*bpàirt*	200	*sorng róy ... etc*
9	*gâo*	1000	*(nèung) pun*
10	*sìp*	10,000	*mèun*
11	*sìp-et*	100,000	*sairn*
12	*sìp-sorng ... etc*	1,000,000	*láhn*

Index

Titles available in the Footprint *Focus* range

Latin America	UK RRP	US RRP
Bahia & Salvador	£7.99	$11.95
Brazilian Amazon	£7.99	$11.95
Brazilian Pantanal	£6.99	$9.95
Buenos Aires & Pampas	£7.99	$11.95
Cartagena & Caribbean Coast	£7.99	$11.95
Costa Rica	£8.99	$12.95
Cuzco, La Paz & Lake Titicaca	£8.99	$12.95
El Salvador	£5.99	$8.95
Guadalajara & Pacific Coast	£6.99	$9.95
Guatemala	£8.99	$12.95
Guyana, Guyane & Suriname	£5.99	$8.95
Havana	£6.99	$9.95
Honduras	£7.99	$11.95
Nicaragua	£7.99	$11.95
Northeast Argentina & Uruguay	£8.99	$12.95
Paraguay	£5.99	$8.95
Quito & Galápagos Islands	£7.99	$11.95
Recife & Northeast Brazil	£7.99	$11.95
Rio de Janeiro	£8.99	$12.95
São Paulo	£5.99	$8.95
Uruguay	£6.99	$9.95
Venezuela	£8.99	$12.95
Yucatán Peninsula	£6.99	$9.95

Asia	UK RRP	US RRP
Angkor Wat	£5.99	$8.95
Bali & Lombok	£8.99	$12.95
Chennai & Tamil Nadu	£8.99	$12.95
Chiang Mai & Northern Thailand	£7.99	$11.95
Goa	£6.99	$9.95
Gulf of Thailand	£8.99	$12.95
Hanoi & Northern Vietnam	£8.99	$12.95
Ho Chi Minh City & Mekong Delta	£7.99	$11.95
Java	£7.99	$11.95
Kerala	£7.99	$11.95
Kolkata & West Bengal	£5.99	$8.95
Mumbai & Gujarat	£8.99	$12.95

For the latest books, e-books and a wealth of travel information, visit us at: www.footprinttravelguides.com.

Africa & Middle East	UK RRP	US RRP
Beirut	£6.99	$9.95
Cairo & Nile Delta	£8.99	$12.95
Damascus	£5.99	$8.95
Durban & KwaZulu Natal	£8.99	$12.95
Fès & Northern Morocco	£8.99	$12.95
Jerusalem	£8.99	$12.95
Johannesburg & Kruger National Park	£7.99	$11.95
Kenya's Beaches	£8.99	$12.95
Kilimanjaro & Northern Tanzania	£8.99	$12.95
Luxor to Aswan	£8.99	$12.95
Nairobi & Rift Valley	£7.99	$11.95
Red Sea & Sinai	£7.99	$11.95
Zanzibar & Pemba	£7.99	$11.95

Europe	UK RRP	US RRP
Bilbao & Basque Region	£6.99	$9.95
Brittany West Coast	£7.99	$11.95
Cádiz & Costa de la Luz	£6.99	$9.95
Granada & Sierra Nevada	£6.99	$9.95
Languedoc: Carcassonne to Montpellier	£7.99	$11.95
Málaga	£5.99	$8.95
Marseille & Western Provence	£7.99	$11.95
Orkney & Shetland Islands	£5.99	$8.95
Santander & Picos de Europa	£7.99	$11.95
Sardinia: Alghero & the North	£7.99	$11.95
Sardinia: Cagliari & the South	£7.99	$11.95
Seville	£5.99	$8.95
Sicily: Palermo & the Northwest	£7.99	$11.95
Sicily: Catania & the Southeast	£7.99	$11.95
Siena & Southern Tuscany	£7.99	$11.95
Sorrento, Capri & Amalfi Coast	£6.99	$9.95
Skye & Outer Hebrides	£6.99	$9.95
Verona & Lake Garda	£7.99	$11.95

North America	UK RRP	US RRP
Vancouver & Rockies	£8.99	$12.95

Australasia	UK RRP	US RRP
Brisbane & Queensland	£8.99	$12.95
Perth	£7.99	$11.95

footprinttravelguides.com

Join us on facebook for the latest travel news, product releases, offers and amazing competitions: www.facebook.com/footprintbooks.